T0361210

APPLIED GENERAL EQUILIBRIUM ANALYSIS OF INDIA'S TAX AND TRADE POLICY

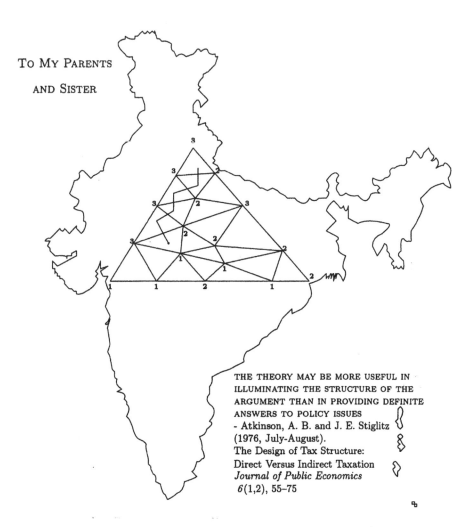

TO MY PARENTS

AND SISTER

THE THEORY MAY BE MORE USEFUL IN
ILLUMINATING THE STRUCTURE OF THE
ARGUMENT THAN IN PROVIDING DEFINITE
ANSWERS TO POLICY ISSUES
- Atkinson, A. B. and J. E. Stiglitz
(1976, July-August).
The Design of Tax Structure:
Direct Versus Indirect Taxation
Journal of Public Economics
6(1,2), 55–75

Applied General Equilibrium Analysis of India's Tax and Trade Policy

SAMEER R. REGE

Larsen & Toubro Limited, India

Routledge
Taylor & Francis Group

LONDON AND NEW YORK

First published 2003 by Ashgate Publishing

Reissued 2018 by Routledge
2 Park Square, Milton Park, Abingdon, Oxon OX14 4RN
711 Third Avenue, New York, NY 10017, USA

Routledge is an imprint of the Taylor & Francis Group, an informa business

Copyright © Sameer R. Rege 2003

Publisher's Note
The publisher has gone to great lengths to ensure the quality of this reprint but points out that some imperfections in the original copies may be apparent.

Disclaimer
The publisher has made every effort to trace copyright holders and welcomes correspondence from those they have been unable to contact.

A Library of Congress record exists under LC control number: 2003041916

ISBN 13: 978-1-138-71189-1 (hbk)
ISBN 13: 978-1-315-19947-4 (ebk)

Contents

Preface and Acknowledgements

The monograph is written from the perspective of a policy analyst as well as a student who requires an introduction into the field of applied general equilibrium modelling. The focus in the monograph has been exclusively on India's Tax and Trade policy; however, for the student the models used in the thesis are fairly standard and have been used for policy applications in many countries. It is hoped that the student will gain from the chapters on literature survey and the various appendices which, in addition to mathematical derivations, also give an explanation for construction and solution of applied general equilibrium models. From the perspective of a policy analyst, the monograph outlines the various assumptions and delves into the possible explanations on the nature of results. It highlights the importance of sensitivity analyses and elucidates the limitations of the modelling methodology on the nature of results.

Acknowledgements

First I would like to thank Dr. Parikh who gave me an opportunity to study economics, since I had no formal training of the subject. Everything contained in this book is an outcome of the valuable comments I received from my advisers Dr. Parikh, Dr. Shikha Jha and Dr. P. V. Srinivasan.

The thesis has its origins in the self study I did under Dr. Shikha Jha in public finance. During the course I came across the article by Harberger (1962) which fuelled my interest in analysing the impacts of capital taxation. Another article by Shoven and Whalley (1984) led to an interest in computable general equilibrium. Later I was fortunate to spend some time at the SOW-VU (Centre for World Food Studies) at the *Vrije Universiteit Amsterdam*. Here, under the watchful eye of Dr. Keyzer, I learnt the basic building blocks that go to make a CGE model. Under the tutelage of Mr. Geert Overbosch I learnt the nuances of creating data sets and the patience and tenacity required to build them. Mr. Overbosch also continued to lend his expertise long after my departure from the centre, for which I am truly grateful.

No applied work is complete without data, and obtaining data is one of the important and difficult tasks. In obtaining the latest data sets of the Indian economy, I am grateful to Mr. Veervart Negi, without whose help I would have never got access to the Planning Commission. At the Planning Commission I was generously helped by Dr. A.B. Negi, Mr. Malik, Mr. Datta and Mr. Mohan Chutani who, despite their busy schedule during the budget work in February

95, found some of their valuable time for me. I also thank Dr. Hashim who gave permission for the data set to be released. I owe my sincere thanks to these gentlemen.

The thesis topic that I chose requires knowledge from different subjects, which should be available to the researcher at the shortest time. A good library solves this problem to a large extent. I thank Mr. Railkar, the chief librarian of the institute from its inception, who procured books at the shortest possible time. This tradition was commendably followed by the new chief librarian Mr. Manjunath who also spared no efforts to procure books. I am also indebted to Mrs. Sushma Karnik, Mrs. Usha Rani and Mr. Rizvadkar who were very helpful in introducing me to various methods of procuring literature and statistical data sets. I also thank Pratibha, Ananthi, Sangeeta, Vinita, Aparna who were very helpful during my stay. I also thank Mr. Sarang who was very prompt in locating books in the library. I thank the library committee, especially Dr. P. G. Babu who endorsed good books. I have to mention a special thanks to Mr. Ron-Lane Smith who also helped in procuring books.

My thesis required computer inputs in terms of software and programming. I have to thank Ms. P. Pushpa who helped me in honing my programming skills in FORTRAN that had rusted since my engineering days. I also thank Mr. Lingaraj Panda who had the patience to help me debug some of my programs when I got stuck. I am grateful to Dr. Kankar Bhattacharya and Piyush who were always there to lend their expertise in FORTRAN/GAMS and attended to some of my frivolous problems with alacrity.

I have to thank Dr. John Piggott who was kind enough to point out nuances in his book Piggott and Whalley (1985). The thesis was typeset in LaTeX for which I am grateful to Dr. Ranade who lent me his personal copy of the manual by Goosens, Mittelbach, and Samarin (1994) and was always willing to debug problems. I learnt about DTP from Dr. Hemant Datye and the formatting in the document is a result of my conversations with him.

A part of this thesis was presented at the IFAC Symposium on *Computation in Economics, Finance and Engineering Economic Systems* at the University of Cambridge. I gratefully acknowledge the funding from Review of Economic Studies Travel Grant and Mr. Deepak H. Parekh, Chairman, Housing Development Finance Corporation. I am indebted to Prof. Heracles Polemarchakis and Churchill College, Cambridge for their hospitality during my stay at the conference in July 1998.

Finally I have to thank my seniors Piyush, Deb, Saumen, Rajendra, Mukesh, classmates Raghu, Pradheepa and juniors Sagar, Haripriya, Rajeev, Vinish, Jesim, Mandira, Ibo, Jayatu and Puneet.

My friends Chotu and Bobby deserve a special mention for their support and help to my family.

I owe my greatest debt to my parents and sister without whose support none of this would have been possible.

I sincerely appreciate the co-operation from the editorial team at Ashgate, Mary Savigar, Carolyn Court, Pam Bertram and Peter Waterhouse.

List of Figures

List of Tables

Chapter 1

Introduction

Overview

Reducing the incidence of poverty, increasing productive employment, achieving sustainable high rates of growth and laying the foundations of an egalitarian society have been the aims of governments. To achieve these goals it is important to have an efficient resource allocation and use. Since independence successive governments have followed policies to achieve these goals. Yet poverty persists coupled with unemployment and a mediocre rate of growth. The country faced a major balance of payments crisis in 1991. It is worthwhile to investigate the causes that led to this crisis in the background of the policy framework that existed.[1]

The Indian policy regime can be broadly classified into the external front comprising of trade policies and the domestic front comprising of tax-subsidy policies, industrial policy and fiscal policy of the government. The country followed an inward looking import substitution policy along with the creation of a large public sector. To achieve import substitution there was a very complex trade policy consisting of an import regime, tariff structure and an export regime. Each will be described in brief.

- Import regime – This consisted of non-tariff barriers which were used to protect and regulate domestic industries. These controls included:

  a. import licensing,

  b. "actual user" policy that allowed only the user to import,

  c. canalised imports which implied monopoly of public sector and government organisations to import,

  d. phased manufacturing programmes which require a firm to progressively phase out imported components,

  e. industrial regulatory system primarily to protect domestic capital goods industry from competing imports, and

  f. government purchase preference which gave priority to domestic suppliers a price preference equivalent to 25% of CIF price plus duties.

- Tariff structure – The tariff structure consists of three parts:

  a. basic customs duties applied to the CIF price of imports,

  b. auxiliary duty applied to the CIF price, and

---

[1] A part of this section is based on Aksoy (1990).

   c. countervailing duties (CVD) applied to the CIF price plus customs and auxiliary duties. Auxiliary duties are ad valorem in nature, customs duties are both specific and ad valorem while CVDs are equal to excise duties and are a mixture of ad valorem and specific taxes.

- Export regime – Similar to a complex import regime the government had an elaborate export regime to compensate the exporters for high duties on inputs. These arrangements took on various forms from administrative controls to economic incentives. The regime used the following to promote exports:

   a. cash compensatory support (CCS) compensating for the unrebated indirect taxes paid by exporters on export goods,

   b. duty drawback (DD) which reimbursed exporters for duties paid on imported inputs and excise duties on domestic inputs,

   c. replenishment (REP) licenses under which an exporter could import raw materials items under the canalised list,

   d. advanced licenses (AL) applicable to items on the restricted list, which could not be imported using REP licenses, thus allowing exporters to import raw materials duty free,

   e. free trade zones (FTZ) and export oriented units (EOU), which are outside domestic tariff area and can import raw materials free of licenses and duties,

   f. profits tax and credit subsidies which gave concessions to profits on exports and interest rebate upto 20% on long term loans for firms exporting more than 25% of their output, and

   g. subsidies on domestic raw materials which refunded exporters the difference between domestic and imported price of raw materials.

The outcome of this inward looking policy was the creation of a diversified and self sufficient industrial sector. However the problems started to surface by the end of the 1970s. The growth rate of the industrial sector was disappointing despite the high investment. The technology was inefficient and outdated partly due to the protection from foreign competition and partly due to the industrial policy of the government. The imports were reduced to such an extent that any disruption affected domestic production. This also resulted in a slow growth of exports with the consequence of a reduction in India's share in world trade.

The policies followed on the domestic front were also responsible for the poor industrial performance. The government had effectively controlled entry into industrial sectors by introducing licenses, and had also prevented upgradation of technology for firms already operating within an industry. Moreover certain commodities were restricted to the small scale sector, thus preventing larger firms to achieve economies of scale. In sectors where the commodities were produced by the small scale sector as well as large firms there were tax incentives for the small scale sector as opposed to high level of indirect taxes on larger firms. There were a myriad of indirect taxes, often on the same base which resulted in cascading. This level of high indirect taxation of inputs negated the effects that high tariffs on imports had on the effective protection rates (EPR). One of the reasons is the high rate of excise taxes on capital goods, which make the domestic industry non competitive due to higher output prices. The more serious outcome is that high capital costs are not accounted for in calculating EPRs and are not compensated under GATT rules. For details of domestic resource costs and effective protection refer to Bruno (1972).

The lower growth rate of industry prompted the government to relax the controls on the external and internal front. The import controls were relaxed with easier access to select imports. Restrictions on domestic firms to expand and gain access to technology were lowered. As a result the manufacturing sector grew with part of the growth being attributed to a fall in the incremental capital output ratio (ICOR). Growth in manufacturing output, appreciation of the rupee in the early 1980s, increasing fiscal deficit, relaxation of the import regime led to a deterioration of the macro balances position at the end of 1980s. It culminated in the balance of payments crisis in 1991.

This crisis led to an initiation of a process of structural reform. Under its auspices the government is trying to liberalise the economy with an outward looking approach to globalisation. Moreover the Uruguay round of talks and subsequent entry of India into the world trade organisation (WTO) implies cutting of tariffs in a phased manner to international levels. The immediate outcome of cut in tariffs will be a fall in the revenues of the government. The importance of tariff revenues can hardly be undermined as is evident from Table 1.1.

Table 1.1: **Share of Various Taxes in Total Taxes (%)**

Year	Direct Taxes	Customs	Union Excise	State Excise	Sales Taxes	Other Indirect Taxes	Total	Total Taxes Rs. Crores
88-89	13.73	24.36	28.33	4.45	20.30	8.84	100	64146.8
89-90	14.37	23.21	28.84	5.22	20.16	8.19	100	77692.4
90-91	13.98	23.53	27.95	5.69	20.78	8.08	100	87722.6
91-92	16.14	21.57	27.24	5.54	20.88	8.63	100	103198.4
92-93	16.98	20.83	27.01	5.79	21.05	8.34	100	114165.4
93-94	18.43	18.45	26.04	5.57	22.67	8.85	100	121929.9
94-95	18.89	18.32	25.56	5.35	20.95	10.93	100	144371.8
95-96	19.45	17.83	25.86	4.96	20.98	10.93	100	165434.5

Source: Computed from Table 1 of Burgess and Stern (1993) and IES-PF (1995)

The share of customs duties has more than doubled in the past two decades and as per Table 8 of Burgess and Stern (1993) the share of duties in total imports has been rising for the last three decades. The substantial increase in the rise of customs duties as a percentage of imports is a cause for concern. The other impact will be on the prices of domestic industries. The domestic tax structure which has multiple levels of indirect taxes result in cascading and non competitive prices in the international markets. For Indian companies to compete in the international markets or with import substitutes they require a level playing field. For this purpose the tax structure will have to be rational. The current levels of high indirect taxes and subsidies will have to be changed to eliminate distortions. It is imperative to reform tax rates.

The government raises revenue from direct as well as indirect taxation. The relative importance of direct taxes is evident from Figure 1.1 whose share has been falling. It is only since 1986 that the trend has been reversing with a marginal increase in direct tax collections.

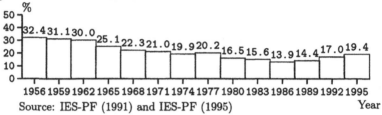

Source: IES-PF (1991) and IES-PF (1995)

Figure 1.1: **Share of Direct Taxes in Total Taxes (%) (1956/57–1995/96)**

Hence the government has relied primarily on a multitude of indirect taxes to raise revenues. Their share has been increasing as depicted in Figure 1.2. Despite the fact that the share of indirect taxes has fallen since 1986, it still is the major source of revenue for the government.

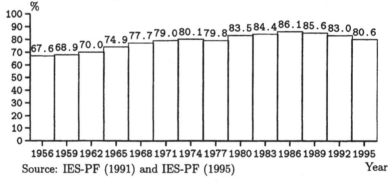

Source: IES-PF (1991) and IES-PF (1995)

Figure 1.2: **Share of Indirect Taxes in Total Taxes (%) (1956/57–1995/96)**

The dependence on indirect taxes results in a lack of transparency and it becomes difficult to evaluate the incidence of taxes. As mentioned earlier it is detrimental to competition and exports. The government, realising this, introduced a Modified Value Added Tax (MODVAT) in 1986. Under the MODVAT, some commodities were exempted from excise duties, thus lowering input costs of some commodities. However, this scheme was not extended to all goods with capital goods, petroleum being major exceptions. The major fallout of not extending

MODVAT to capital goods is the direct increase in price of output on account of high capital costs along with no compensation under GATT for exports.

Revenue forms one part of government budget and expenditure the other. Components of expenditure are also important as they may introduce distortions. Subsidies are an important part of annual government spending and are one of the major factors contributing to deficit. Table 1.2 shows the provision for subsidies in the central government budget for the 1980s.

Table 1.2: **Provision for Subsidies in Central Government** *(Rs. Crores)*

	1989-90	1990-91	1991-92	1992-93	1993-94	1994-95	1995-96
Food	2476	2450	2850	2800	5200	5100	5250
Fertilizer	4542	4400	4800	5796	4400	5166	5400
Total	10862	10728	10326	10126	11485	12268	12323

Source: IES-PF (1991) and IES-PF (1995)

A major fraction is consumed by food and fertilizer subsidies. Fertilizer subsidy was first given in 1977. It is difference between the retention price given to manufacturers of fertilizers and price paid by farmers on the domestic front. On the imported front it is the difference between the import price plus transportation costs and the price charged to farmers. Food subsidy is the difference between the price charged to consumers at the fair price shops through the public distribution system and the cost of procuring, storing and distributing these commodities.

Another important subsidy is the subsidy given to the agriculture in the form of cheaper credit for irrigation purposes along with power at lower tariffs for the same purpose.

Taxes can introduce distortions in the behaviour of agents and the current indirect tax system is highly distortional. From the view point of efficiency, equity and an evolution of a competitive environment, it is necessary to reform the tax structure. The other strong motivation to reform taxation is the current level of macro economic imbalances, which is evident from the level of fiscal deficit which stood at 9.28% of the GDP in 1988-90 having risen from 1.21% since 1950-51.

The dilemmas faced by the policy makers are to correct the macro imbalances, lower tariff rates, reform the tax system such that it fosters an environment of competition at the same time have a taxation structure that achieves equity and efficiency. Given the difficulties faced by the government in raising taxes through direct taxation to achieve equity, it has to use indirect taxes to obtain these goals. Moreover to control the deficit the government has to raise revenues or cut expenditure or both. Given that revenues have to be raised a tax structure has to be designed which minimises welfare losses. The other issues are administrative involving the costs and benefits of government machinery to collect direct and indirect taxes and an ability to enforce rules to achieve an equitable income distribution.

The objective of the study is to study the impact of current tax reforms undertaken by the government and to explore other tax reforms. Also, having outlined the importance of tariff revenues on the macro balances of the economy, trade policy becomes an important element which one cannot afford to neglect.

What the Theory has to Say

Theory has a very important role to play and is useful in defining the domain of the analyses. It is not always that theory can provide unambiguous answers to all problems faced by policy makers. At the same time the assumptions made by theory to build elegant models abstracted from reality do not render it insignificant. Theoretical models offer valuable insight into the underlying process. In what follows the qualitative insights from theory will be pitted against the need to analyse policy questions beyond the limitations of theory and used to highlight the need for empirical work. This section highlights the various policy questions addressed and is structured as follows. The first part deals with trade related issues, while the second with tax related ones.

Trade Issues

An important concept of the theory of trade is the principle of comparative advantage as a reason for mutually beneficial trade between two countries. In a simple two country, two commodity model, benefits accrue from trade as long as the terms of trade lie between the autarky price ratios existing between the two countries. Thus the classical theory identifies comparative advantage to be the driving force to trade. Thus with a small country assumption, policy instruments like tariffs may lead to welfare loss by reducing the volume of trade taking place. However a large country can influence the terms of trade gains by levying optimal tariffs on imports.

The Heckscher–Ohlin theorem states that a country will export that good which uses the relatively more abundant factor more intensively. It assumes non-reversal of factor intensities, identical demand structure in both countries and over lapping of ranges of relative factor prices in the two countries. This has strong implications of factor price equalisation across countries and implies that free trade in goods will equalise both goods and factor prices.

The Stolper–Samuelson theorem states that increase in relative price of a commodity favours (raises the marginal product) the factor used intensively in the production of that commodity.

Rybczinski's theorem states that, at unchanged commodity and factor prices, an increase in the quantity of one factor (given the other) will increase the output of the commodity which uses this factor more intensively.[2]

The gains from trade for a small country are illustrated using Figure 1.3. Here PP is the production possibility frontier of a country which produces two goods X and Y. Initially in autarky it consumes what it produces at relative prices p_1p_1, achieving utility u_1u_1. After indulging in trade at world prices given by p_2p_2, it

---

[2]For details on trade theory literature refer to Chapter 2.

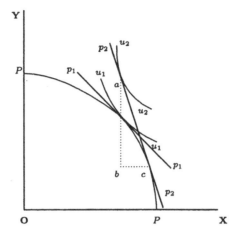

Figure 1.3: **Gains from Trade for a Small Country**

produces at c but consumes at a exporting bc of commodity X and importing ab of commodity Y, achieving utility $u_2 u_2$. Indulging in trade is welfare improving as utility $u_2 u_2$ lies above $u_1 u_1$.

The small country case assumes that the country cannot influence the price of its exports or imports or it has no monopoly, monopsony power in exports and imports. However, there might be gains from tariffs if the country is large. This is illustrated using Figure 1.4. In the figure OC_F is the foreign offer curve while OC_{H1} is the domestic offer curve before imposing tariffs. The intersection of the two offer curves gives the terms of trade and gives utility $U_1 U_1$. By imposing tariffs a large country can improve welfare and it will be maximum if the tariffs are optimum. In the figure the welfare is maximised at a where the indifference curve $U_m U_m$ is tangent to the foreign offer curve OC_F. At a the new domestic offer curve OC_{H2} intersects the foreign offer curve OC_F resulting in favourable terms of trade. Any further tariffs or tariff reduction will lead to a welfare loss as the indifference curves will pass below a.

The structure of Heckscher–Ohlin model is illustrated in Figure 1.5.[3] The factor intensity by industry as a function of the wage-rental ratio is shown in the upper quadrant and the ratio of relative prices of output (p) as a function of wage-rental ratio ($\frac{w}{r}$) is shown in the lower quadrant. For any wage-rental ratio *industry 1* is more capital intensive than *industry 2*. The factor intensity endowment ratios for the two countries are denoted by $\overline{\left(\frac{K}{L}\right)}_A$ and $\overline{\left(\frac{K}{L}\right)}_B$. The country A can produce both commodities with factor allocations in the range of ZY. At Z only commodity 1 is produced while at Y only commodity 2 is produced. As the real wages rise the wage-rental ratio increases implying a higher cost of labour intensive commodity 2 and a higher relative price ratio

---

[3] Figure 2.5 of Whalley (1985).

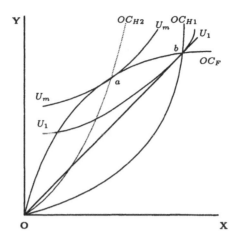

Figure 1.4: **Impact of Tariff on Terms of Trade for a Large Country**

p. Before trade country A produces commodity 1 corresponding to YW and commodity 2 corresponding to WZ at the relative prices p_A^A, while country B produces commodity 1 corresponding to DF and commodity 2 corresponding to GF at relative prices p_B^A. After trade the common price ratio is p_W^{FT}. This results in country A produces corresponding to YQ of commodity 1 (corresponding to QZ of commodity 2). Country B produces corresponding to EG of commodity 2 (corresponding to DE of commodity 1). Thus relatively more capital abundant country A exports commodity 1 from *industry 1* which is capital intensive and relatively more labour abundant country B exports commodity 2 from *industry 2* which is labour intensive. Now a tariff on commodity 2 by country B will raise the price of commodity 2 and the corresponding wage-rental ratio will go up. This would result in substitution of labour (abundant factor in country B) by capital. Increased capital implies a fall in the marginal product of capital (less abundant factor) and decreased labour implies a rise in the marginal product of labour (more abundant factor) proving the Stolper–Samuelson theorem.

However all these models have their limitations. They do not account for intermediate inputs of commodities as means of producing commodities. Also they assume the number of factors are equal to the number of goods. Any inequality implies redundancy of either factors or goods, whichever is in excess. The results from theoretical models with two commodities may not necessarily hold in the multi commodity case, which calls for an empirical analysis of the same. Policy instruments like tariffs as handled in theory are restricted to small changes, but large changes in tariffs warrant multi sector empirical general equilibrium models. The trade model in this monograph is used to address some trade related issues which are of importance for India in its process of liberalisation.

From the policy perspective it is important to analyse the implications of trade liberalisation. These implications are studied using a modelling exercise.

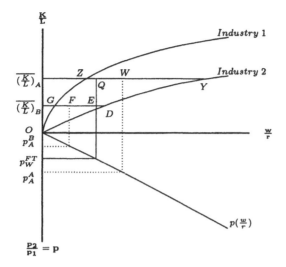

Figure 1.5: **"Harrod–Johnson" diagram for a Heckscher–Ohlin Trade Model**

A caveat is due here. Just as a chain is strong as its weakest link, results from a model are as robust as its strongest assumption. There might be a possibility of policy conclusions being wrongly drawn due to strong assumptions. However, if the model results are insensitive to assumptions and parameters, then drawing policy guidelines is relatively robust.

- *Impact of tariff cuts under constant returns to scale.*
  Tariff cuts of various magnitudes across all commodities is implemented with constant returns to scale assumption which implies perfect competition and zero profits under various export elasticities and Armington imports. This falls under the realm of neoclassical trade theory which attributes comparative advantage as the basis of trade. It primarily deals with inter industry trade.

  From the Indian perspective this is an important exercise in order to evaluate the welfare implications of the Uruguay round under the provisional GATT treaty which has now paved a way for the World Trade Organisation (WTO). To draw policy conclusions the model is subjected to extreme values of parameters and policy tools. If the conclusions remain invariant it can be safely assumed that for any parameters and policy tools with intermediate values the conclusions will hold.

- *Do tariff cuts under increasing returns to scale show larger welfare changes as compared to constant returns?*
  The assumption of perfect competition is relaxed for a select set of sectors. These sectors have either average cost pricing or have profits (losses) in the short run or entry (exit) in the long run. The tariff cuts are as in the

constant returns to scale case. This falls in the domain of "new" trade theory, which incorporates ideas from industrial organisation literature. Here, the emphasis is on intra industry trade rather than inter industry.

The "new" trade theory has implications for developing countries like India which predominantly followed an import substitution policy. If due to liberalisation there is a contraction of domestic sectors it implies higher average costs and higher prices leading to welfare loss. This is partly compensated by increased imports at lower price leading to welfare gain. Which effect dominates needs to be evaluated empirically.

- *Impact of real exchange rate devaluation on welfare, trade deficit and export performance.*
  The exchange rate is devalued allowing the trade deficit to adjust while tariffs are cut. From the Indian perspective this is interesting to analyse as the Indian rupee has been devalued after the reform began. Though this devaluation was with respect to the nominal exchange rate which has no existence in real general equilibrium models, it is worthwhile to investigate the real exchange rate devaluation from a welfare perspective.

Tax Issues

The long run growth of an economy depends on its capacity to accumulate capital generated from savings of individuals and firms. The accumulation of savings also results in inter-generational transfers leading to a skewed distribution of wealth. To fulfil the objective of equity, the government resorts to taxation. This besides attempting to reduce inequity, is a source of revenue for the government. Tax policy designed to achieve these objectives has its impact on labour supply, income, savings, risk taking, bequests by people and investment decisions by firms.

Consider the impact of taxation on labour supply.[4] This is shown in Figures 1.6A and B. The agent is assumed to have non-wage income I and supplies labour L at a wage rate w. Before taxation the income Y is $wL + I$. The utility is maximised at P where the utility curve $u_n u_n$ is tangent to the income line. The amount of leisure consumed is denoted by 1. After a proportional tax rate t the budget constraint shifts to $I'b$ from Ia with income $(wL + I) \times (1 - t)$. The income effect is shown by PQ, while the substitution effect (change in labour supply that would have occurred due to change in wages to keep the individual at the same level of utility) equals QP'. The amount of leisure consumed (labour supplied) depends on which effect dominates. In the Figure 1.6A the income effect (change in the labour supply due to decrease in wages makes individuals worse off) dominates and more labour is supplied at the cost of decreased leisure as denoted by 2.

In Figure 1.6B, the substitution effect dominates the income effect which leads to a decrease in the labour supply with leisure increasing from 1 to 2. As

---

[4]This follows Chapter 2 of Atkinson and Stiglitz (1987).

seen in Figures 1.6A and B the impact of uniform taxation on leisure (labour) is ambiguous and depends on the utility function. This means that the labour–leisure choice of individuals needs to be investigated empirically.

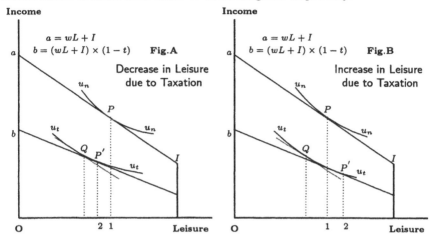

Figure 1.6: **Impact on Leisure due to Taxation**

Governments often have to decide between choices of different taxation systems. To compare between various systems the concept of equal yield is used. The yield from a tax is the distance between the two budget constraints, one without tax and the other with tax. Figure 1.7 shows the impact on labour supply (leisure consumption) of an equal yield tax. The pre tax budget line is denoted by Ia, while the proportional post tax budget line by $I'b$. The revenue to the government is given by ef. A lump sum tax leaves the wage rate unchanged. So the budget line is parallel to the no tax line Ia through f. The consumption occurs at r where the utility u_2u_2 is tangent to the new budget line. The equal yield income tax has resulted in smaller consumption of leisure at q as opposed to larger consumption of leisure at f from an proportional income tax if utility has to be kept constant at u_1u_1. To analyse intertemporal issues a simple life cycle model is used as an illustration. The consumption choice is illustrated in Figure 1.8. Here an individual lives for two periods, consuming C_1 in period 1 and C_2 in period 2. Consumption in period 2 requires saving in period 1 which offers an interest rate r (price of period 2 consumption is $\frac{1}{1+r}$). The budget constraint for this period model is Xa such that $C_1 + \frac{C_2}{1+r} = w$. The individual maximises lifetime utility $U(C_1, C_2)$ to consume at P. Now assume a tax on interest rate which reduces the rate from r to $r1$. This increases the price of consumption in period 2 ($\frac{1}{1+r_1} > \frac{1}{1+r}$). The effect of this price rise is to lower consumption C_2 unambiguously. The impact on consumption in period 1 is not clear. Due to the substitution effect there is an increase in consumption, but due to the income effect (will save more as period 2 consumption has become expensive) there is a fall in C_1. Which effect dominates depends on the utility function and the

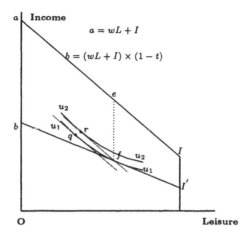

Figure 1.7: **Impact on Leisure due to Equal Yield Taxation**

elasticity of substitution. As shown in Figure 1.8A there is a fall in period 1 consumption C_1 with income effect dominating the substitution effect. Figure 1.8B shows the case where there is a rise in the consumption C_1. As opposed to the earlier case the substitution effect dominates the income effect leading to greater consumption in period 1, mainly due to high elasticity of substitution. To resolve this ambiguity an empirical analysis is necessary. Theoretical models built to analyse savings behaviour with perfect and imperfect capital markets for two and multi periods find that savings increase (decrease) depending on whether the elasticity of substitution is greater (smaller) than wealth elasticity of consumption. In models which analyse issues in a life cycle hypothesis savings depend on the timings of wage tax or consumption tax. The demand for risky assets is affected by the type of taxation *viz.* income or wealth. Models have also analysed labour leisure choice of individuals given the tax structure. For firms the debt equity choice is affected by taxation and theory attempts to explain the existing structure of corporate investment.

Theoretical models are elegant constructs and offer insights into very specific problems. However their use from the policy perspective is somewhat limited. A policy maker is concerned with the impacts of the policy on all the decision variables of individuals and not on each variable in isolation. The objective of a policy maker reforming indirect taxes is to minimise (maximise) welfare loss (gain) while raising revenue needed to meet various social objectives. While levying income taxes the attempt is to select a rate which will generate desired revenues but at the same time minimise incentives to evade or disincentive to supply optimal level of labour. Other problems are to select a tax structure given the presence of a large number of taxes. All these point to the fact that tax rates and structure have economy wide implications, and in designing them theoretical results are of limited use. Empirical analysis can provide richer insight.

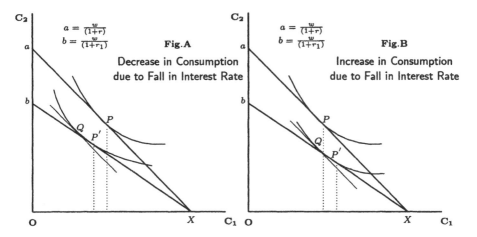

Figure 1.8: **Impact on Consumption due to Change in Interest Rate**

The policy issues addressed by the tax model are as follows. All simulations are carried out under the condition of revenue neutrality. This helps in focussing on the issue of structure, rather than levels of taxes.

- *What is the impact of removal of input subsidies viz. agriculture and fertilizer in the agriculture sector?*
  The input subsidies on agriculture and fertilizer are reduced to zero. To maintain revenue neutrality there is a reduction in the sales tax rates across all commodities either in a uniform or differentiated manner. The objective is to find out whether reducing subsidies which results in lower tax revenue requirements and lower tax rates, lead to welfare gains.

- *Is it welfare improving to remove these input subsidies and give a corresponding food subsidy?*
  These input subsidies are reduced to zero and only food subsidy is increased with other tax rates untouched. The aim is to find out which subsidy structure is more distortional and if possible to reduce these distortions to achieve higher welfare.

- *Does MODVAT (MODified Value Added Tax) improve welfare?*
  MODVAT falls under the jurisdiction of the central government which imposes central excise. MODVAT enables firms to claim refund on excise duties and countervailing duties on their inputs. Other indirect taxes still remain. Here the excise duties on sectors under MODVAT is reduced to zero. To maintain revenue neutrality rates are increased for sales taxes.

  This is simulated in two ways. One is the way it currently operates in India with elimination of excise duties for MODVAT sectors and increase in excise duties for non MODVAT sectors. The other is to substitute it by a sales tax structure. Conceptually there is no difference from the earlier regime without MODVAT as both sales taxes and excise are distortional. This is carried out only to compare with the case of extension of MODVAT to capital goods, where the only degree of freedom left to meet revenue neutrality are the sales taxes. The point of the exercise is to compare the relative levels of distortions of sales and excise taxes.

- *Impact of extending MODVAT to the capital goods sectors.*
  Currently MODVAT is applicable only to a particular set of industries. To extend MODVAT to capital goods sectors, the excise taxes on these sectors are also reduced to zero with imposition of compensating sales taxes.

- *Will the introduction of a full VAT be welfare improving?*
  A full VAT implies complete elimination of taxes on intermediate use with taxes on final consumption. The tax rates on intermediate use are reduced to zero and VAT rates computed such that revenue neutrality is maintained. One set of simulations is carried out with total elimination of indirect taxes and subsidies as in the case of a consumption type VAT. The other case the subsidies are maintained while the taxes are eliminated.

- *Is it beneficial to go to a full VAT at one go or gradually implement a VAT by cutting indirect taxes over a period of time?*
  To implement VAT reform one can change the structure at one go or gradually move to a VAT at the end of a certain time period. The gradual implementation involves uniform reduction in indirect taxes with compensating sales taxes to maintain revenue neutrality with complete elimination of indirect taxes at the end of the period. The gradual implementation of VAT means that in the intermittent years cascading prevails but to a lower extent due to reduction of indirect taxes.

- *What will be the impact of exempting certain sectors in the implementation of a VAT?*
  Exempted sectors are not a part of the VAT and have to pay taxes on inputs with zero taxes on their outputs. Zero rated sectors get a refund on their inputs and have zero tax rate on final consumption. In the exempt case the indirect tax rates on these sectors is maintained while putting rates of final consumption to zero. To implement these simulations the sales taxes for the exempt sectors are set to zero while for the non exempt sectors is calculated endogenously.

Choice of Methodology

The goal to analyse India's tax policy is not achievable without a suitable tool. Since the arguments outlined above point to an economy wide ramifications a computable general equilibrium (CGE) approach was selected to tackle the problem on hand. Previous studies have used an econometric approach, with the objective of tackling only select tax issues in mind or studied the tax system of some of the states in the country. The centre state politics plays a major role in the design and operation of the tax system but analysing fiscal federalism is beyond the scope of the study.

The computable general equilibrium models used in the study are calibrated to the latest data set relating to the Indian economy. The economic analysis is at a fairly disaggregated level of 19 sectors. The approach followed is to use a theoretical specification for behaviour of agents and calibrate it to the base case. This is preferred over empirical estimation due to the non-availability of data required to undertake satisfactory estimations. However wherever possible parameters have been estimated from data and then used in calibration. To overcome the limitations of calibration the models are subjected to a sensitivity analysis. The base year of analysis is 1989 − 90 which is the latest data set available on the Indian economy when this study was carried out. The study incorporates all the major indirect taxes and subsidies currently in existence.

The study uses two general equilibrium models. One to analyse trade policy and the other to analyse tax policy. Both the models have the same sectoral classification but differ in the consumption and production structure. Besides the structural differences in the two models, the main reason to build separate models was prompted by policy issues. It is not that one model cannot and could not handle both the issues, but each model has a specific purpose. Under the WTO treaty, India has to cut tariffs in a phased manner. This does not mean that an overhauled tax structure will be implemented along with it. At the same time tariff cuts lead to revenue loss and hence an increased deficit. The trade model just analyses tariff cuts and its corresponding revenue loss or gain maintaining a constant trade deficit in foreign currency. The tax model on the contrary operates on a revenue neutral framework under the assumption that the government will be able to or plan to implement a new indirect tax structure which encompasses both domestic taxes and tariffs.

Approach of the Monograph

Governments have to take policy decisions that will reduce the fluctuations in the economy with an aim to improve welfare. If theory was sufficient to address these issues and offer solutions, the need for empirical work would not arise. Also, to deliberate on normative issues one requires the help of the positive part of the subject. The monograph is used as an attempt to validate theory using an empirical methodology. The potential pitfalls of such an attempt are numerous. The assumptions in theory may be violated in empirical studies. The data set available may itself impose limits to the extent of empirical modelling.

Computable General Equilibrium modelling is one such empirical tool used in this monograph. This tool is built on a foundation of behaviour of agents derived from microeconomic theory. It lacks statistical rigour. The numerous parameters required to validate these models may not be readily amenable to estimation. Even if they are estimated, the estimation is based on a subset of the total data set. This may bias the estimates. To make an attempt to tackle these limitations, the models are subjected to a limited sensitivity analysis, with the objective of obtaining a range of values for the objective variable, in this case, welfare.

Structure of the Monograph

This section briefly describes the contents of the subsequent chapters and will motivate the flow of the monograph.

Chapter 2 deals with the literature survey and traces the development of the subject in a very brief manner. The objective is to put the work in perspective and to justify the choice of models used in the monograph. Wherever necessary, references to other surveys is given to prevent repetition.

Chapter 3 describes the mathematical models used for trade and tax policy analysis. The chapter describes the equations and structure of the basic model along with modelling extensions to this structure. The simulations performed using the trade model are documented and explained in Chapter 4, while simulation results and description from the tax model follow in Chapter 5.

Chapter 6 is the concluding chapter before the appendix chapters begin. It summarises the work done, limitations and outlines extensions for further research.

There are five appendices. Appendix A deals with the mathematical derivation of the expressions used throughout the monograph. Appendix B outlines the methodology used in the construction of the benchmark data set, while documenting the various data sources used in the construction of the SAM. Appendix C tabulates the econometric estimations undertaken along with calibration procedures. It also tabulates the selection of exogenous parameters used in the models. Appendix D provides a brief introduction to fixed point nomenclature. It explains the details of Merrill's algorithm and its application for building a prototype CGE model. Appendix E is the last in the monograph and provides a brief background on the Indian political system and major economic indicators.

Chapter 2

Literature Survey

Introduction

The objective here is not to give a detailed literature survey of applied general equilibrium models, public finance and trade literature. There are many excellent surveys already available and will be cited when necessary. The main objective of the chapter is to highlight the work undertaken in the perspective of development in the literature. It is also necessary to explain the choice of models from the vast array of models available and its relevance to the analysis undertaken.

The chapter is organised as follows. The next section deals with the classification of general equilibrium models, using various criteria for classification. This is followed by a survey of public finance and trade literature. The final section concludes with the relevance of the choice of model.

Computable General Equilibrium

The study uses computable general equilibrium as a tool to analyse various policy issues mentioned in the previous chapter. This section gives a brief introduction to the literature.

Classification

The pioneering work in CGE modelling was done by Johansen (1974) for Norway, in which he analysed the impact of various policies on the growth of various sectors in a general equilibrium framework. More influential was the article by Harberger (1962) who investigated tax policy questions in a two-sector general equilibrium framework. The solutions obtained were analytical in nature and suited to the analysis of only small changes in tax policy. A major impetus to the implementation of more complex models analysing tax policy was provided by the development of a fixed point algorithm by Scarf (1973). Table 2.1 shows a scheme of classification of general equilibrium (GE) models based on various attributes such as, tradition, treatment of time, areas of application, modelling of production structure and solution methods. The above classification is used to put the literature in perspective and as will be shown later, each model in literature belongs to more than one category in the above list. Each of the criteria will be taken up and dealt with in brief.

Table 2.1: **Different Classifications of General Equilibrium Models**

A	B	C	D	E
Tradition	Modelling of Time	Areas of Application	Production Structure	Solution Methods
• Multi-Sectoral Growth or Johansen	• Static	• Public Economics	• Constant Returns to Scale	• Linearisation
• Yale (HSSW)	• Sequentially Dynamic	• International Economics	• Increasing Returns to Scale	• Mathematical Programming
• World Bank	• Fully Dynamic	• Resource Economics	• Sunk Costs	• Simultaneous Non-linear Equations
		• Development Economics		
		• Agricultural Economics		

Source: Author

Tradition

The classification of general equilibrium models based on tradition primarily refers to the place of origin and to the pioneers of the particular method of application.

Multi-sectoral Growth or Johansen   This tradition is adopted by a group of researchers who follow the linearisation approach proposed by Johansen (1974). The most widely quoted example of this tradition is the ORANI model for Australia.

Yale or Harberger–Scarf–Shoven–Whalley (HSSW)   This approach was developed at Yale by applying Scarf's algorithm to the capital taxation problem proposed by Harberger by Shoven and Whalley (1972). The models in literature based on this tradition had studied problems related to tax issues in developed countries with some applications for developing countries. New models address much wider issues than just tax policy but still fall under the Yale tradition as they were built by students of Scarf or students of students of Scarf.

World Bank   This approach was first developed at the World Bank under various research projects and tend to closely follow the early work of Dervis, deMelo, and Robinson (1982) and Adelman and Robinson (1978). Most of these works are associated with evaluation of trade related issues such as tariff cuts, import quotas, exchange rates, protection, resource pulls and foreign exchange shortages to name a few. This approach also differs from the *HSSW* or *Yale* approach in terms of the solution strategies used. Though both use the simultaneous solution approach, the *Yale* tradition used the fixed point approach of Scarf. The World Bank tradition used either the Gauss–Seidel method or updated prices using the Jacobian of excess demand functions.

Modelling of Time

Many of the issues addressed in these models are functions of time and not all issues can be addressed without effectively incorporating the dynamic behaviour of agents. Models can be classified in three groups using this attribute.

Static Approach This is the easiest of all the applied general equilibrium models with only one time period. Inter-temporal decisions of saving and investment are not a result of any optimisation on the part of the agents but are specified arbitrarily.

Sequentially Dynamic Approach This is the logical extension of static models and involves the non-optimal movement of the economy over time. Here time is important only for consumption decisions. Thus there is a choice between present and future consumption, which determines savings in any period. Investment adjusts passively to savings, thus augmenting the capital stock. The economy grows along a path formed by the evolution of capital stock and this forms the link between various static equilibria. The equilibrium in period $t+1$ is dependent on the equilibrium in period t only.

Fully Dynamic Approach In this approach, the decisions of agents follow explicit inter-temporal optimisation. The consumers maximise the discounted present value of the lifetime utility subject to the lifetime budget constraint. The producers maximise the value of the firm or the inter-temporal net cash flow. The government in general plays a passive role of running a balanced budget in each period.

The producer behaviour is based on the specification of investment dynamics based on the q theory of Tobin (1969), where q is the value of capital relative to its replacement cost. Tobin in his article referred to marginal q. However in practice one observes average q and it was Hayashi (1982) who derived a relation between average and marginal q which is the basis for implementation of general equilibrium models with explicit investment dynamics.

Based on the above one can have various permutations and combinations of fully dynamic general equilibrium models. One approach is to have dynamic behaviour for both consumers and producers in a multi-sectoral framework with either a closed economy (Pereira and Shoven (1988)) or open economy (Goulder and Summers (1989)). The other is to have similar behaviour for producers but consumer behaviour is modelled in an overlapping generations (OLG) framework as pioneered by Auerbach and Kotlikoff (1987), in which they have a single sector producing one good consumed by 55 overlapping generations. The *OLG* framework in a two country framework for single sector is tackled in Bettendorf (1994).

Areas of Application

General equilibrium models differ in their structure depending on the issues they are addressing. The areas of application can be broadly classified as follows.

Public Economics   Perhaps this is the oldest area of application dealing with tax reforms. The issues tackled are related to direct taxes, indirect taxes, integration of corporate and personal income taxes, introduction of consumption taxes and impact of value added taxes to name a few. The model of Ballard, Fullerton, Shoven, and Whalley (1985) analyses in detail the US tax system and has been used in other applications for the UK – Piggott and Whalley (1985) – and Finland – Tørmä and Rutherford (1992) – and is the model used in this monograph for analysing India's tax reform. The model has constant returns to scale production functions with a static behaviour of producers. The consumers have myopic expectations and in each period make a choice between current and future consumption. The economy is assumed to be on the balanced growth path with savings augmenting capital stock. Another model using the structure of Ballard, Fullerton, Shoven, and Whalley (1985) is Fehr, Rosenberg, and Wiegard (1995) where they analyse the impacts of VAT harmonisation in Europe. This model differs from Ballard, Fullerton, Shoven, and Whalley (1985) in the following ways. It is a static multicountry model not dealing with investments, but incorporates labour leisure choice. Serra-Puche (1984) analysed the income distribution and resource allocation of a Mexican VAT, when Mexico shifted from an indirect turnover tax to a consumption VAT in 1980. A comparison of methodologies used in various general equilibrium models in the 1980s is given in Fullerton, Henderson, and Shoven (1984). Studies incorporating fully dynamic behaviour analysing VAT issues are Perraudin and Pujol (1991) and Frenkel, Razin, and Symansky (1991).

International Economics   Impacts of trade negotiations carried out during the various rounds of the General Agreement on Tariffs and Trade (GATT) have also been studied. Predominantly tariff and non-tariff barriers to trade have been analysed using multi country models. Analysis of the Tokyo round in a multi country framework has been done by Whalley (1985) and Deardorff and Stern (1986), though the model by Deardorff and Stern is not in the general equilibrium framework. Analyses generally include unilateral and multilateral cutting of tariffs. Models have also been constructed to study the impact of non-tariff barriers such as voluntary export restrictions (VERs) and quantity restrictions (QRs). deMelo and Tarr (1992) study the efficiency costs of quotas, capture of quota rents, costs of protection under imperfect competition to name a few. Apart from these issues, impacts of trade liberalisation on agriculture has also been a focus of study. Studies of this kind are Fehr and Wiegard (1996) and Guzel and Kulshreshtha (1995). A survey of GE models for taxation and trade is given in Shoven and Whalley (1984).

Resource Economics Modellers have attempted to study the impact of shocks to price of oil on the long term growth in the economy, given the fact that oil is one of the important sources of energy. Hence any policy decision involving energy inputs will have an impact on prices, output, consumption and welfare. Since general equilibrium models are best equipped to study the complex interactions in any economy, they were also used to study energy policy issues. The earliest study was done by Hudson and Jorgenson (1974) after the first oil shock. Since then many other studies have been done analysing energy issues. Borges and Goulder (1984) studied the impact of higher energy prices on long-term growth. The production structure used is *KLEM* allowing for substitutability between various energy inputs and capital.

Increasing awareness about the potential impacts of emissions of greenhouse gases has prompted researchers to analyse the economic impacts of policies aimed to reduce greenhouse gas emissions. The main focus of greenhouse gas reduction has been CO_2, which is a global pollutant. Various economic instruments proposed to reduce CO_2 emissions, such as carbon taxes, taxes on energy content of fuels and taxes on use of fuels have been analysed by Jorgenson and Wilcoxen (1990) for the US economy. For a survey of GE models related to energy and environment issues refer to Bhattacharya (1996).

Development Economics Rapid growth and structural changes in the 1970s were unable to reduce poverty, with little or no benefits reaching a large strata of low income people. As a result GE models for developing economies focussed primarily on income distribution issues and policy prescriptions were designed with an aim to alleviate poverty and reduce income disparity. The first attempt was by Adelman and Robinson (1978) for Korea. Less developed countries also faced a paucity of foreign exchange reserves and were highly susceptible to external shocks. After the first oil shock in the 1970s GE models were built to analyse these shocks and the corresponding structural adjustments. These models were developed under the auspices of the World Bank and follow its tradition. An excellent reference is given by Bandara (1991) and Decaluwé and Martens (1988).

Agriculture Economics Perhaps this section is tautological as many general equilibrium models have been built to analyse issues related to agriculture like trade liberalisation. However this classification has been earmarked to outline some of the models in literature which explicitly model agricultural production within the general equilibrium framework. These models have an explicit agricultural production sub model and are used to analyse the policy issues like operation of buffer stocks, procurement, public distribution system, input subsidies, terms of trade and agricultural trade liberalisation to name a few. The production of agricultural commodities is based on physical area allocated, the number of times the crops are harvested per year, fertilizer input, type of seed (local or high yield) and area allotted to each type, irrigation, investment in irrigation in previous periods and relative prices of crops in the earlier period. An important contribution using this approach is Narayana, Parikh, and Srinivasan (1991) and the models built under the International Institute of Applied Systems Analysis (IIASA) food and agriculture programme. They built a sequentially dynamic model to analyse various agriculture policies incorporating 9 agriculture and allied sectors and 1 non-agriculture sector. Storm (1993) is another study that accounts for the short and medium term impacts of agriculture policies on sectoral growth rates, inflation, deficit, balance of payments and income distribution. The model by Keyzer (1990) studies the inter-linkages between agriculture and non-agriculture sectors for Indonesia. The model has two types of sectors. The input–output (IO) sectors which can increase outputs within limits and have mark-up pricing. The non-IO sectors which have fixed production and work with a lag of one year. Price clears the markets for these sectors. There are multiple technologies to produce some of the goods. The agriculture sectors are further divided based on type of products, investment and technology along with different land types.

Production Structure

The production structure plays an important role in determining the type of results and has implications for solution strategy.

Constant Returns to Scale   This assumption is the most widely used in general equilibrium models. It also helps in reducing the dimensionality of the problem. Product prices are determined from factor prices through unit cost functions.

Increasing Returns to Scale   With the emergence of "new" trade theory which analyses trade on the basis of imperfect competition, increasing returns to scale has become an important aspect of general equilibrium models analysing trade. Incorporating increasing returns however comes at a price of increased dimensionality. The prices are no longer equal to unit costs but also depend on the level of output. The other reason to model increasing returns for trade models is to assess whether this assumption results in larger welfare changes as opposed to the constant returns case and enquire into the probable causes of these type of results. The seminal paper by Harris (1984) showed large gains by incorporating increasing returns. Since then there have been various studies for the developed countries with one exception for Cameroon a developing country by Devarajan and Rodrik (1989). The result has been mixed with some studies Harrison, Rutherford, and Tarr (1997), deMelo and Tarr (1992) showing marginal welfare changes between increasing and constant returns to scale. Norman (1990) used numerical model experiments to compare various modelling assumptions and found that increasing returns plays an important role in welfare levels. Similar results of large welfare changes have been observed for Spain by Roland-Holst, Polo, and Sancho (1995).

Sunk Costs   Larger magnitudes of welfare changes with models of increasing returns have been attributed to several factors like the pricing hypothesis, elasticities of demand, product differentiation and perfectly mobile fixed costs. Mercenier and Schmitt (1996) have attributed the high welfare changes to the recoverable nature of fixed costs. They find that with sunk costs the gains or losses are not magnified while incorporating increasing returns. This is because sunk costs act as exit barriers and firms will continue to stay in the market despite below market level returns. With recoverable nature of fixed costs, the firms would exit allowing the remaining firms in the market to increase output while travelling down the average cost curves, thus achieving efficiency gains. These efficiency gains are not possible with sunk costs and hence a lower level of welfare changes.

Solution Methods

General equilibrium models possess a rigourous structure derived from sound microeconomics, usually optimising the behaviour of agents in an economy to analyse economy wide impacts of exogenous shocks on complex interactions in the economy in a tractable and coherent way. They are not built for the purpose of forecasting and are generally concerned with the impact on welfare of various policies. Putting it succinctly, a general equilibrium modeller is primarily concerned with the amount of change a particular shock or policy will induce in the system. The absolute amount of change, though important, is not as important as the direction of change in which the system moves due to external forces. Thus, the fundamental need to investigate the direction of change has led researchers to apply various methods to achieving this end.

In mathematical and computational terms, any general equilibrium model involves the solution of n number of simultaneous non-linear equations in n variables. Due to Walras' law, one equation becomes redundant, and to determine the solution to the system another equation is added to determine one price known as the numéraire. This, however, does not change the mathematical or computational structure of the problem. Thus, putting in mathematical notation any general equilibrium problem seeks the solution to

$$F(X) = 0 \qquad (2.1)$$

where X is a vector of endogenous variables. The various methods of solution are outlined below.

The Linearisation Approach In this approach,[1] a solution is sought for a system of equations as in equation (2.1), where X is a vector of dimension n and the function F in general, is a vector function of dimension m. Here n may exceed the number of equations m. The vector function F is assumed to be differentiable. In the above system when the number of equations m is less than the number of variables n, there are $n - m$ variables, which can be made exogenous to solve for the m endogenous variables. The linearisation approach involves the

---

[1] This paragraph follows Chapter 3 in Dixon, Parmenter, Powell, and Wilcoxen (1992).

transformation of equation (2.1) into

$$A(X)x = 0 \tag{2.2}$$

where $A(X)$ is an $m \times n$ matrix whose entries are derived from X and x is an n vector of changes in either percentage or logarithmic forms.

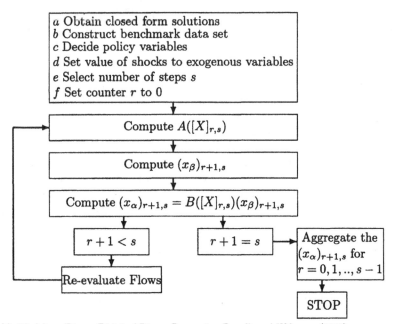

Modified from Figure E3.8.1 of Dixon, Parmenter, Powell, and Wilcoxen (1992)

Figure 2.1: **Solution Strategy using Linearisation Approach**

The entries in $A(X)$ are evaluated at the initial values of X, namely X^I. To evaluate the impact of changes on the m endogenous variables due to changes in $n - m$ exogenous variables, equation (2.2) is reformulated as

$$A_\alpha(X^I)x_\alpha + A_\beta(X^I)x_\beta = 0 \tag{2.3}$$

where x_α are the changes in the m endogenous variables required to be evaluated and x_β are the changes in the $n - m$ exogenous variables. The above equation is solved for x_α in terms of x_β Thus

$$x_\alpha = -A_\alpha^{-1}(X^I)A_\beta(X^I)x_\beta = B(X^I)x_\beta \tag{2.4}$$

In the above equation $-A_\alpha^{-1}(X^I)$ is assumed to exist and is evaluated at the initial values of X. The disadvantage of this method is that it is suitable for only small changes in exogenous variables and introduces large errors when the system is subjected to large shocks. The advantages are that very large scale general equilibrium models can be constructed and solved using the above approach. The linearisation errors mentioned above can be reduced to a major extent by performing the procedure outlined in equation (2.4) in a multi step fashion rather than in a single step. Thus at each step the matrices A_α and A_β are evaluated by using values of X obtained in the previous iteration. Similarly, the vector of exogenous changes x_β is also evaluated at each step based on the value in the previous step.

To solve general equilibrium models, first the closed form solutions to the agents optimisation problem are obtained. These sets of equations are then converted to percentage-change form depending on whether they involve products, exponents or sums of variables. This percentage-change is then arranged in the form as depicted in equation (2.1). The iterative structure of the linearisation approach is shown in Figure 2.1.

The Simultaneous Equations Approach   This method of solution of general equilibrium problems was pioneered by Scarf (1984) using the concept of the fixed point. Using Shashkin (1991), a fixed point can be explained briefly as follows. Consider an equation in a single variable x of the form

$$f(x) = 0 \qquad (2.5)$$

over the interval $[a, b]$. The objective is to find x such that it satisfies the above equation. The above equation can also be written as

$$\lambda f(x) + x = x \qquad (2.6)$$

where $\lambda \neq 0$. Let $\lambda f(x) + x = F(x)$. Thus the above equation simplifies to

$$F(x) = x \qquad (2.7)$$

Here λ is chosen such that $F(x) \in [a, b]$. If x_0 is a solution such that it stays where it is under the transformation and is termed as a fixed point. If a differentiable function is shown to map onto itself over the relevant range of importance it is said to possess a fixed point, which is a solution to the problem.

To solve the general equilibrium system modellers always try to reduce the dimensionality of the system. Mostly the approach is to reduce the system to a set of non-linear equations in factor prices. Using the constant returns to scale technology, the commodity prices are independent of the output and can be solely determined from the factor prices. The solution strategy using a simultaneous equation approach is illustrated below.

In Figure 2.2 the most important part is the algorithm used to solve the system. There are three types of algorithms.

1. Fixed point algorithms pioneered by Scarf (1984), with modifications by Merrill and van der Laan and Talman. These are explained in Shoven and

Whalley (1992). The advantage is that these methods are guaranteed to converge but are very slow in convergence.

2. Newton methods which use the Jacobian of excess demand functions to update prices. Care has to be taken that the Jacobian is non-singular near the solution. It has a limitation that it is not guaranteed to converge, however this has rarely been a problem in practice. This method has been used by Dervis, deMelo, and Robinson (1982).

3. Tatonnement method which uses the Gauss–Seidel algorithm. Various methodologies for solution of general equilibrium models are outlined in Manne (1985).

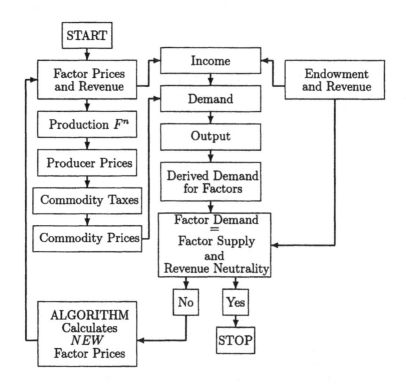

Figure 2.2: **Solution Strategy using Simultaneous Equation Approach**

The Mathematical Programming Approach   This method of solution is based on the paper by Negishi (1960) wherein a weighted utility function is maximised subject to the budget constraints and a minimum feasible utility level, with the sum of the weights normalised to unity. It has been proved that non-negative welfare weights exist which satisfy the constraints such that a competitive equilibrium is obtained. Mathematically one can represent the Negishi format as maximise welfare

$$W = \max \; \sum_i \alpha_i U_i(x_i) \tag{2.8}$$

$x_i \geq 0, \; y_j, i = 1, ..., m, \; j = 1, ..., n \;\; \sum_i \alpha_i = 1$
subject to

$$\sum_i x_i = \sum_j y_j + \sum_i \omega_i \quad y_j \in Y_j \tag{2.9}$$

where x_i is the consumption vector, ω_i is the endowment vector of the ith agent and y_j is the output of the jth firm. Different mathematical programming formats along with their merits are given in Gunning and Keyzer (1993) and Ginsburgh and Keyzer (1997).

For illustration purposes an example from Dixon (1991) is used. Consider an economy with k consumers indexed $1, ..., r$, in which an equilibrium is a nonnegative vector of prices p and outputs X with consumption $c(k)$ and income $Y(k)$ such that $c(k), k = 1, ..., r$ maximises

$$U(c[k]) \tag{2.10}$$

subject to

$$p'c[k] = Y[k] \tag{2.11}$$

demand is less than or equal to supply

$$\sum_{k=1}^{r} c[k] \leq \sum_{k=1}^{r} z[k] + Ax \tag{2.12}$$

and any commodity in excess supply has zero price

$$p'\left[\sum_{k=1}^{r} c[k] - \sum_{k=1}^{r} z[k] - Ax\right] = 0 \tag{2.13}$$

No activity is operated at positive profits

$$p'A \leq= 0 \tag{2.14}$$

and any activity involving losses is operated at zero level

$$p'Ax = 0 \tag{2.15}$$

setting up of the numéraire

$$p'z(1) = 1 \tag{2.16}$$

$$p'z(k) = Y[k], \quad k = 1, ..., r \tag{2.17}$$

The mechanics of the solution process for one consumer can be explained as follows. Let the utility function be of a linear form $U[k] = a\gamma$, where a is a $n \times h$ matrix of n goods and h vectors of preferences. Each of the h preference vectors can be consumed in proportion γ, where γ is a vector of h variables. The γs will be non-negative with at least one positive value. The objective is to find values of γ which will maximise the utility function. The process of maximising utility for an economy with linear technology is enumerated below.

1. Since the technology is linear with one factor of production, the no profit condition coupled with the numéraire determine the prices of the n goods and one factor.

2. With the prices the income can be calculated, since factor endowments are exogenous.

3. Maximise the h vector γ subject to the income and $a\gamma = c$ constraints to obtain γs.

4. From the values of γ the consumption vector c is calculated.

5. Aggregating individual consumption vectors and using supply = demand equation calculate outputs of goods.

For the multiple consumer case, the solution strategy is similar. The problem to be tackled is as follows. Maximise the utility of one consumer subject to the utility levels of the remaining (in this case) $r - 1$ consumers. The program will iterate on the utility level of the remaining consumers from iteration to iteration, but within each iteration the utility level of the $r - 1$ consumers will be fixed. The equilibrium will be found when the utility level of the $r - 1$ consumers does not change beyond some iteration, i.e. $U^{[s-1]} = U^{[s]}$, where s is the iteration counter.

Public Finance

The analysis of welfare effects of different tax policies falls under the domain of public finance. It is important to survey the theoretical and empirical literature in the field to justify the need for the study and highlight the strength and weaknesses of the approach. This section briefly describes the public finance literature.[2]

Introduction

The objective of every government is to maximise welfare by implementing policies that are least distortional or are efficient (least welfare loss) and result in a

---

[2]The structure of this section is based on the 2 volumes on public finance by Atkinson (1991).

more desirable distribution of income. The first welfare theorem states that if a competitive market allocation of goods is in equilibrium it is Pareto optimal. The second welfare theorem states that if transfers can be mobilised, distributional objectives can be achieved through a competitive market equilibrium and the resulting equilibrium will be Pareto efficient, though not necessarily Pareto superior to the earlier one. It is the second welfare theorem that plays a pivotal role in the justification of government intervention and creates the need to study public finance.

The government, to achieve its objectives of distribution and efficiency, is involved in taxation and transfers. The very act of taxation leads to distortions of behaviour of agents and may have an impact on household behaviour, cost of capital for firms, differential tax burden on different firms and households and the provision of public goods. Evaluation of these effects falls in the category of positive economics which deals with the quantification of policy impacts. On the normative or prescriptive side one is concerned with optimal levels of taxation, process of tax reform, national debt, macroeconomic fiscal policy, public choice and public spending. Some of these will now be dealt in brief.

Taxation and Household Behaviour

Households take decisions on consumption, savings and labour supply.[3] They also decide the riskiness of the portfolio of assets they want to hold. All these decisions of the households are distorted by taxation. In theory these issues have been tackled by using either two-period models or multi-period models. The results obtained from two-period models with perfect capital markets state that the consumption will unambiguously fall with a rise in price of second period consumption. However, the effect of first period consumption depends on the demand functions. In the presence of wage or expenditure taxes, there is only a pure income effect as opposed to tax on interest income, which increases the price of second period consumption. Since the second period consumption is financed out of saving in period one, savings falls. Incorporating labour supply decisions affects the income and therefore consumption and savings. Taxation of labour income implies that the price of leisure has increased, affecting the labour supply. The final effects on consumption and savings decisions with variable labour supply in presence of taxation are too complex to be tackled by theoretical models.

Risk is another problem to be tackled by households. How much to hold in a risky asset has an impact on household income and capital accumulation in the economy. Taxation affects risk taking in two ways. If losses can be offset against income then the tax liability will be reduced by the extent of loss and will encourage risk taking. The other is the expected income due to taxes on the risky asset. The tax will cause the household to hold more of the risky asset to achieve the same level of income as compared to the no tax case. However the underlying behaviour of households to risk is important and is characterised by the utility function. The portfolio theory is characterised with a risk averse

---

[3]This subsection follows Atkinson and Stiglitz (1987).

investor and two assets, one risk free and the other risky. The amount of risky asset in the portfolio will directly depend on the wealth elasticity of demand for the risky asset. Wealth taxation leads to a fall in the wealth and the proportion of risky asset held depends on the wealth elasticity.

Taxation and the Firm

Taxation affects the investment decision of firms and as per theory is expected to have substantial effects on the cost and structure of capital. Tax deductability of bond financing should bias the firm to raise its funds via debt rather than equity. However, corporate financial structure has not been dramatically altered by taxation policies with both debt and equity existing as a source of funds. Stiglitz (1973) investigates the effect of taxation on corporate financial policy and the cost of capital. For this purpose he uses a multi-period model of T time periods with a representative consumer. In the last period the consumer either consumes the proceeds of the investment or leaves a bequest. This is an outcome of a sequence of investment decisions for which financial policy of funding investment has to be decided on both personal and firm account. The point of the analysis is that the debt equity choice of the firm depends on the level of personal and corporate taxation. A high debt policy is useful if the corporate tax rate is higher than the personal tax rate. Also it is not useful to borrow and invest in equity as tax rates on dividends and residual capital gains tax result in lower savings than bond financing.

Incidence of Taxation

Apart from minimising welfare loss due to imposition of taxes, the government is also concerned with the incidence of taxation. The incidence is important to study as tax affects the price of factors which in turn determine income and welfare. The important point from the policy perspective is whether every agent is able to shift the tax forward or has to bear a part of the burden. This has allocative and dynamic effects on the economy. A seminal contribution by Harberger (1962) gave an impetus to the analysis of incidence of taxation in a general equilibrium framework. He analysed the impact of capital income tax on the corporate sector in the US. The point is that despite attempts of producers to pass the tax forward, the burden is borne by factors depending on the demand schedule and production functions. The short coming of this analysis was that it was restricted to linear changes. This was relaxed by Shoven and Whalley (1972), who built a multi-sector model for the US economy analysing the impact of capital income taxation. The highlight was the use of Scarf's algorithm to solve the set of equilibrium prices. The above analyses neglected the effects of taxation on savings as they were static in behaviour. However savings is an important aspect in that it affects capital accumulation and growth of the economy. The models which included dynamics restricted themselves to a two period economy, with income in period one leading to consumption and saving. The second period involved dis-saving for consumption. In this case the elasticity of savings with respect to interest rate is equivalent to the elasticity of substitution between present and future consumption. Summers (1972) addresses this issue in a life-cycle growth model. The model maximises the discounted value of a time invariant utility function subject to the discounted value of income from labour. This results in a variable propensity to save out of labour income and zero propensity to save out of capital income. The equivalence of wage and consumption taxation in the two-period model does not hold in this case. In the life-cycle model, consumption taxation implies more saving in the earlier periods, to account for higher value of consumption in later years as compared to wage taxation.

Optimal Taxation

The government's aim to achieve a more desirable distribution compels it to undertake taxation. Lump sum taxes exhibit the least distortional effects but may not be feasible due to practical problems. This leads to the residual alternative of taxing goods and services. The problem of optimal taxation can be stated as the level of taxes on commodities required to raise a given revenue with minimum welfare loss. Samuelson (1986) while formulating the theory of optimal taxation maximised a social welfare function to find prices for a given level of government consumption. The point to note is that policy makers often neglect the cross price effects on which the magnitude of welfare loss is dependent. He also points to the fact that in a long run formulation of the problem, incorporating all commodities at all points of time, income taxes need not give rise to a larger welfare loss as compared to commodity taxes.

In another classic paper, Diamond and Mirlees (1971) demonstrate the desirability of production efficiency in the public sector despite the presence of a non Pareto optimal outcome due to commodity and income taxes. The argument is extended for production with intermediate goods and they advocate the presence of taxes on final consumption and not on intermediate goods. With external economies the tax on final consumption of imported goods should be equal to taxes on domestic goods with the absence of tariffs.

The discussion so far has concentrated on the optimality of commodity taxes. However progressive income taxation is an important policy variable at the disposal of the government to achieve the requisite income distribution. Mirlees (1971) formulates optimal income taxation as an optimal control problem with utility composed of consumption and labour inputs. The economy has labour of different ability and the consumer selects the control variable of labour to maximise the state variable of utility from consumption. The conclusions are that high marginal rates are not justified even from the equity viewpoint and are sensitive to the skill levels and labour leisure preferences. However, it neglects to account for capital income, which is a major source of wealth of the rich and concentrates solely on labour. The policy conclusion is that commodity taxes along with income tax are needed to improve welfare.

The above mentioned papers dealt with either commodity or direct taxes in isolation. Atkinson and Stiglitz (1976) have analysed this issue in the presence of both direct and indirect taxation with labour being the only source of income. The conclusion is that income tax is the best tax on efficiency grounds and with a general income tax and a separability between goods and labour, the need for indirect taxes does not arise. However the main point to note from the above discussion is a quote from their article, "the theory may be more useful in illuminating the structure of the argument than in providing definite answers to policy issues".

Theory of Tax Reform

The previous section on optimal taxation dealt with the theoretical arguments about the most efficient tax system. In reality, planners cannot design a tax system from scratch. They have to be contented with modifications to the existing structure and are therefore involved in tax reform and not tax design. Feldstein (1976) deals with the various social choice criteria for optimal tax reform and discusses the pros and cons of the utilitarian versus egalitarian principles.[4] The point for policy makers is that tax reform is an ongoing process with dynamic effects and the efficacy of the current tax policy depends on the effect on behaviour and the subjective probabilities for other changes in the future. An example for the Indian case is the amnesty granted to people who default on their income taxes. The voluntary disclosure scheme followed by successive governments creates an impression that the policy will be followed in the future and makes the exercise ineffective. Optimal tax reforms have to resolve the dichotomy between postponement of taxation versus reduction in tax rates and balancing efficiency and horizontal equity. Postponement gives an opportunity to agents to adjust their behaviour to the impending change and reduces uncertainty and arbitrary losses to consumers. Policy decisions should be taken by accounting for the general equilibrium effects and postponement is better than partial reforms.

Policy makers have to choose between direct and indirect taxes for raising revenues such that the welfare gain(loss) is maximised(minimised). Corlett and Hague (1953) discuss the complementarity and excess burden of taxation by accounting for consumption and leisure in the utility function. The analysis is restricted to small changes around the base case satisfying revenue neutrality. The recommendation is that any change from direct to indirect taxes, which makes the consumer work harder, will take the consumer to a higher indifference curve. This result is a conclusion from the complementarity of leisure and consumption goods. For policy makers the point to note is that direct taxes are better on the assumption of constant supply of labour. However when labour–leisure choice is taken into account the labour supply varies implying income varies. Lower tax rates imply higher incomes which lead to increased inequity.

Pure theory needs to be tested in practice. King (1983) outlines a methodology to simulate the efficiency and distributional aspects of tax reform using

---

[4]Utilitarian approach maximises a social welfare function which may lead to outcomes of increased income at a greater inequality. Egalitarian principle disallows any increase in inequality at the cost of increased income.

empirical data. A reform is defined as a mapping from a vector of old prices and income to a vector of new prices and income. To account for non-linear budget constraints the concept of virtual prices[5] is used. The simulations satisfy revenue neutrality. To measure the effect of reforms the concept of equivalent or compensating variation is used. Equivalent variation is the amount of income that has to be taken away(given) for a welfare gain(loss) to keep the consumer at the same level of utility at old prices. Compensating variation is amount of income to be given away(taken) for a welfare gain(loss) to keep the consumer at the same utility level at new prices. However, the main point to note is that these welfare measures are based on parameters that are statistically estimated. Since they are not accurately known the confidence intervals for welfare gains have to be evaluated.

It is often the case that private and social costs of commodities are different. To improve welfare it may be necessary to impose quotas (+ve if social costs > private costs and -ve if vice versa) to achieve an optimal consumption of commodities.Guesnerie and Roberts (1984) evaluate the policy tools and quantity controls to achieve this end. The policy prescriptions which emerge are that positive quotas have to be implemented on goods when price changes cannot be accompanied with appropriate income change. Also, if prices are constrained while incomes are not, quotas are desirable. This is the case with public distribution system where food grains are available at subsidised price with positive quotas. The point to note is that quotas are desirable and welfare improving in a second best world with prior existence of distortions.

National Debt

Governments run deficits which implies they accumulate debt. The question then arises whether public debt is a burden to society. Tobin (1965) reviews the various views on the burden of public debt. The original view was that no burden exists because the liabilities can be transferred ad infinitum to the future generations. Moreover this has to be met by tax payments to bond holders and implies a transfer form one set of agents to another. The other view that a burden exists uses the argument that taxes per se are a burden and debt just postpones the burden to future generations. This view has the shortcoming that it accounts for the burden due to taxes but fails to take into account the burden due to opportunity costs of lack of funds to the private sector. Modigliani (1961) propagates the view that burden exists and is distortional in nature, with debt affecting investment and taxes affecting consumption. The implicit assumption in this view is that people have fixed shares allotted to saving and consumption and if a larger part is devoted to debt a smaller part is invested for capital formation. The third view is that burden exists due to the excess consumption by the older generation in retirement by selling government paper leaving the younger generation to save.

---

[5]For details refer Neary and Roberts (1980).

Diamond (1965) analyses the role of debt in a neoclassical growth model and is restricted to differential incidence wherein substitution of debt for tax finance is studied for a given level of government expenditure. The economy is assumed to be on the golden rule of expansion where the marginal product of capital is equal to the growth rate. The debt is also assumed to grow at the same rate. Two types of debt are considered, namely internal and external, both playing the role of financing expenditure not covered by taxes. Internal debt implies citizens hold government paper in their portfolios instead of other physical assets as opposed to foreigners holding it in case of external debt. Thus, internal debt lowers physical debt and increases interest debt.

Do people perceive debt to increase wealth or does Ricardian equivalence hold is the objective of Barro (1974). He investigates the effect of finite lives on the value of bonds and taxes, the two instruments to cover deficit in absence of money. The model is an overlapping generations one with the utility of each generation being dependent on consumption in the two periods of life plus the utility of the next generation. Each generation when young accumulates assets out of labour income and bequests from the previous generation and spends them in the next period on consumption and bequests to the next generation. As long as this inter-generational transfer takes place, the consumption values remain unchanged with one generation paying of the principal of debt by taxes and the previous generations paying off the interest.

International Trade

With the emergence of trade blocks and the liberalisation programme that the government has embarked upon, it is interesting to study the theory of trade. Whether the results suggested by theory hold in practice and the theory is consistent in recommending policy decisions remain to be seen. The theory of trade is a subset of microeconomic theory of markets separated by international markets. Here exchange and transfers play a role. What gains are to be achieved by indulging in trade and does market structure affect the outcome? Can trade restrictions be beneficial for the home country? Is the trade policy an independent decision by the government or there is a political process behind it? If so what drives this process? Literature has explored these questions and each of which will be dealt with in brief.[6]

International Exchange

Exchange plays a central role in trade theory and every country strives to improve its terms of trade with its trading partners. The terms of trade are affected by exogenous policy decisions like tariffs, quotas, transfers.

The classical system, as covered by Mundell (1968), deals with the balance of payments problem when an economy is subjected to exogenous shocks, using

---

[6]The structure of this section is based on one of the 2 volumes on international trade by Neary (1995).

a comparative statics approach. For the system to be stable the elasticity of demand for imports has to be greater than the marginal propensity to import. Exogenous policy shocks, like transfer from one country to another, affect the terms of trade. The impacts of terms of trade will be smaller the larger the price elasticity of demand for imports of the country receiving aid. In order to pay back the transfer a fall in terms of trade to achieve balance of payments equilibrium has an effect on the real income and is known as the transfer burden. The real income of a country will be smaller, the larger the propensity to import.

Endogenous changes like productivity increase affect the terms of trade and a country can be worse of due to it. This is primarily due to the negative income effect of changes in relative prices being greater than the positive effect of increased output.

The discussion was restricted to a two-country problem. However, if more than two countries participate in trade and there is a transfer from one country to another, a paradoxical outcome of donor country gaining and recipient country losing is possible. This is proved by Yano (1983) under the presence of a third country whose export supply determines the available resources to the two countries and the volume of trade between the two. Dixit (1983) generalises this result to a multicountry case with the paradoxical result being dependent on the patterns of trade and aid of the recipient country being different with different countries.

Trade Policy and Gains From Trade

Are there many benefits from indulging in trade and does the market structure play a role in these benefits are questions that have to be addressed. If trade offers benefits no matter what the market structure, then an inward looking policy of import substitution in not the right one. Gains from trade under perfect competition, oligopoly and monopolistic competition with increasing returns will each be assessed in brief.

Trade Policy in Competitive General Equilibrium

Ohyama (1972) analyses the benefits of trade in a general equilibrium context. He finds it beneficial to trade with or without tariffs provided the tariffs are self-financing (net tariff revenues are non negative). Any trade that involves a negative income transfer is welfare reducing compared to the autarkic state. Moreover, the larger the deviation of international prices from the domestic one in autarky, the more beneficial it is to trade.

From the policy perspective it is important to know what tool can be used to better the terms of trade and welfare. One of the most commonly used is tariffs with the resultant revenue being distributed. The important result pointed out by Dixit and Norman (1972) is that it is beneficial not to impose tariffs. This transforms into lower producer prices, and hence consumer prices, so improving welfare. There is also an incentive for the people to manipulate their behaviour if the tariff generated revenue is to be distributed in a lump sum manner. By manipulating behaviour if a subset of agents can acquire rents, these rents will not be distributed in a lump-sum manner. Hence there is an incentive for producers to lobby for higher tariffs.

Trade Policy in Oligopoly

Market structure and industrial organisation has an important impact on welfare. This becomes important in trade issues as pricing behaviour of firms in domestic and international markets depends on the market structure. In the earlier section trade policy was discussed with perfectly competitive markets, an assumption not always true. Brander and Spencer (1985) analyse export subsidies in an oligopolistic market existing in a third country with two countries supplying goods to that market. The result that emerges is export subsidies are welfare improving as they enable the firm getting the subsidy to capture a larger share of the foreign market and increase profits due to the deviation of price cost margins existing as a virtue of oligopolistic markets. This results in a worsening of the terms of trade. With both governments involved in granting subsidies, the profits of both firms will decline, but will still generate welfare gains. Eaton and Grossman (1986) study the same problem in a more general setting using a conjectural variation approach, along with extensions incorporating entry and domestic consumption. With Cournot conjectures (the rival firm does not change quantity when the home firm does) an optimal export subsidy can improve home profits, reduce world prices and improve welfare. With Bertrand conjectures (rival firm does not change price when home firm does) as export tax will increase profits, raise world price and lower welfare. With consistent conjectures the optimal policy is neither taxes nor subsidies. When both governments try to do the same by offering subsidies to their respective firms, with Cournot conjectures it will decrease profits and welfare falls due to price rise as neither government will offer subsidies. With Bertrand conjectures both governments will tax so that price rises and welfare falls. In the presence of domestic consumption the policy recommendations are not trivial. Production subsidies are desired to increase output as marginal cost of production and marginal value of consumption differ due to market structure. If conjectures are Bertrand, the optimal policy is laissez faire.

Trade Policy with Entry, Monopolistic Competition and Increasing Returns

The above discussion restricted itself to an oligopolistic market structure where profits could be made and no entry took place to drive profits to zero. Venables (1985) analyses trade policy for identical products with imperfect competition by accounting for entry by firms. Trade is better than autarky as entry would drive profits to zero and improve welfare. From an industrial organisation view point this would lower price by lowering price marginal cost differential. With technical progress a country stands to gain by increasing output and market share at the cost of other country. The main assumption here is that entry takes place at an efficient scale. Horstmann and Markusen (1986) analyse the effect of inefficient entry on protection policy. This is important from the policy view point because the policy may not achieve its goals due to the type of competition. The model uses two imperfectly substitutable products. If positive profits exist, entry drives them to zero. Tariffs on trade may then be welfare reducing if inefficient entry occurs if firms are forced to move up on their average cost curves, driving price higher. With export subsidies also the same can take place with the added effect of worsening of the terms of trade.

Quantitative Trade Restrictions

In order to improve terms of trade, governments often resort to instruments such as tariffs, quotas or negotiate voluntary export restrictions (VERs). Neary (1988) investigates the welfare impacts of these instruments in the presence and absence of international capital mobility. The outcome is that welfare impacts of quotas lie between those from tariffs and VERs under exogenous shocks. Tariffs raise cost of low priced imports and increase domestic output at higher price, thus lowering welfare. As opposed to this extra domestic output lowers quota rents, which are a transfer between different agents thus not affecting welfare. In case of VERs, the rents accrue to foreigners and any policy that reduces rents to them is welfare improving.

Tariffs generate revenues due to the disparity between domestic and imported prices while quotas generate revenues by premia paid due to restricted supply of imports. In case of perfect competition it is easy to determine a tariff level that will generate import demand equal to a particular quota level and vice versa. This implies that tariffs and quotas are equivalent. Whether this conclusion holds under all market structures was investigated by Bhagwati (1965). The result was that the two are not equivalent if monopoly markets exist in either domestic production or imports. An important implication for policy is that quotas are effective in setting only an upper limit on the level of imports. The other point to note is the mechanism in which the quotas are allocated. If auction of quotas leads to a monopoly situation it will have different implications for import demand than when quotas are allocated to a large number of agents.

The remaining policy instrument to curtail imports is to negotiate voluntary export restrictions (VERs). Harris (1985) analyses why VERs are voluntary and foreign firms choose to restrict their output to a particular level. The reason for this behaviour is the change in market structure from a perfect competitive case to a price setter (domestic firm), price follower (foreign firm) case. This holds under the imperfect substitutability of domestic and foreign goods. The outcome is that domestic firms raise price to maximise profits and the foreign firms also do the same with the detrimental effect of same imports at a higher price. If the own price elasticity of demand is quite high it might also lead to a fall in the share domestic output. From the policy perspective VERs is not the best form of restricting imports and an undesirable form of protection.

Political Economy of Trade Policy

As mentioned before, tariffs, quotas and VERs are used to restrict imports. However, what is the process that determines the decision to use these tools. If these instruments lead to welfare loss, why and how are these instruments used? Kreuger (1974) analyses the political economy of rent seeking due to quantitative restrictions. The welfare loss as estimated equals the welfare loss from tariffs plus that due to rent seeking. The reason being, a part of society is excluded from receiving rents resulting in welfare loss for which resources were spent to acquire these rents. This strong result is negated by Bhagwati and Srinivasan (1980) who agree that though lobbying for rent goes on their share in private hands is small and largely lies with the state. An example is the canalised imports in India, where the government is the monopoly importer. The other point assumed by Kreuger is that lobbying goes on only for quotas and reverse lobbying for tariffs and the subsequent rents from it are ignored. Another paradoxical result of improving welfare due to rent seeking depends on the shadow price of the factor used for the purpose of seeking rents. Findlay and Wellisz (1982) point out that a factor which has a negative social opportunity cost if used to seek rents will generate positive welfare. However if a factor with positive social cost is used the welfare will fall, as happens in Kreuger's model. The other major point is, despite low tariff levels, if a major part of a factor with positive social cost is used it leads to welfare losses.

Choice of Models

To achieve the goal it was decided to implement computable general equilibrium models of the Indian economy, which had all the major flavours of the Indian tax and tariff system without digressing unnecessarily in the minutiae of tax structure at a cost which was not too prohibitive in terms of data collection, implementation and analysis.

The monograph includes two general equilibrium models, one analysing trade policies (cutting tariffs) and the other analysing tax policies (various indirect tax reforms). The two models were built separately as empirical counterparts to the theoretical developments in the trade and public finance literature. The other reason to build two separate models was the differential pace of developments on the external and internal fronts. The trade model only incorporates effects due to tariff cuts inevitable due to the WTO pact. The tax model analyses indirect tax reforms and potential tax reforms on the agenda, which have not been implemented.

In a pioneering general equilibrium study on India, Narayana, Parikh, and Srinivasan (1991) restrict themselves to a detailed analysis of the agricultural policy. They build a sequentially dynamic model to analyse various agriculture policies incorporating 9 agriculture and allied sectors and 1 non-agriculture sector. This model has an explicit agricultural production sub-model and is used to analyse the policy issues such as operation of buffer stocks, procurement and subsidies, to name a few. The production of agricultural commodities is based on physical area allocated, the number of times the crops are harvested per year, fertilizer input, type of seed (local or high yield) and area allotted to each type, irrigation, investment in irrigation in previous periods and relative prices of crops in the earlier period. Other notable models on India are by Taylor, Sarkar, and Rattso (1984) in which they analyse the macro economic effects of short term policy instruments in a 5 sector framework. DeJanvry and Subbarao (1986) analyse income distribution and sectoral growth effects of alternate agriculture policies using a 7 sector model. Sarkar and Panda (1991) investigate the effects of changes in foodgrain buffer stocks and prices and exchange rates using an 8 sector model. Storm (1993) is another study that accounts for the short and medium term impacts of agriculture policies on sectoral growth rates, inflation, deficit, balance of payments and income distribution. Mitra and Tendulkar (1986) analyse the impact of oil price shock and harvest failure on the economy with a 5 sector dynamic model for the period between 1973–74 to 1983–84. None of these models address tax or trade issues for the industrial sectors.

The choice of tax and trade models is elucidated in the perspective of the requirements of general equilibrium models. The successful interpretation of any policy depends on the ability of models to capture the underlying processes. Implementation of a model depends on three inputs, namely

1. availability of data

2. computation skills or packages to solve complex non-linear equations

3. the most important, the relevance of the underlying microstructure to the current state of the economy.

⸱Tax Models

In order to achieve objectives of equity and efficiency, the government is involved in taxation and transfers. The very act of taxation leads to distortions in behaviour of agents and has an impact on household behaviour, the behaviour of producers, the cost of capital for firms, the incidence of taxation and the provision of public goods. These fall in the category of positive economics which deals with the quantification of policy impacts. On the normative or prescriptive side, one has to deal with optimal taxation, the theory of tax reform, national debt, macroeconomic fiscal policy, public choice and public spending.

The computable general equilibrium models restricted themselves to differential tax incidence. The literature has grown from simple two-sector static models to multi-sector sequentially dynamic models to fully dynamic models of open economies. The fully dynamic models incorporate overlapping generations and dynamic optimisation behaviour of firms, with foundations in optimal control. They have a richer structure and are better suited to analyse issues such as deficits. However, the cost is much higher than that of sequentially dynamic models adopting static behaviour of producers. The reason being installation costs of capital which do not allow the exploitation of constant returns to scale to work in the realm of factor prices. This increases the dimensionality of the problem. Also there are two processes at work in these models. The outer is a solution to differential equations of a two-point boundary value problem to trace the path of the economy. The inner is the solution to each period's markets based on price expectations in the outer solution. Besides the computational requirements, the data requirements are also greater as more estimates of average q (value of the firm to the replacement price of capital), which is the basis of the dynamics in these models.

It was difficult to implement the fully dynamic models in the desired context for the following reasons. In India, manufacturing value added accounts for roughly 33% of the total value added. In the manufacturing sector alone approximately 50% is accounted by the unorganised sector. Thus, the relevance of the maximising the stock market value of firms is a little difficult to justify in the present context. Even if this point is to be overlooked, data availability is a major hurdle. Since the main aim is to analyse the tax system in some detail, the economy had to be somewhat disaggregated. This raises a dimensionality problem with the approach outlined above.

The next best solution was to incorporate limited dynamics. For this the structure of Ballard, Fullerton, Shoven, and Whalley (1985) was adopted. Here the producer behaviour is static while the consumer behaviour is dynamic with a choice of present and future consumption decisions in each period. The expectations are myopic and the economy is assumed to be on the balanced growth path with savings augmenting capital stock. This model has balanced trade with imports scaled to match exports. This was an inappropriate assumption in the Indian context and was relaxed to incorporate a trade deficit (kept constant across scenarios) with exchange rate as the clearing variable. This structure is widely applied for analysing the economies of the US, UK, Finland and the problem of multi-country VAT harmonisation in the EU.

Trade Models

The theory of trade primarily addresses the issues of gains from trade under different policy tools at the disposal of governments such as tariffs, quantity restrictions in the form of quotas or voluntary export restrictions or the option to be a part of a customs union. The modern trade theory has investigated the effects of industrial policy and market structure on decisions related to trade by governments. The industrial organisation approach has succeeded in explaining the discrepancies of welfare implications of neoclassical trade policy. It is therefore important to incorporate industrial organisation literature into an empirical analysis of trade policy. In the literature on general equilibrium modelling of trade issues either a single or a multi-country modelling is done. In single-country modelling, the imports and exports are parametrically modelled as opposed to multi-country modelling where the trade across all countries is balanced with total surplus equal to total deficit. This implies that it is more expensive and difficult to implement multi-country models. A comprehensive and unifying treatment of computable general equilibrium modelling of trade policy was done by deMelo and Tarr (1992). They analysed the welfare implications of the removal of voluntary export restrictions on steel and automobiles in the US economy under Increasing Returns to Scale (IRS) with perfect and imperfect competition. This model was chosen because of its harmonious balance between theoretical and empirical issues. Since the objective of the exercise was not to study the economic implications of India being part of a customs union like APEC, multi-country general equilibrium models were not considered.

Chapter 3
Tax and Trade Models

Overview of Model

This chapter explains the basic structure of the general equilibrium tax and trade model used in the monograph. The models with this basic structure are later extended to incorporate other modelling extensions. The chapter is outlined as follows. The description of the trade model and its extensions is followed by that of the tax model.

Sectoral Classification

For analysing the various tax and trade issues the economy is aggregated into 19 sectors, the details of which are given in Table B.1. This sectoral classification was chosen to achieve a compromise between the non-availability of data and econometric estimates and the policy issues at stake. From the taxation view point the disaggregation of industries is appropriate given the data availability. The services are all clubbed into one sector since the updated input–output table as supplied by the Planning Commission contains only one service sector. The presence of only one service sector is not detrimental to the analysis as there are no taxes levied on them. The agriculture sector is also combined into one as there are no major taxes levied. The data on various agricultural subsidies is also not available especially irrigation subsidy. The amount of subsidy on fertiliser both domestic and imported, however, is documented and fertiliser is a separate sector.

Notation

The model equations are described in the next two sections. The models follow the following format. There are N sectors, denoted by either i or j. Of the N sectors, m sectors are traded sectors and the remaining $N - m$ sectors are non-traded. NT refers to the set of non-traded sectors while T refers to traded sectors the union of both equals N. Exogenous parameters are shown by either Greek letters or uppercase Latin letters with bars over them. Variables are uppercase Latin letters with no bars over them.

Trade Model

The basic trade model is influenced by the work of deMelo and Tarr (1992). The model begins with perfect competition, and later introduces increasing returns to scale. The trade model does not deal with investment decisions nor the consumption decisions by the government and all final consumption is attributed to a *representative* consumer. In the model, the government is confined to collecting and distributing trade-related revenues and any surplus or deficit is adjusted by a lump-sum transfer or tax-payments from the consumer.

The basic model is used to analyse various trade related issues of cutting tariffs as required by the former GATT (General Agreement on Tariffs and Trade) or the new WTO (World Trade Organisation). India has had a history of levying very high tariffs partly to protect the domestic industry and partly to discourage imports which would have led to an unfavourable balance of payments position. Under the auspices of the WTO, India has to cut tariffs to international levels. *A priori* this implies an increase in the amount of imports. To keep the imports at a reasonable level one option is to allocate quotas which is also not permitted under the WTO rules. The other option is to negotiate voluntary export restrictions (VERs) with those countries with whom India has an adverse trade flow. Quotas and VERs serve the same purpose of restricting imports but has different impacts as far as accrual of rents due to restriction of imports go. In case of quotas the rents accrue to domestic agents while in case of VERs the rents are dependent on the market structure and may accrue to foreigners. Tariff reduction accompanied by devaluation can restrict imports and promote a more desirable pattern of imports. It will also encourage exports and can improve trade balance.

The Economic Agents

The model deals with unbalanced trade in the base case[1] with the real exchange rate being the equilibrating variable. The excess of imports over exports is financed from capital inflows from the *rest of the world (ROW)* which is kept constant in foreign currency. This prevents a free lunch from the *ROW*.

In the model producers maximise profits subject to a constant returns to scale (CRTS) technology. The technology is a Leontief technology with value added as a fixed proportion of the output. Given the technology and prices, the producers buy inputs to minimise costs. The representative consumer sells factor endowments in the market thus endogenously generating income. Given income and endogenous transfers, the consumer consumes various commodities based on the demand system. At any set of prices the consumer's income and expenditure are equal implying that Walras' law is satisfied. Thus only relative prices matter.

General equilibrium is achieved when both factor and product markets clear with the balance of trade at the benchmark in foreign currency. It is assumed that the economy is in equilibrium in the benchmark. The replication of the benchmark data set is realised by adjusting parameters in a process known as calibration.

---

[1]Base case assumes that the economy is in equilibrium before any policy shock is administered.

Specification of Producer and Consumer Behaviour

The functional structure used in the trade model is shown in Figure 3.1. The production process is a Leontief function between intermediates and value added. The value added is a Cobb–Douglas function of the primary factors of labour and capital. Each intermediate input is a Cobb–Douglas function of domestic and imported goods. More flexible functional forms (e.g. translog) can be included in principle. However the use of such forms requires the availability of estimates which are difficult to obtain and complicates calibration.

Consumption follows a Cobb–Douglas demand system. There are substitution possibilities between domestic and imported commodities within each good. A linear expenditure system (LES) could also be used but the parameters are not available in the literature for the sectoral classification in the model, nor are data available to estimate one.

The description of exogenous variables is given in Table 3.1 while that of the endogenous parameters is in Table 3.2

Equations of the Basic Trade Model

Production

Production is characterised by a two-level nesting structure (see Figure 3.1)

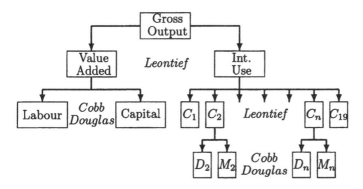

Figure 3.1: **Production Structure in Trade Model**

The top level is a Leontief input–output production function. At the top level, composite inputs (*IUse*) and primary factors (*Labour and Capital*) are combined in fixed proportion to produce output. At the second level each composite input $(C_1, .., C_n)$ is a Cobb–Douglas aggregate between domestic (D_i) and imported good (M_i). The inputs are combined to produce output (X_i) according to the following top level production function

$$X_i = \min\left[\frac{F_i(K_i, L_i)}{a_i^0}, \frac{Int_i^1}{a_i^1}, ..., \frac{Int_i^n}{a_i^n}\right] \tag{3.1}$$

where F_i is the function of primary factors in value added, $a_i^0, .., a_i^n$ is the coefficient of use of good $0, .., n$ per unit of good i.

Cost

The industry is assumed to minimise variable cost CV_i, which is the sum of primary costs PVC_i and intermediate costs Int_i. The cost function is

$$CV_i \equiv PVC_i + Int_i \tag{3.2}$$

$$CV_i = a_i^0 \frac{X_i}{\phi_i^A} \left[\frac{w(1+tl_i)}{\delta_i} \right]^{\delta_i} \left[\frac{r(1+tk_i)}{(1-\delta_i)} \right]^{(1-\delta_i)} + \sum_{i=1}^{n} a_{ij} X_j PV_{ij} \tag{3.3}$$

where, w is wage rate, r is price of capital, PV_{ij} is the unit price of composite input, tl_i, tk_i are tax rates on labour and capital inputs, δ_i is share parameter in production function and ϕ_i^A is normalising constant in the production function.

Factor Markets

The producers minimise primary costs subject to the value added resulting in their demand for primary factors of labour and capital. The factor demands are reflected below.

$$L_i = X_i \frac{PVC_i \delta_i}{w(1+tl_i)} \tag{3.4}$$

$$K_i = X_i \frac{PVC_i (1-\delta_i)}{r(1+tk_i)} \tag{3.5}$$

where L_i and K_i are labour and capital inputs in sector i. The total demand for factors equals their total supply, $\overline{LT}$ and $\overline{KT}$. This is as shown below.

$$\sum_{i=1}^{n} L_i = \overline{LT} \quad \sum_{i=1}^{n} K_i = \overline{KT} \tag{3.6}$$

Demand for Intermediate Products

The producers minimise the sum of the costs of the composite inputs V_{ij} which are Cobb–Douglas aggregates of domestic VD_{ij} and imported inputs, VM_{ij}.

$$V_{ij} = \phi_{ij}^B [VD_{ij}^{\delta_{ij}^B} VM_{ij}^{(1-\delta_{ij}^B)}] \tag{3.7}$$

In case of non-tradable goods the demand for imported goods is zero and demand equals domestic supply.

$$VM_{ij} = 0, \quad V_{ij} = VD_{ij}, \quad i \in NT, j \in N \tag{3.8}$$

The level of composite inputs V_{ij} is obtained from the Leontief technology assumption in the top level of the production function nesting.

$$V_{ij} = a_{ij} X_i, \quad i, j \in N \tag{3.9}$$

The price of composite input PV_{ij} is equal to the unit cost function as per equation (3.10).

$$PV_{ij} = \frac{1}{\phi_{ij}^B} \left(\frac{PDI_{ij}}{\delta_{ij}^B} \right)^{\delta_{ij}^B} \left(\frac{PMI_{ij}}{(1 - \delta_{ij}^B)} \right)^{(1 - \delta_{ij}^B)} \tag{3.10}$$

where PDI_{ij} is the domestic price of intermediate input i in sector j while PMI_{ij} is the imported price of intermediate input i in sector j. Equation (3.11) describes the demand for domestic intermediate inputs

$$VD_{ij} = \frac{PV_{ij} V_{ij} \delta_{ij}^B}{PDI_{ij}}, \quad i, j \in N \tag{3.11}$$

while the demand for imported intermediate inputs is described by equation (3.12)

$$VM_{ij} = \frac{PV_{ij} V_{ij} (1 - \delta_{ij}^B)}{PMI_{ij}}, \quad i \in T, j \in N \tag{3.12}$$

Price of Traded Goods

The domestic price of exports equals the world price of exports (PWE_i) times the exchange rate (ER). This assumes no export taxes or quotas.

$$PE_i = PWE_i \, ER, \quad i \in T \tag{3.13}$$

The intermediate import price is depicted in equation (3.14)

$$PMI_{ij} = PWM_i \, (1 + t_{ij}^{MI}) \, ER, \quad i \in T, j \in N \tag{3.14}$$

while the import price for final demand imports is given by equation (3.15)

$$PMF_i = PWM_i \, (1 + t_i^{MF}) \, ER, \quad i \in T \tag{3.15}$$

Import Supply and Export Demand

The world demand for exports (E_i) is given by

$$E_i = \overline{E_i} \, (PWE)^{\eta_i}, \quad i \in T \tag{3.16}$$

where η_i is the price elasticity of demand for exports.[2] While the country is not able to influence the price of its imports thus implicitly making the small country assumption for imports.

$$PWM_i = \overline{PWM_i}, \quad i \in T \tag{3.17}$$

---

[2]Which is same for all sectors due to lack of estimates.

Final Demand

Final demand is characterised by a two level tree structure as shown in Figure 3.2. At the first stage the demand for the good is made which is an aggregate of domestic and imported good. At the second stage a choice between domestic and imported good is made.

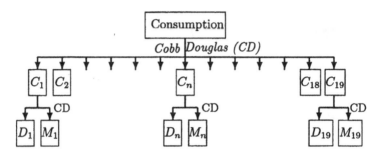

Figure 3.2: **Consumption Structure in Trade Model**

$$C_i = \left(\frac{\alpha_i}{PC_i}\right)Y, \quad i \in N \tag{3.18}$$

$$C_i = \phi_i^1 \left[CD_i^{\delta_i^1} CM_i^{(1-\delta_i^1)}\right] \tag{3.19}$$

$$PC_i = \frac{1}{\phi_i^1}\left(\frac{PDF_i}{\delta_i^1}\right)^{\delta_i^1}\left(\frac{PMF_i}{(1-\delta_i^1)}\right)^{(1-\delta_i^1)} \tag{3.20}$$

Equation (3.21) describes the final domestic demand (CD_i).

$$CD_i = \frac{PC_i\, C_i\, \delta_i^1}{PDF_i}, \quad i \in N \tag{3.21}$$

while the demand for final imports (CM_i) is described by equation (3.22)

$$CM_i = \frac{PC_i\, C_i\, (1-\delta_i^1)}{PMF_i}, \quad i \in T \tag{3.22}$$

Total import of good i (M_i) is

$$M_i = \sum_{j=1}^{n} VM_{i,j} + CM_i, \quad i \in T \tag{3.23}$$

while use of domestic good (D_i) barring exports is

$$D_i = \sum_{j=1}^{n} VD_{i,j} + CD_i, \quad i \in N \tag{3.24}$$

Income, Revenue and Trade Balance

Income (Y) accrues from selling factor endowments of labour and capital which are exogenously fixed along with revenue collection and the benchmark trade deficit.

$$Y = w\overline{LT} + r\overline{KT} + \overline{TD}\,ER + REV \tag{3.25}$$

The government collects revenue from taxing intermediate and final domestic and imported goods along with direct taxes, provident fund from industries and exports. This revenue (REV) is distributed in a lumpsum manner to the representative consumer.

$$\begin{aligned}
REV = \;& \sum_{i=1}^{n}\sum_{j=1}^{n} PWM_i\, ER\, VM_{ij}\, t_{ij}^{MI}, && i \in T, j \in N \\
+ \;& \sum_{i=1}^{n}\sum_{j=1}^{n} PX_i\, VD_{ij}\, t_{ij}^{DI}, && i,j \in N \\
+ \;& \sum_{i=1}^{n} PE_i\, E_i\, t_i^{E}, && i \in T \\
+ \;& \sum_{i=1}^{n} PVC_i\, X_i\, \delta_i \left(\frac{tl_i}{(1+tl_i)} \right), && i \in N \\
+ \;& \sum_{i=1}^{n} PVC_i\, X_i\, (1-\delta_i) \left(\frac{tk_i}{(1+tk_i)} \right), && i \in N \\
+ \;& \sum_{i=1}^{n} PWM_i\, ER\, CM_i\, t_i^{MF}, && i \in T \\
+ \;& \sum_{i=1}^{n} PX_i\, CD_i\, t_i^{DF}, && i \in N
\end{aligned} \tag{3.26}$$

The trade deficit $(\overline{TD})$ is the difference between imports and exports valued in foreign currency.

$$\overline{TD} = \sum_{i=1}^{n} PWM_i\, M_i - \sum_{i=1}^{n} PWE_i\, E_i, \quad i \in T \tag{3.27}$$

Equilibrium

In the basic model all industries have constant returns to scale and follow the price equals marginal cost rule resulting in zero profits.

$$PX_i = \frac{CV_i}{X_i} \tag{3.28}$$

Welfare Measure

Let $IU(P, I)$ denote indirect utility in terms of prices P and income I and let $E[P, IU(P, I)]$ denote the expenditure function which stands for the minimum income required to achieve utility IU. The equivalent variation is defined as[3]

$$EV = E[P^0, IU(P^1, I^1)] - E[P^0, IU(P^0, I^0)] \qquad (3.29)$$

When old prices are a constraint a positive EV means higher income is necessary to reach the consumers utility level, implying welfare gains. Then equivalent variation is measured as

$$EV = Y^1 \left[\prod_{i=1}^{n} \frac{P_i^0}{P_i^1} \right]^{\alpha_i} - Y^0 \qquad (3.30)$$

Numéraire

The solution of the model entails solving a set of simultaneous non-linear equations. Because of Walras' law, one equation gets dropped. To solve the system another equation is introduced and this is termed as the numéraire. The numéraire can be anything like setting wage rate or price of capital to unity or their sum to unity *etc.* The model is a real model and all prices are relative prices. The real exchange rate is defined as the ratio of the price of tradeable to non tradeable. The numéraire is chosen such that the percentage change in the variable ER is equal to the percentage change in the real exchange rate (RER).

$$1 = \frac{\sum_{i=1}^{n} PX_i X_i^0}{\sum_{i=1}^{n} PX_i^0 X_i^0} \qquad (3.31)$$

The proof follows *Appendix 3B: The Real Exchange Rate* of deMelo and Tarr (1992). The real exchange rate as defined above can be expressed as

$$RER = \frac{\sum_{i \in T} (\alpha_i PWE_i \times ER + \beta_i PWI_i \times ER + \gamma_i PWM_i \times ER)}{\sum_{i=1}^{n} \tau_i PX_i} \qquad (3.32)$$

where $\sum_{i \in T} (\alpha_i + \beta_i + \gamma_i) = \sum_{i=1}^{n} \tau_i = 1$, with α_i, β_i and γ_i are > 0. The expression for RER can be simplified as

$$RER = \left(\frac{ER}{\sum_{i=1}^{n} \tau_i PX_i} \right) \sum_{i \in T} (\alpha_i PWE_i + \beta_i PWI_i + \gamma_i PWM_i) \qquad (3.33)$$

where $\sum_{i \in T} (\alpha_i PWE_i + \beta_i PWI_i + \gamma_i PWM_i)$ is fixed due to exogenously fixed world prices of tradeable. Therefore percentage change in real exchange rate reduces to the percentage change in the variable ER and the percentage change in the index of domestic prices PX. Expressing in percentage terms

$$\widehat{RER} = \widehat{ER} - \left(\sum_{i=1}^{n} \tau_i \widehat{PX_i} \right) \qquad (3.34)$$

---

[3]For derivation of welfare measures refer to Section A.4, of Mathematical Appendix.

where the $\hat{}$ indicates percentage change. If the numéraire $\tau_i PX_i$ is chosen as unity, the percentage change in real exchange rate is reflected in the percentage change in the variable ER.

Transformation between Exports and Domestic Sales

Incorporating a constant elasticity of transformation (CET) function between domestic sales and exports is depicted in the Figure 3.3.

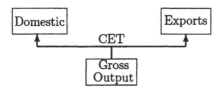

Figure 3.3: **Transformation of Output Between Domestic and Export Sales**

This enables the producers to shift resources between domestic output and exports which are qualitatively different so as to maximise revenues. The following changes are done to the model. Output (X_i) is now a CET function of exports (E_i) and domestic sales (D_i).

$$X_i = \phi_i^T \left[\gamma_i E_i{}^{\rho t_i} + (1 - \gamma_i) D_i{}^{\rho t_i} \right]^{1/\rho t_i}, \qquad \rho t_i > 1, \ i \in T \tag{3.35}$$
$$X_i = D_i, \qquad E_i = 0, \qquad i \in NT$$

The output is equal to the domestic sales for non tradeable (NT) and the ratio of domestic sales to exports is

$$\frac{D_i}{E_i} = \left[\left(\frac{1 - \gamma_i}{\gamma_i} \right) \left(\frac{PE_i}{PD_i} \right) \right]^{-\sigma t_i}, \qquad i \in T \tag{3.36}$$
$$\sigma t_i = \frac{1}{\rho t_i - 1}$$

The price of output PX is a CET function of export and domestic sales price.

$$PX_i = \phi_i^{T-1} \left[\gamma_i{}^{-\sigma t_i} PE_i{}^{(1+\sigma t_i)} + (1 - \gamma_i)^{-\sigma t_i} PD_i{}^{(1+\sigma t_i)} \right]^{1/(1+\sigma t_i)} \qquad i \in T \tag{3.37}$$

With the transformation function, there is a change in the numéraire. The ratio of price index of domestic goods in benchmark and counterfactual scenarios is normalised to unity.

$$1 = \frac{\sum_{i=1}^{n} PD_i D_i^0}{\sum_{i=1}^{n} PD_i^0 D_i^0} \tag{3.38}$$

Terms of Trade

Let p_m and p_x be the price indices of imports and exports respectively. The the net terms of trade (ToT_N) is defined as

$$ToT_N = 100\frac{p_x}{p_m} \tag{3.39}$$

where price index of exports p_x is defined as

$$p_x = \frac{\sum_i PWE_i^1 X_i^0}{\sum_i PWE_i^0 X_i^0} \tag{3.40}$$

and price index of imports p_m is defined as

$$p_m = \frac{\sum_i PWM_i^1 M_i^0}{\sum_i PWM_i^0 M_i^0} \tag{3.41}$$

Extensions to the Basic Trade Model

This section deals with the extensions to the basic model. The "new" trade theory advocates market imperfections and scale economies as the basis for intra-industry trade as opposed to the "old" theory which believes in comparative advantage as the cause for trade. What is more important is that the "new" theory claims to have larger welfare impacts than traditional theory. The objective is to find out whether this hypothesis holds for India and delve into the probable reasons for its presence or absence in the Indian case. This is achieved by relaxing the assumption of CRS in production and introducing increasing returns to scale under different market structure assumptions.

Imperfect Competition

Under increasing returns to scale the cost is no more independent of the level of output. The level of output depends on the number of firms in an industry given the demand function. For modelling imperfect competition the following assumptions are made (a) no entry in the short run and (b) entry/exit in the long run so that entry occurs if there are pure profits and exit when there are losses. For computation purposes five firms are taken in each industry and the number of firms entering or exiting is a continuous function.

The costs definitions are as follows. Total Costs (TC) are a sum of fixed costs (FC) and variable costs (CV) as defined in equation (3.3). Average costs is the ratio of total costs to total output. Thus

$$TC = FC + CV, \quad AC = \frac{TC}{X} \tag{3.42}$$

Fixed costs are defined as

$$FC = \overline{KF} \times r + \overline{LF} \times w \tag{3.43}$$

where $\overline{KF}$ is the fixed capital cost and $\overline{LF}$ is the fixed labour costs. The fixed capital and labour costs are weighed equally as in the constant returns to scale case.

With increasing returns to scale, marginal cost pricing leads to losses since marginal cost is less than average costs. So the way firms price their outputs matter and one pricing hypothesis used is the contestable market assumption. Here low cost of entry (exit) forces firms to price at average costs such that there are no pure profits and to bring about an equilibrium, equation (3.28) is modified to

$$PX_i = \frac{CV_i}{X_i} \tag{3.44}$$

In the second case each industry is assumed to have an oligopolistic structure, with each firm maximising its profits. For this, firms anticipate the reactions of other firms' output decisions and accordingly decide their output. The conjecture of a firm is the change in the industry's output given the change in the firm's own output. Thus the total industry output $Q = Q_i N_i$, where N_i is the number of firms. Thus conjecture $\Omega_i \equiv dQ/dQ_i$. All firms are assumed to have the same conjectures $\Rightarrow \Omega = \Omega_i$ Let the market elasticity of demand be $\epsilon^d \equiv -(dQ/dP)(P/Q)$. Profit maximisation by each firm $\Rightarrow$

$$\Pi_i = P(Q)Q_i - TC_i \tag{3.45}$$

$$\frac{d\Pi}{dQ_i} = P(Q) + Q_i \frac{dP}{dQ}\frac{dQ}{dQ_i} - \frac{dTC_i}{dQ_i} = 0 \tag{3.46}$$

Marginal costs are given by $dTC_i/dQ_i = CV_i/Q$. Thus, the above expression simplifies to

$$P = \frac{CV}{Q} + \frac{Q}{N}\frac{1}{\epsilon^d}\frac{PD}{Q}\Omega \tag{3.47}$$

which can be further simplified as

$$\frac{P_i - C_i'}{P_i} = \frac{\Omega}{N_i \epsilon^d_i} \tag{3.48}$$

where $C_i' = CV/Q$.

Based on the value of the conjecture the market structure will be determined. $\Omega = 0$ implies competitive behaviour and that change in the output of the firm has no impact on industry output and price equals marginal cost. If $\Omega = 1$ there are Cournot conjectures with firms believing that change in their output equals change in output of industry. $\Omega = N_i$ implies the existence of monopoly. In the model the market elasticity of demand is unity as a Cobb–Douglas utility function is used.[4] Market imperfections give rise to pure profits which have to

---

[4]To calculate the elasticity of demand for CES utility function refer to Appendix 7A in deMelo and Tarr (1992).

be incorporated in the income. Thus the income equation changes to

$$Y = w\,\overline{LT} + r\,\overline{KT} + \overline{TD}\,ER + REV + \sum_{i=1}^{n} PROF_i \tag{3.49}$$

where $PROF_i$ is profit in industry with market imperfection. Factor constraints are also modified to

$$\sum_{i=1}^{n} L_i + \overline{LF} = \overline{LT}, \quad \sum_{i=1}^{n} K_i + \overline{KF} = \overline{KT} \tag{3.50}$$

In long-run modelling where profits go down to zero due to entry/exit, an added equation mentioned below is required.

$$PROF_i = 0 \tag{3.51}$$

Table 3.1: **Description of Exogenous Parameters for the Trade Model**

Parameter	Description
ϕ_i^A	Normalising constant for value added/primary cost function
$\overline{LT}$	Fixed supply of labour
$\overline{KT}$	Fixed supply of capital
δ_i	Share parameter in value added/primary cost function
a_{ij}	Fixed coefficient input of good i consumed by sector j in Leontief production function
ϕ_{ij}^B	Normalising constant for composite commodity consumption of good i in sector j
δ_{ij}^B	Share parameter in composite commodity consumption of good i in sector j
t_{ij}^{MI}	Tax rate on imported intermediate good i used by sector j
t_i^{MF}	Tax rate on imported good i used for final consumption
η	Foreign elasticity of demand for exports
α_i	Parameter of Cobb–Douglas demand system for good i
ϕ_i^1	Normalising constant for composite commodity consumption of good i in final demand
δ_i^1	Share parameter in composite commodity consumption of good i in final demand
t_{ij}^{DI}	Tax rate on domestic intermediate good i used by sector j
t_i^{DF}	Tax rate on domestic good i used for final consumption
t_i^E	Tax rate on exports of good i
tl_i	Tax rate on use of labour by sector i
tk_i	Tax rate on capital of sector i
$\overline{TD}$	Exogenous value of trade deficit expressed in foreign currency
ϕ_{Ti}	Normalising constant for transformation function
σt_i	Elasticity of transformation function between exports and domestic goods

Source: Author

Table 3.2: **Description of Endogenous Variables for the Trade Model**

Variable	Description	No. of variables
X_i	Gross output of sector i	n
CV_i	Unit Costs	n
PVC_i	Primary Costs	n
Int_i	Intermediate Costs	n
w, r	Wage and rental rates	2
PV_{ij}	Unit price of composite input of good i used in sector j	n^2
L_i	Demand for labour in sector i	n
K_i	Demand for capital in sector i	n
V_{ij}	Demand for composite input good i by sector j	n^2
VD_{ij}	Intermediate demand for domestic good i by sector j	n^2
VM_{ij}	Intermediate demand for imported good i by sector j	nm
PDI_{ij}	Price of domestic intermediate input i in sector j	n^2
PMI_{ij}	Price of imported intermediate input i in sector j	nm
PE_i	Price of export good i	m
PD_i	Price of Domestic good i	n
PX_i	price of output of good i	n
PWE_i	World price of exports	m
ER	Real exchange rate	1
PWM_i	Exogenous world price of imports	m
PC_i	Unit price of composite final demand good i	n
C_i	Final demand for composite good i	n
Y	Disposable income	1
CD_i	Final demand for domestic good i	n
CM_i	Final demand for imported good i	m
M_i	Total import of good i	m
E_i	Total supply of good i for exports	m
D_i	Total supply of good i for domestic sales	n
REV	Government revenue	1
EV	Equivalent Variation	1
ToT_N	Net Terms of Trade	1
p_x	Price index of exports	1
p_m	Price index of imports	1
TC_i	Total Costs	n
FC_i	Fixed Costs	n
$\overline{LF_i}$	Fixed Labour Costs	n
$\overline{KF_i}$	Fixed Capital Costs	n
Π_k	Profit of firm k in industry with increasing returns	5
Q_k	Output of firm k in industry with increasing returns	5
Q_i	Output of industry i with increasing returns	4
Ω_k	Conjecture of firm k	5
$PROF_i$	Profit of industry i with increasing returns	4

Source: Author

Tax Model

This section explains the basic structure of the general equilibrium tax model used in the monograph. The model with this basic structure is later extended for a dynamic setting.

The tax model has two agents. First, the government which collects taxes and tariffs and redistributes its budget surplus as a lump-sum payment to a *representative* consumer. The investment decisions by the representative consumer are modelled on the lines of Ballard, Fullerton, Shoven, and Whalley (1985) in their tax analysis of the US economy. Since there is only one *representative* consumer the questions of tax incidence are not analysed. Mathematically or computationally the problem of different income classes is similar to the representative consumer case. However in the Indian case, it is not possible to construct income classes from expenditure classes using a log-normal assumption of income and consumption. The reason is the sectoral disaggregation used in the model is not compatible with expenditure class data on different commodities.

The basic tax model is used to analyse various direct and indirect tax issues with more emphasis on the indirect taxation side. All major indirect taxes and subsidies are accounted and various simulations are run on lowering excise, sales taxes as well as MODVAT (MODified Value Added Tax) extension to capital goods sectors. The welfare implications of a VAT (Value Added Tax) is studied with exemption and zero rating of various sectors.

Both models deal with unbalanced trade in the benchmark with real exchange rate being the equilibrating variable. The excess of imports over exports is financed from capital inflows from the *rest of the world (ROW)* which is kept constant in foreign currency. This prevents a free lunch from the *ROW*.

In the model producers maximise profits subject to a constant returns to scale (CRTS) technology. The technology is a Leontief technology with value added as a fixed proportion of the output. Given the technology and prices, the producers buy inputs to minimise costs. The representative consumer sells factor endowments in the market thus endogenously generating income. Given income and endogenous transfers, the consumer consumes various commodities based on the demand system.

Description of exogenous variables is given in Table 3.3 while that of the endogenous parameters is in Table 3.4.

Equations of the Basic Tax Model

Production

Production is characterised by a two-level nesting structure as shown in Figure 3.4. The outer level is similar to the trade model having a 19 sector Leontief input–output production function. The second level is also a fixed coefficient structure with zero substitutability between domestic (d_{ij}) and imported (m_{ij}) intermediate inputs. The zero profit condition is outlined in the equation below.

$$P_j = \sum_{i=1}^{n} P_i \left(1 + t_{ij}^{DI}\right) d_{ij} + \sum_{i=1}^{n} PWM_i\, ER\left(1 + t_{ij}^{MI}\right) m_{ij}$$
$$+\ w\left(1 + tl_j\right) L_j + r\left(1 + tk_j\right) K_j \tag{3.52}$$

where P_i is the price of commodity i, t_{ij}^{DI} is tax on use of domestic intermediate good i in sector j, t_{ij}^{MI} tax on use of imported intermediate good i in sector j

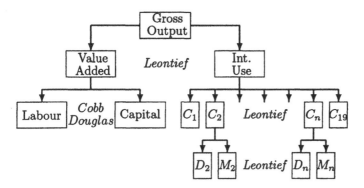

Figure 3.4: **Production Structure in Tax Model**

and PWM_i is the world price of imports of good i.

Factor Demands

The producers minimise cost subject to value added resulting in their demand for factors. The factor demands are as shown below with labour L_i and capital K_i, with factor prices w and r respectively.[5]

$$L_i = (\frac{a_i^0 X_i}{\phi_i})\left(\frac{\delta_i r}{(1-\delta_i)w}\right)^{(1-\delta_i)} \qquad i \in N \qquad (3.53)$$

$$K_i = (\frac{a_i^0 X_i}{\phi_i})\left(\frac{(1-\delta_i)w}{\delta_i r}\right)^{\delta_i} \qquad i \in N \qquad (3.54)$$

Demand for factors equals supply of factors $\overline{LF}$ for labour and $\overline{KF}$ for capital.

$$\sum_{i=1}^{n} L_i = \overline{LF} \qquad \sum_{i=1}^{n} K_i = \overline{KF} \qquad i \in N \qquad (3.55)$$

Demand for Intermediate Goods

Since the second level in the production function is also Leontief the demand for intermediate goods both domestic and imported is a fixed proportion of the output. Hence the demand for domestic goods (VD_{ij}) is

$$VD_{ij} = d_{ij} X_j \qquad i, j \in N \qquad (3.56)$$

The demand for imported intermediates (VM_{ij}) is

$$VM_{ij} = m_{ij} X_j \qquad i \in T, j \in N \qquad (3.57)$$

where X_i is output of commodity i.

---

[5]For derivation of factor demands see Sections A.2.1 and A.2.2.

Price of Traded Goods

The domestic price of exports (PE_i) equals the world price of exports (PWE_i) times the exchange rate (ER).

$$PE_i = PWE_i\,ER, \qquad\qquad i \in T \tag{3.58}$$

The price of intermediate imports (PMI_i) is as below, with tariffs (t^{MI})

$$PMI_{ij} = PWM_i\,(1 + t_{ij}^{MI})\,ER, \qquad i \in T,\ j \in N \tag{3.59}$$

while the price for final demand imports (PMF_i) is, with tariffs (t^{MF})

$$PMF_i = PWM_i\,(1 + t_i^{MF})\,ER, \qquad i \in T \tag{3.60}$$

Import Supply and Export Demand

The small country assumption is dropped in the case of exports.

$$E_i = \overline{E_i}\,(PWE)_i^{\eta}, \qquad\qquad i \in T \tag{3.61}$$

While the country is not able to influence the price of its imports thus implicitly making the small country assumption for imports.

$$PWM_i = \overline{PWM_i}, \qquad\qquad i \in T \tag{3.62}$$

Structure of Final Demand

The final demand is composed of 4 nests as shown in Figure 3.5. The demand for commodities is obtained from solving the optimisation problems of this nested utility function at various nests.

Savings Choice

The savings decision is based on the maximisation of a nested utility function. The outer nest offers a choice between present (H) and future consumption (C_F). The future consumption is the composite of the stream of consumption in the future periods. The *representative* consumer is infinitely lived and the decision made at the outer nest results in the incremental consumption in the future period due to savings made today. The expectations are myopic and hence the choice of future consumption is based on current prices. Symbolically $U \equiv U(H, C_F)$, and has the following CES structure.

$$U = (\alpha^{(\frac{1}{\sigma_3})} H^{(\frac{(\sigma_3-1)}{\sigma_3})} + (1-\alpha)^{(\frac{1}{\sigma_3})} C_F^{(\frac{(\sigma_3-1)}{\sigma_3})})^{(\frac{\sigma_3}{(\sigma_3-1)})} \tag{3.63}$$

The consumer starts with an income I_{Max}, which is the sum of capital endowments and labour endowments inclusive of leisure time. The present consumption costs P_H while future consumption costs P_G. The consumer buys a homogeneous

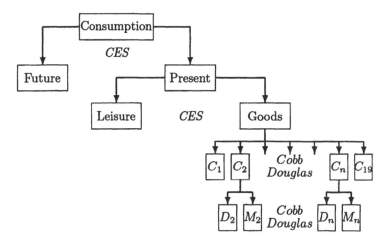

Figure 3.5: **Consumption Structure in Tax Model**

savings good S which is rented directly to the industries. The cost of buying this good is P_S. Capital endowment of the consumer is measured in service units and not in physical units, while the savings good is measured in physical units. Each unit of savings good yields a flow of capital which fetches a price in future periods. Each unit of savings is assumed to yield γ units of capital services. Each unit of capital service earns r in each period. With myopic expectations the price of the basket of consumption good P_G (described later) is expected to remain same in each period. Incremental future consumption C_F will thus cost $P_G C_F$. This is financed from savings $r\gamma S$. This $\Rightarrow r\gamma S = P_G C_F$. Multiplying both sides with P_S and rearranging

$$P_S S = \frac{P_S P_G}{r\gamma} C_F \tag{3.64}$$

A given value of savings $P_S S$ earns a return $r\gamma S$. Hence the rate of return is $\frac{r\gamma}{P_S}$. The income is spent on savings S costing P_S and present consumption H costing P_H. The consumers budget constraint is therefore

$$I_{Max} = P_H H + \left(\frac{P_S P_G}{r\gamma}\right) C_F \tag{3.65}$$

At the outer nest the consumer maximises the utility U subject to the budget constraint. Let,

$$\Delta_1 = \alpha P_H{}^{(1-\sigma_3)} + (1-\alpha)\left(\frac{P_S P_G}{r\gamma}\right)^{(1-\sigma_3)} \tag{3.66}$$

A closed form solution to the maximisation problem in the outer nest results in the demand for present consumption H as,

$$H = \frac{\alpha I_{Max}}{P_H{}^{\sigma_3} \Delta_1} \tag{3.67}$$

Similarly future consumption C_F is

$$C_F = \frac{(1-\alpha)I_{Max}}{(\frac{P_S P_G}{r\gamma})^{\sigma_3}\Delta_1} \tag{3.68}$$

The demand for savings works out to be,

$$S = \frac{(1-\alpha)I_{Max}}{P_S(\frac{P_G}{r\gamma})^{(\sigma_3-1)}\Delta_1} \tag{3.69}$$

Leisure Choice

At the second stage the consumer decides between consumption of goods X_G and consumption of leisure l. The present consumption H takes the CES form mentioned below.

$$H = (\beta^{(\frac{1}{\sigma_2})}l^{(\frac{(\sigma_2-1)}{\sigma_2})} + (1-\beta)^{(\frac{1}{\sigma_2})}X_G^{(\frac{(\sigma_2-1)}{\sigma_2})})^{(\frac{\sigma_2}{(\sigma_2-1)})} \tag{3.70}$$

The income left to meet present consumption is $I_1 = I_{Max} - P_S S$, since part of the maximum income is allocated to purchasing the savings good. This income is spent in buying goods X_G costing P_G and leisure l costing P_l. Working one additional unit of time gets the consumer $w(1-\tau)$, where τ is the tax rate and w the wage rate. This is the opportunity cost of leisure. Hence the price of leisure $P_l = w(1-\tau)$.

$$I_1 \equiv I_{Max} - P_S S = P_l l + P_G X_G \tag{3.71}$$

At the second nest the consumer maximises the utility H subject to the budget constraint. Let,

$$\Delta_2 = \beta P_l^{(1-\sigma_2)} + (1-\beta)P_G^{(1-\sigma_2)} \tag{3.72}$$

The solution to the maximisation problem at the second nest results in the demand for leisure,

$$l = \frac{\beta(I_{Max} - P_S S)}{P_l^{\sigma_2}\Delta_2} \tag{3.73}$$

and demand for goods

$$X_G = \frac{(1-\beta)(I_{Max} - P_S S)}{P_G^{\sigma_2}\Delta_2} \tag{3.74}$$

Demand for Consumption Goods

The demand for consumption of goods from the second nest is composed of demand for 19 individual goods produced by the sectors. At the third nest the consumer maximises a Cobb–Douglas utility function X_G

$$X_G = \prod_{i=1}^{n} C_i^{\lambda_i}, \qquad i \in N \tag{3.75}$$

$$\sum_{i=1}^{n} \lambda_i = 1, \qquad i \in N \tag{3.76}$$

The income left to meet the consumption of goods is $I_2 = I_1 - P_l l$, since part of the income is lost due to leisure consumption. This income is used to buy the 19 consumption goods, the composite of who is X_G. Therefore the budget constraint is

$$I_2 \equiv I_{Max} - P_S S - P_l l = \sum_{i=1}^{n} C_i P C_i, \qquad i \in N \tag{3.77}$$

Solving the maximisation problem at nest 3, the demand for individual goods is

$$C_i = \frac{\lambda_i (I_{Max} - P_S S - P_l l)}{P C_i}, \qquad i \in N \tag{3.78}$$

The price index for the goods is

$$P_G = \prod_{i=1}^{n} \left(\frac{P C_i}{\lambda_i} \right)^{\lambda_i}, \qquad i \in N \tag{3.79}$$

Choice Between Domestic and Imported Goods

At the last nest each good is a composite of domestic and imported good. The consumer has decided from nest three the aggregate expenditure on each good, but the choice of domestic and imported depends on the prices. So at the last level the consumer minimises the expenditure cost on each good. The expenditure is given below.

$$PDF_i \, CD_i + PMF_i \, CM_i = PC_i \, C_i, \qquad i \in N \tag{3.80}$$

Each good is a Cobb–Douglas between domestic and imported good.

$$C_i = CD_i^{\epsilon_i} CM_i^{(1-\epsilon_i)} \tag{3.81}$$

Demand for domestic and imported goods is,

$$CD_i = \epsilon_i \frac{PC_i C_i}{PDF_i} \qquad CM_i = (1 - \epsilon_i) \frac{PC_i C_i}{PMF_i} \tag{3.82}$$

Revenue, Income and Trade Balance

The government collects revenue from taxing intermediate and final domestic and imported goods along with direct taxes and the provident fund from industries and exports. This revenue is distributed in a lump sum manner to the representative consumer.

$$REV = \sum_{i=1}^{n} \sum_{j=1}^{n} PWM_i \, ER \, VM_{ij} \, t_{ij}^{MI}, \qquad i \in T, j \in N$$

$$+ \sum_{i=1}^{n} \sum_{j=1}^{n} P_i \, VD_{ij} \, t_{ij}^{DI}, \qquad i, j \in N$$

$$+ \sum_{i=1}^{n} PE_i \, E_i \, t_i^{E}, \qquad i \in T$$

$$+ \sum_{i=1}^{n} w \, tl_i \, L_i + \sum_{i=1}^{n} r \, tk_i \, K_i \qquad i \in N$$

$$+ \tau(w \sum_{i=1}^{n} L_i + r \sum_{i=1}^{n} K_i) \qquad i \in N$$

$$+ \sum_{i=1}^{n} PWM_i \, ER \, CM_i \, t_i^{MF}, \qquad i \in T$$

$$+ \sum_{i=1}^{n} P_i \, CD_i \, t_i^{DF}, \qquad i \in N \tag{3.83}$$

Income accrues from selling factor endowments of labour and capital which are exogenously fixed along with revenue collection and the benchmark trade deficit.

$$I_{Max} = (1 - \tau)(wE + r\overline{KF}) + \overline{TD} \, ER + TR \tag{3.84}$$

The trade deficit is the difference between imports and exports valued in foreign currency.

$$\overline{TD} = \sum_{i=1}^{n} PWM_i \, M_i - \sum_{i=1}^{n} PWE_i \, E_i, \qquad i \in T \tag{3.85}$$

Numéraire

As in the trade model described earlier, the numéraire is kept the same for reasons cited as follows. The numéraire is chosen such that the percentage change in the variable ER is equal to the percentage change in the real exchange rate (RER). Hence the model can be solved only for relative prices.

$$1 = \frac{\sum_{i=1}^{n} P_i X_i^0}{\sum_{i=1}^{n} P_i^0 X_i^0} \tag{3.86}$$

Welfare Measure

Let $IU(P, I)$ denote indirect utility in terms of prices P and income I and let $E[P, IU(P, I)]$ denote the expenditure function which stands for the minimum income required to achieve utility IU. The equivalent variation is defined as

$$EV = E[P^0, IU(P^1, I^1)] - E[P^0, IU(P^0, I^0)] \tag{3.87}$$

When old prices are a constraint a positive EV means higher income is necessary to reach the consumers utility level, implying welfare gains. Let H^0 and H^1 be the quantities of present consumption before and after the policy change. Let the corresponding prices be $P_H{}^0$ and $P_H{}^1$ respectively. Then $H^1 P_H{}^0$ is the expenditure to consume H^1 at prices $P_H{}^0$. $H^0 P_H{}^0$ is the expenditure to consume H^0 at prices $P_H{}^0$. Then equivalent variation is measured as[6]

$$EV = (H^1 - H^0) P_H{}^0 \tag{3.88}$$

Revenue Neutrality

Let the original tax revenues collected be R^0 and after the policy change be R^1. The government is interested in knowing how these to revenues are equal. If the new revenue R^1 is corrected by a laspeyre's price index Q_L, then for differential tax incidence $R^1 = R^0 Q_L$, where

$$Q_L = \frac{\sum_{i=1}^{n} q_i^1 X_i^0}{\sum_{i=1}^{n} q_i^0 X_i^0} = \frac{\sum_{i=1}^{n} PC_i^1 X_i^0}{\sum_{i=1}^{n} PC_i^0 X_i^0} \tag{3.89}$$

and X_i^0 is the consumption of commodity i in the base case and q_i^0 and q_i^1 are consumer prices of commodity i in the base and revised case respectively equal to PC_i^0 and PC_i^1 respectively.

Extension to the Basic Tax Model

The basic tax model is static. The impact of tax reforms on welfare in the static and dynamic case will vary since the path of consumption will be altered in the dynamic case. Welfare loss in the static case due to immediate fall in consumption and increased saving may convert to a welfare gain in the dynamic case due to capital augmentation and increased income in the future. The basic model is extended to incorporate limited dynamics.

Sequential Dynamics

In the base case, the economy is said to be on a balanced growth path with all variables growing at the rate of growth of capital stock, which equals the growth rate of effective labour. Growth rate of effective labour is composed of population growth and labour productivity growth. Hence growth rate z_t is

$$z_t = \frac{\dot{E}}{E} = \frac{\dot{K}}{K} \tag{3.90}$$

---

[6]For derivation of equivalent variation and compensating variation refer to Appendix A.

Capital endowments grow based on the level of investment in the previous period. Total capital endowment in any year is the sum of capital in the previous year and the investment in the previous year. For modelling purposes, equilibria are calculated at time intervals greater than unity. In this case it is necessary to calculate the investment in the intermediate years. To calculate this, the rate of investment (ratio of total investment to capital endowment) for intermediate years is equal to the endogenously determined rate of investment calculated at the beginning of the period. Thus, if K_t is the capital at time t and $z_{(t-1)}$ is the rate of investment at time $t - 1$, then

$$K_t = K_{(t-1)} \times \left(1 + z_{(t-1)}\right)^s \tag{3.91}$$

where s is the number of intermediate years.

Capital endowment is measured in service units while investment is measured in physical units. To determine the rate of investment z it is necessary to convert the physical investment into service units. The parameter γ converts physical units of investment into capital service. Thus one physical unit of investment will yield γ units of capital services. Thus total capital services added due to investment I is

$$z_t = \frac{\gamma I_t}{K_t} \tag{3.92}$$

where I_t is the level of investment in period t.

The economy is assumed to be on the balanced growth path where all endowments and income grow at the benchmark growth rate. As a result, the transfers also grow at the same rate since the consumer is given a share of the revenue. Exports and imports grow proportionately, implying that trade deficit grows as a difference between the two in the benchmark. All factor and commodity prices are unity in the base case for all years.

Table 3.3: **Description of Exogenous Variables for the Tax Model**

Parameter	Description
σ_3	Elasticity of substitution between present and future consumption
α_3	Share parameter at nest 4
γ	Real rate of return to capital in benchmark
σ_2	Elasticity of substitution between leisure and goods
β	Share parameter at nest 3
λ_i	Share parameter for composite good i at nest 2
σ_1	Elasticity of substitution between domestic and imported
ϵ	Share parameter at nest 1
δ_i	Share parameter in value added function
η_i	Foreign elasticity of demand for exports
d_{ij}	Fixed coefficient input of domestic good i consumed by sector j in Leontief production function
m_{ij}	Fixed coefficient input of imported good i consumed by sector j in Leontief production function
t_{ij}^{MI}	Tax rate on imported intermediate good i used by sector j
t_i^{MF}	Tax rate on imported good i used for final consumption
t_{ij}^{DI}	Tax rate on domestic intermediate good i used by sector j
t_i^{DF}	Tax rate on domestic good i used for final consumption
t_i^{E}	Tax rate on exports of good i
tl_i	Tax rate on use of labour by sector i
tk_i	Tax rate on capital of sector i
$\overline{TD}$	Exogenous value of trade deficit expressed in foreign currency
$\overline{PWM}$	Exogenous world price of imports

Source: Author

Table 3.4: **Description of Endogenous Variables for the Tax Model**

Variable	Description	No. of variables
U	Utility of representative consumer.	1
H	Present Consumption composed of leisure and goods	1
S	Consumption of savings good in physical units	1
C_F	Incremental future consumption aggregated over time	1
P_S	Price of savings good	1
P_H	Price of composite current consumption	1
P_G	Price index of composite good X_G	1
w, r	Wage and rental rates	2
ER	Real exchange rate	1
I_{Max}	Maximum Income plus transfers net of taxes	1
l	Quantity of leisure consumed	1
X_G	Consumption of composite good	1
P_l	Price of leisure	1
P_i	Producer Price of good i	n
X_i	Output of good i	n
L_i	Labour demand by sector i	n
K_i	Capital demand by sector i	n
E_i	Exports of good i	n
M_i	Imports of good i	n
C_i	Quantity of good i consumed as final demand	n
VD_{ij}	Demand for domestic good i in sector j	n
VM_{ij}	Demand for imported good i in sector j	n
PC_i	Price of good i consumed as final demand	n
PDF_i	Price of domestic good i for final demand	n
PMF_i	Price of imported good i for final demand	n
PC_i	Price of good i consumed as final demand	n
PDF_i	Price of domestic good i for final demand	n
PMF_i	Price of imported good i for final demand	n
CD_i	Quantity of domestic good i for final demand	n
CM_i	Quantity of imported good i for final demand	n

Source: Author

Chapter 4
Results from the Trade Model

Introduction

This chapter explains the simulations performed using the trade model. The model is primarily used to address the impact of tariff cuts under various production and market structure assumptions.

The chapter is outlined as follows. First the simulations are performed for various tariff cuts under perfect competition and constant returns to scale technology. Following this, the impact of real devaluation on trade deficit and welfare is studied. Later the constant returns to scale assumption is relaxed and increasing returns to scale is modelled, with perfect competition and imperfect competition in the short run and long run. The last section concludes.

Tariff Cut Under CRS

Simulations are carried out to estimate the impact on welfare due to across-the-board tariff cuts keeping trade deficit constant in units of foreign currency. Different export elasticities ranging from low (-1), medium (-2) and high (-5) are used for this purpose. The value of these elasticities are kept uniform across all sectors, mainly due to the lack of availability of estimates for the commodity classification used in the study. The ability of producers to shift resources between the domestic and export market is studied using a constant elasticity of transformation (CET) function.[1] The elasticities of substitution in the CET function would have different impacts on the composition of exports and domestic goods in the output leading to real exchange rate changes, domestic price of imports and welfare. The model uses an array of CET elasticities from very low to very high to evaluate the sensitivity of the results. To evaluate welfare gains the terms of trade play a major role. Simulations are run using both the small country (exogenous terms of trade) and the large country assumption (endogenous terms of trade).

Modelling Constraints in Empirical Trade Models

Before proceeding to tabulate the results of trade liberalisation, the various methodologies used in literature are briefly summarised. The results are then explained in light of the methodologies/assumptions outlined.

The welfare impacts of trade liberalisation depend on the modelling methodology used. Which methodology is adopted depends on the data availability and

---

[1]For details refer to Powell and Gruen (1968).

the nature of study. The theory says that there are gains in unilateral trade liberalisation, provided the country is a small country for which the terms of trade are exogenously given. If however the country can influence the terms of trade, it is no longer a small-country and trade liberalisation may lead to welfare losses. In empirical modelling of trade liberalisation, there are two kinds of approaches.

- *Single-country modelling*

    1. Without trade deficit – This approach is followed by Ballard, Fullerton, Shoven, and Whalley (1985). For the year of construction of the model or the social accounting matrix (SAM), in which the economy is assumed to be in equilibrium, the value of exports and imports are matched. This eliminates the trade deficit and both imports and exports are parametrically modelled using export demand and import supply equations. The exposition of external sector closing rules as outlined in Whalley and Yeung (1984) is used here. The foreign export demand equation is given by $E = E_o(\frac{p_E}{e})^{-\eta}$ $(0 < \eta < \infty)$ while the domestic import supply equation is given by $M = M_o(\frac{p_M}{e})^{\mu}$ $(0 < \mu < \infty)$. Here the exchange rate is denoted by e can be substituted out by using the trade balance condition $p_M.M = p_E.E$. Thus one can get exports and imports in terms of elasticities, prices of exports and imports and parameters E_o and M_o, the base case exports and imports respectively.

    2. With trade deficit – In the case of developing countries such as India, the approach to scaling exports to match imports to achieve a trade balance while constructing a social accounting matrix (SAM) has little cause for justification. It becomes even more difficult to adopt this procedure, given the fact that India landed in a serious balance of payments crisis in 1991 and had to devalue its currency.

        This implies a trade deficit or surplus while constructing the base case. In terms of simulation of trade policy, the trade deficit has to be fixed in terms of units of foreign currency equivalent to the base case trade deficit. The absence of such constraints implies change in trade deficit and free lunch from the rest of the world. This would lead to unambiguous welfare gains following trade liberalisation. The structure of general equilibrium models do not account for money and are "real" models. Thus there is no role for a nominal exchange rate. but there is a role for the real exchange rate. Also, to solve the system, an equation termed as the numéraire has to be added. To keep the trade deficit fixed in units of foreign currency the following methodology is adopted. In the base case the numéraire is chosen such that the percentage change in real exchange rate is reflected in the change in a variable ER, which is introduced to achieve trade balance. This ensures that trade deficit is fixed in terms of foreign currency and there is no free lunch from the rest of the world.

- *Multi-country modelling:* In this case the terms of trade are endogenous, and unilateral trade liberalisation may lead to welfare losses due to adverse terms of trade. However, multilateral trade liberalisation may lead to welfare gains due to the increase in the volume of trade. The modelling methodology adopts an Armington function in both the domestic and foreign country demands. Here one country's trade deficit is another's trade surplus. The trade deficit in one country is financed by capital inflows from the other. The welfare gains from two-country trade liberalisation are shown in Figure 4.1.

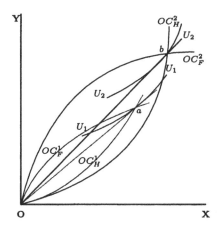

Figure 4.1: **Welfare Impacts of Multi-country Trade Liberalisation**

The terms of trade before liberalisation is shown by Oa, with home offer curve OC_H^1 and foreign offer curve OC_F^1. The maximum utility achieved is shown by the indifference curve U_1U_1. After liberalisation by both countries, the terms of trade shifts to Ob, with home offer curve OC_H^2 and foreign offer curve OC_F^2. The maximum utility achieved is shown by the indifference curve U_2U_2. This is above the pre liberalisation indifference curve U_1U_1 implying a welfare gain from trade liberalisation.

Trade Liberalisation with a Small-Country Assumption

This section analyses the effects of trade liberalisation using a small-country assumption. Here the terms of trade are kept constant, by exogenously setting the world price of exports and imports. The CET function is then responsible for determining the amount of exports and domestic sales so as to maximise revenues for the producers. Table 4.1 tabulates the impact of various tariff cuts under different CET elasticities, on wage rate (w), rental price of capital (r), real exchange rate (er) and welfare (ev).

The factor prices increase with larger tariff cuts, but exhibit a marginal decline with increased CET elasticities. The real exchange rate depreciates with larger tariff cuts, but appreciates with increased CET elasticities. There are welfare gains across all simulations which increase with larger tariff cuts and with higher CET elasticities.

The probable reasons for the welfare gains are as follows. The larger the tariff cuts, the larger is the amount of cheaper imports available to the domestic consumer. Constant terms of trade imply domestic producers still continue to get the same international price before trade liberalisation. To maintain a constant trade deficit, increased imports have to be matched with increased exports or a depreciation of exchange rate to reduce imports and boost exports. The constant terms of trade implies that higher exports are achieved at relatively lower volume of exports, given the fixed pre liberalisation price of exports. Lower CET elasticities imply less homogeneity of domestic and export goods. This further implies smaller change in composition of output between domestic and exportable as compared to the high elasticity case, for the same change in relative prices. The demand for domestic and imported goods depends on their relative prices and Armington elasticity of demand between the two. Low Armington elasticity will not allow a large change in consumption pattern between domestic and imported goods, despite a fall in domestic price of imports. This demand for domestic goods has to be met from domestic production, where there is a trade off between domestic and exportable. The fall in demand for domestic goods (now substituted by cheaper imports) is matched with less supply, by a fall in price of these goods. The increase in imports is matched with increased exports, whose supply increases with a price rise. The exchange rate (price ratio of tradable to non-tradeable) depreciates. The greater the tariff cuts, the greater is the amount of imports and therefore larger fall in domestic demand and greater rise in exports. This is achieved with a larger depreciation of the exchange rate. At low elasticities of transformation, the change in composition being relatively small. At very high elasticities, a small change in the relative price of domestic and exports leads to a large change in their composition. Demand for domestic goods is determined from the Armington elasticities. Small change in domestic demand will lead to small change in supply. At high elasticities the only way this comes about is with an appreciation of the exchange rate. This appreciation leads to higher price of domestic goods, increasing their supply. Makes exports expensive reducing their demand curtailing imports, and bringing demand and supply in equilibrium. The main reason for the appreciation at high CET elasticities is the small country assumption implying constant terms of trade. This allows infinite exports at the given world price. The appreciation of the exchange rate at high elasticities, coupled with cheaper imports leads to larger welfare gains as compared to the low CET elasticity case.

Table 4.1: **Impact of Trade Liberalisation with Small Country Assumption**

Cut (%)	0.25	0.50	1	2	5	10	50
Wage Rate [Rs.]							
25	1.007	1.007	1.007	1.007	1.007	1.007	1.006
50	1.016	1.016	1.015	1.015	1.015	1.014	1.013
75	1.026	1.025	1.025	1.024	1.023	1.023	1.022
100	1.038	1.037	1.036	1.035	1.033	1.032	1.033
Rental of Capital [Rs.]							
25	1.008	1.008	1.008	1.008	1.008	1.008	1.009
50	1.017	1.017	1.017	1.017	1.017	1.017	1.018
75	1.028	1.028	1.027	1.027	1.027	1.027	1.029
100	1.042	1.041	1.040	1.039	1.038	1.039	1.040
Real Exchange Rate							
25	1.043	1.035	1.025	1.015	1.005	1.001	0.996
50	1.100	1.081	1.058	1.036	1.014	1.005	0.990
75	1.176	1.142	1.101	1.062	1.025	1.008	0.976
100	1.281	1.224	1.158	1.096	1.039	1.013	0.957
Equivalent Variation [Rs. 000s Crores]							
25	1.257	1.356	1.482	1.618	1.798	1.967	3.006
50	2.289	2.480	2.724	2.985	3.333	3.663	5.902
75	3.122	3.385	3.720	4.082	4.579	5.080	8.394
100	3.536	3.813	4.169	4.566	5.151	5.809	9.532

Source: Computed

Trade Liberalisation with a Large-Country Assumption

As mentioned in the previous subsection, a two- or multi-country modelling will lead to endogenous terms of trade. If the terms of trade movement is adverse, it may lead to welfare losses despite trade liberalisation. In this section, simulations are carried out to assess the impacts of trade liberalisation using the large country assumption.

The simulations use two sets of assumptions. One uses a CET function between exports and domestic goods and the other does not. The absence of a CET function not only leads to endogenous terms of trade, but also assumes perfect homogeneity between domestic and export markets. In both cases, the volume of exports depends on endogenously determined domestic price of exports, which through the exchange rate translates into a variable international price. The foreign price elasticity of demand for domestic exports plays a role in determining exports.

Welfare impacts due to various tariff cuts under no CET and CET function are depicted in Table 4.3.

The results show a larger fall in welfare for larger tariff cuts with the same foreign price elasticity of demand (η) for exports without a CET function. There is welfare improvement with increasing elasticities of exports for the same level of tariff cut for both CET and no CET cases. The impact on factor prices is minimal at low tariff cuts and increase with higher tariff cuts and larger values of export elasticities. The real exchange rate depreciates with tariff cuts. The larger the

Table 4.2: **Glossary of Abbreviations – Trade Model**

Y	Income (Rs 000 Crores)
M	Imports (Rs 000 Crores)
X	Exports (Rs 000 Crores)
ev	Equivalent Variation (Rs 000 Crores)
td	Trade Deficit (Units of Foreign Currency)
inv	Investment Expenditure (Rs 000 Crores)
w	Wage rate Rs
r	Price of capital Rs
er	Real Exchange Rate
η	Export Elasticity
P_d	Domestic Price
O/P	Output (Rs 000 Crores)

Source: Author

Table 4.3: **Tariff Cuts Under CRS**

Cut %	η	Y	M	X	er	w	r	tot	ev
0		456.174	48.903	37.011	1.000	1.000	1.000	1.000	0.000
No CET									
25	−1	454.255	51.684	39.116	1.057	1.001	1.002	0.945	−1.236
	−2	454.895	51.393	39.168	1.028	1.004	1.005	0.971	0.219
	−5	455.334	51.243	39.228	1.010	1.006	1.007	0.988	1.172
50	−1	451.492	55.408	41.934	1.133	1.002	1.004	0.881	−3.416
	−2	452.912	54.706	42.048	1.064	1.008	1.010	0.937	−0.151
	−5	453.870	54.352	42.180	1.024	1.012	1.014	0.974	1.984
75	−1	447.582	60.431	45.736	1.236	1.002	1.005	0.807	−6.810
	−2	449.952	59.138	45.920	1.112	1.013	1.015	0.896	−1.308
	−5	451.526	58.508	46.138	1.040	1.019	1.022	0.957	2.281
100	−1	441.681	67.666	51.212	1.384	1.001	1.005	0.720	−12.304
	−2	445.277	65.461	51.479	1.176	1.017	1.021	0.846	−3.919
	−5	447.614	64.431	51.800	1.062	1.026	1.030	0.935	1.534
CET [Elasticity $\eta_{cet} = 1$]									
25	−1	455.941	51.476	39.201	1.032	1.007	1.007	0.968	1.109
	−2	456.353	51.323	39.241	1.016	1.008	1.009	0.984	1.981
	−5	456.740	51.277	39.314	1.006	1.009	1.010	0.993	2.625
50	−1	455.321	54.909	42.145	1.073	1.014	1.015	0.931	2.012
	−2	456.209	54.550	42.228	1.036	1.018	1.019	0.964	3.943
	−5	457.031	54.441	42.391	1.013	1.020	1.022	0.986	5.370
75	−1	454.192	59.521	46.119	1.127	1.023	1.025	0.888	2.587
	−2	455.642	58.875	46.247	1.062	1.029	1.031	0.941	5.828
	−5	456.958	58.684	46.527	1.022	1.033	1.036	0.977	8.218
100	−1	452.130	66.136	51.852	1.201	1.034	1.037	0.834	2.487
	−2	454.273	65.064	52.022	1.097	1.042	1.046	0.912	7.416
	−5	456.146	64.756	52.461	1.034	1.048	1.053	0.966	11.026

Source: Computed

For abbreviations refer to the glossary in Table 4.2

reduction in tariffs the greater the depreciation of the real exchange rate. Also the depreciation is higher for lower elasticities than for higher elasticities.

For the CET case the welfare effects are positive with tariff cuts and exhibit larger gains with larger tariff cuts for the same elasticity of exports. The welfare gains also increase with higher export elasticities. The impact on factor prices is larger in the CET case than the no CET case. The rise in factor prices is greater with larger tariff cuts and with larger export elasticities. The real exchange rate depreciates but to a lesser extent as compared to the no CET case.

The probable reasons for the fall in welfare due to tariff cuts needs to be analysed. It also is important to determine the reasons for welfare gains in the CET case as opposed to welfare losses in the no CET case for the same level of tariff cut.

Tariff cuts imply that imports become cheaper and hence commodities using imported intermediates should have a lower price resulting in increased exports and welfare gains. The sectors which were import competing should contract and exporting sectors should expand. In the Indian case, with endogenous terms of trade, there are large welfare losses with tariff cuts.

The welfare effects can be explained using Figure 4.2.

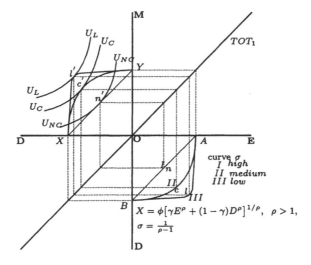

Figure 4.2: **Welfare Effects of CET Under Various Elasticities of Substitution**

As the figure shows, there are 3 commodities, namely tradable (exportable E), non-tradable (domestic good D) and importable (M). The output of commodity X is a CET function of the exportable (E) and domestic good (D). The consumption is an Armington function between domestic good (D) and imported commodity (M). The country indulges in trade and is assumed to be a small country with fixed terms of trade as shown by the line TOT_1 at 45° to the x-axis implying trade is balanced. The south-east quadrant EOD depicts the CET

Table 4.4: **Tariff Cuts without CET – Change in Prices (%)**

Sector	P_d	$\eta = -1$				$\eta = -2$				$\eta = -5$			
		25	50	75	100	25	50	75	100	25	50	75	100
AGRI	1	0.3	0.5	0.7	0.8	0.5	1.0	1.5	2.0	0.6	1.3	1.9	2.7
CCNG	1	0.1	0.1	0.2	0.2	0.2	0.4	0.6	0.8	0.2	0.5	0.8	1.1
MINES	1	0.1	0.2	0.3	0.4	0.3	0.6	0.9	1.3	0.4	0.8	1.3	1.8
FDPR	1	0.1	0.2	0.2	0.2	0.2	0.5	0.7	0.9	0.3	0.6	1.0	1.3
TEXT	1	-0.2	-0.4	-0.7	-1.0	-0.2	-0.5	-0.7	-1.0	-0.2	-0.5	-0.7	-1.0
PAPER	1	0.2	0.4	0.8	1.2	0.1	0.2	0.4	0.6	0.0	0.1	0.2	0.3
CHEM	1	-0.7	-1.4	-2.2	-3.0	-1.0	-2.0	-3.2	-4.5	-1.1	-2.4	-3.8	-5.4
PETRO	1	0.5	1.1	2.0	3.2	0.2	0.4	0.8	1.4	0.0	0.0	0.1	0.3
FERT	1	-0.1	0.0	0.2	0.7	-0.4	-0.8	-1.2	-1.5	-0.6	-1.3	-2.0	-2.8
CEMENT	1	0.4	1.0	1.7	2.8	0.2	0.4	0.8	1.3	0.0	0.1	0.2	0.4
METLS	1	-0.4	-0.7	-0.9	-0.8	-0.9	-1.9	-2.8	-3.7	-1.3	-2.6	-3.9	-5.3
MECHMC	1	-0.6	-1.0	-1.3	-1.3	-1.1	-2.2	-3.2	-4.2	-1.4	-2.8	-4.3	-5.9
ELECMC	1	-0.7	-1.4	-2.1	-2.8	-1.1	-2.2	-3.3	-4.5	-1.3	-2.6	-4.1	-5.6
VEHCL	1	-0.4	-0.8	-1.0	-1.2	-0.8	-1.5	-2.3	-3.1	-1.0	-2.0	-3.1	-4.2
OTHMFG	1	-0.9	-1.9	-2.8	-3.8	-1.3	-2.7	-4.1	-5.7	-1.5	-3.2	-4.9	-6.8
TRNSP	1	-0.3	-0.7	-1.2	-1.9	-0.4	-0.9	-1.4	-2.2	-0.4	-1.0	-1.6	-2.4
ELEC	1	0.4	0.9	1.7	2.8	0.0	0.2	0.4	0.7	-0.1	-0.3	-0.4	-0.4
CONSTR	1	0.2	0.5	1.0	1.7	0.1	0.1	0.3	0.5	0.0	-0.1	-0.1	-0.1
SRVCE	1	0.0	0.0	0.0	-0.2	0.2	0.4	0.6	0.8	0.3	0.7	1.0	1.4

Source: Computed

transformation function for different elasticities of substitution. The curves I, II and III have *high*, *medium* and *low* elasticities respectively. To find the point of consumption corresponding to a point on the CET function the following is done. For a point c on curve II, the imports are obtained via the terms of trade (TOT_1; [assumed =1 here]). The domestic consumption is obtained from the point c and mapped to the north-west quadrant which depicts the consumption choice to point c'. Thus the CET curve AB is mapped to the consumption frontier XY. The point of production will be the one where the utility function is tangent to the consumption frontier or the price ratio (not shown in figure and set to -1). To obtain the consumption trade off in the north-west quadrant the following is done. The producers maximise profits using the CET function to arrive at an optimal mix of domestic and export goods. The export goods then are traded for imports through the terms of trade. The consumers optimise to achieve highest utility, given prices of domestic and imported goods. The shape of the curve in the north-west quadrant is dependent on the terms of trade.

The curve with the lowest elasticity shows the highest level of utility. This is because for a given level of domestic consumption the value of exports and therefore imports is higher resulting in greater consumption of the imported good at a higher indifference curve.

The impact on prices for various tariff cuts under the no CET case is tabulated in Table 4.4.

The impact on prices for various tariff cuts under the CET case is tabulated in Table 4.5.

Table 4.5: **Tariff Cuts with CET = 1 – Change in Prices (%)**

Sector	P_d	$\eta = -1$				$\eta = -2$				$\eta = -5$			
		25	50	75	100	25	50	75	100	25	50	75	100
AGRI	1	0.7	1.5	2.3	3.3	0.8	1.7	2.8	4.0	0.9	2.0	3.1	4.5
CCNG	1	0.3	0.7	1.1	1.7	0.3	0.8	1.3	2.0	0.3	0.8	1.3	1.9
MINES	1	0.5	1.0	1.7	2.5	0.6	1.2	2.0	3.0	0.6	1.3	2.1	3.2
FDPR	1	0.3	0.7	1.0	1.5	0.4	0.8	1.3	2.0	0.5	1.0	1.7	2.5
TEXT	1	-0.2	-0.4	-0.6	-0.8	-0.2	-0.4	-0.6	-0.8	-0.2	-0.4	-0.6	-0.8
PAPER	1	0.2	0.5	0.9	1.4	0.2	0.4	0.7	1.1	0.1	0.3	0.6	0.9
CHEM	1	-1.0	-2.0	-3.2	-4.5	-1.2	-2.4	-3.8	-5.4	-1.4	-2.9	-4.6	-6.5
PETRO	1	0.3	0.7	1.3	2.2	0.1	0.3	0.6	1.2	0.0	0.0	0.1	0.3
FERT	1	-0.4	-0.7	-1.0	-1.3	-0.6	-1.2	-1.9	-2.5	-0.8	-1.7	-2.6	-3.6
CEMENT	1	0.2	0.5	0.9	1.6	0.1	0.2	0.4	0.8	0.0	0.1	0.2	0.4
METLS	1	-0.9	-1.7	-2.4	-3.0	-1.2	-2.3	-3.5	-4.6	-1.4	-2.7	-4.2	-5.7
MECHMC	1	-1.0	-1.9	-2.8	-3.6	-1.3	-2.6	-3.9	-5.2	-1.6	-3.2	-4.8	-6.6
ELECMC	1	-1.0	-1.9	-2.9	-3.8	-1.2	-2.4	-3.6	-4.9	-1.4	-2.8	-4.3	-5.8
VEHCL	1	-0.7	-1.3	-1.9	-2.4	-0.9	-1.8	-2.6	-3.5	-1.1	-2.1	-3.3	-4.5
OTHMFG	1	-1.2	-2.4	-3.6	-4.8	-1.4	-2.8	-4.3	-5.9	-1.6	-3.2	-4.9	-6.7
TRNSP	1	-0.3	-0.6	-0.9	-1.3	-0.3	-0.7	-1.1	-1.6	-0.4	-0.8	-1.2	-1.8
ELEC	1	0.2	0.6	1.1	1.9	0.1	0.2	0.4	0.8	-0.1	-0.1	-0.1	0.1
CONSTR	1	0.0	0.2	0.4	0.7	-0.1	0.0	0.0	0.1	-0.1	-0.2	-0.2	-0.2
SRVCE	1	0.4	0.9	1.4	2.1	0.5	1.1	1.8	2.6	0.6	1.2	2.0	3.0

Source: Computed

The results on price changes show mixed behaviour with rise in price of some sectors and fall in price of the remaining. Those sectors who show a rise in prices exhibit the trend of increasing prices with increased tariff cuts and increased export elasticities. The sectors which show a fall in prices exhibit the trend of decreasing prices with increased cuts and higher price elasticities of exports. The only exception to this trend are the PAPER, PETRO and CEMENT sectors. These sectors exhibit a price rise with increased tariff cuts, which falls with higher export price elasticities. The price rise or price fall in more in the case with a CET of 1 as opposed to the no CET case (means elasticity of ∞).

The reasons for this price behaviour is as follows. The greater the tariff cut, the lower will be the domestic cost of imports, for the same *cif* price. The larger the share of imports in production and consumption, the lower will be the expenditure due to tariff cuts. The lower cost of imports would lead to a price fall. However, this does not lead to a price fall for all commodities. The model specifies the trade balance in units of foreign currency. Cheaper cost of imports leading to their greater demand has to be compensated with a combination of increased exports, depreciation of the exchange rate and the deterioration in the terms of trade. The Armington demand elasticity also puts a limit to the substitutability between domestic and import goods. Low Armington elasticities lead to a smaller change in the relative composition of imports and domestic goods in consumption. The CET elasticity determines the composition of domestic and export supply. The export supply is determined by the foreign price elasticity of demand for domestic exports. Higher the elasticity greater is the supply of exports and lower supply of domestic goods. To achieve trade balance if the exchange rate depreciates and or terms of trade worsen, then the domestic cost of imports rises. If this cost is greater than the tariff inclusive cost in the base case, the cost of imported inputs rises leading to a price rise. If this cost is less than the tariff inclusive cost in the base case, the price would fall. The other component leading to price rise is the domestic cost of goods after liberalisation. Larger export elasticity leads to greater exports and less domestic output. The demand for domestic goods is determined via the Armington function. If this demand is greater than the supply of domestic goods, the price would rise making consumption of domestic goods expensive and escalating cost. This causes the prices to rise with higher export elasticities. To achieve equilibrium, the exchange rate, terms of trade would have to adjust such that the demand equals supply in the domestic, foreign markets with the same trade deficit.

The producer price is higher for the low CET case (1) than the no CET case (∞), for the following reasons. The higher the CET elasticity, the larger is the change in composition of domestic and exports good in output for the same change in relative price of domestic and exports. In other words for the same change in composition of domestic and exports, the relative price of exports to domestic goods is lower in the low CET case than in the high CET case. This means a lesser depreciation of the exchange rate in the low CET case. Smaller depreciation of the exchange rate leads to larger imports and lower domestic demand. The low Armington elasticity (1) as opposed to a higher one implies a smaller change in demand for domestic goods. On the production side, the low CET leads to a smaller decrease in output of domestic goods. The producer price rises on account of the greater share of domestic goods in the production process and the fixed coefficient technology which prevents substitution of expensive domestic goods with cheaper imports.

The level of output will depend on the domestic demand for intermediates and final consumption, exports and imports. A fall in domestic demand can be compensated with greater exports leading to a higher level of output. The demand is a function of the relative prices and elasticity of substitution. Lower the elasticity of substitution, smaller will be the change in demand, despite a large change in relative prices. The model uses a fixed coefficient production function for a composite intermediate good, with a Cobb–Douglas between domestic and imported goods. The final consumption is again a Cobb–Douglas composite between domestic and imported goods.

Table 4.6 shows the impacts on output for tariff cuts under the no CET case. Certain sectors show an increase in output, while the remaining a decrease. Most of the sectors which experience an increase in price exhibit a fall in output and vice versa. There are some sectors which exhibit a fall in both price and output. As mentioned before, if the share of imports in output is high and that of exports low, then trade liberalisation would lead to added imports. Thus demand will be satisfied through imports. Though exports might increase, the increase will not be sufficient to compensate for higher imports. The demand for domestic good would fall due to lower price of imports. The level of fall or rise would depend

Table 4.6: **Tariff Cuts without CET – Change in Output (%)**

Sector	O/P	$\eta=-1$				$\eta=-2$				$\eta=-5$			
		25	50	75	100	25	50	75	100	25	50	75	100
AGRI	180.98	-0.4	-0.9	-1.4	-2.1	-0.5	-1.0	-1.7	-2.5	-0.6	-1.2	-1.9	-2.9
CCNG	10.87	0.4	1.0	1.8	2.8	-0.1	-0.2	-0.3	-0.3	-0.4	-0.9	-1.4	-2.1
MINES	2.21	1.9	4.5	8.2	13.7	1.1	2.8	5.2	8.9	0.4	1.1	2.4	4.3
FDPR	34.79	-0.3	-0.6	-1.0	-1.6	-0.3	-0.6	-1.1	-1.7	-0.3	-0.7	-1.2	-1.9
TEXT	64.50	0.8	1.7	2.9	4.5	0.9	2.0	3.4	5.2	1.0	2.3	3.8	5.7
PAPER	11.37	-0.1	-0.1	-0.2	-0.3	-0.1	-0.1	-0.2	-0.3	-0.0	-0.0	-0.1	-0.1
CHEM	28.32	0.1	0.3	0.5	1.1	0.1	0.2	0.5	1.1	0.4	1.0	1.8	3.4
PETRO	19.54	-0.6	-1.4	-2.5	-3.9	-0.7	-1.5	-2.7	-4.2	-0.7	-1.5	-2.6	-4.1
FERT	7.31	4.9	9.0	12.7	16.2	4.6	8.2	11.2	13.9	4.3	7.6	10.2	12.3
CEMENT	10.80	2.1	4.9	8.6	13.8	2.2	5.1	9.0	14.5	2.2	5.0	8.7	13.8
METLS	21.45	-0.9	-1.9	-2.9	-4.0	-1.1	-2.4	-3.7	-5.1	-1.1	-2.2	-3.5	-4.7
MECHMC	13.57	0.8	1.7	2.7	3.7	1.3	2.8	4.4	6.4	2.0	4.4	7.2	10.8
ELECMC	16.87	0.5	0.9	1.4	1.8	0.9	1.8	2.8	3.9	1.4	2.9	4.7	6.9
VEHCL	16.18	0.5	1.0	1.4	1.9	0.8	1.7	2.7	3.7	1.2	2.5	4.0	5.9
OTHMFG	17.00	0.1	0.1	0.2	0.1	0.3	0.5	0.8	1.2	0.6	1.4	2.4	3.7
TRNSP	41.78	0.6	1.3	2.1	3.4	0.7	1.5	2.6	4.0	0.8	1.8	3.1	4.9
ELEC	21.52	0.2	0.3	0.4	0.4	0.2	0.5	0.7	0.9	0.4	0.7	1.1	1.5
CONSTR	56.20	-0.5	-1.3	-2.3	-3.9	-0.3	-0.7	-1.4	-2.4	-0.1	-0.4	-0.8	-1.5
SRVCE	183.18	0.1	0.2	0.3	0.5	0.1	0.1	0.2	0.3	-0.0	-0.0	-0.0	-0.1

Source: Computed

on the Armington elasticity and relative price. Thus a sector with low export share and high import share METLS would still experience a fall in output with lower domestic price. The reverse is true for sectors with high export and low import share such as CEMENT, where despite increase in domestic price, there is an increase in output. The rise or fall in output is proportional to the level of tariff cut, for the same export elasticity. Also greater the export elasticity, for the same level of tariff cut, the rise or fall in output is proportional.

Table 4.7 shows the impacts on output for tariff cuts under the CET case. The change in level of output will be compared to the no CET case to analyse the impacts of low CET elasticities on output. Lower CET elasticities as explained earlier lead to lesser worsening of the terms of trade and smaller depreciation of the real exchange rate. This leads to lesser exports and larger imports. For sectors which have a high import share this leads to greater imports. The Armington elasticity determines domestic and imported demand. Low Armington elasticities will not permit a large change in the composition of domestic and imported goods in consumption. To meet domestic demand, the price of domestic commodity falls, leading to higher output. For sectors with low import share, the level of import demand after tariff cut does not rise very high. The result is a smaller fall in the share of domestic demand, leading to higher prices. On account of low CET elasticity, the composition of exports and domestic goods changes to a smaller extent than the high CET case, leading in general rise or a smaller fall in output. The exception being CEMENT where there is a smaller rise in output in the CET case (low elasticity) as opposed to the no CET case (high elasticity).

Table 4.7: **Tariff Cuts with CET – Change in Output (%)**

Sector	O/P	$\eta = -1$				$\eta = -2$				$\eta = -5$			
		25	50	75	100	25	50	75	100	25	50	75	100
AGRI	180.98	-0.4	-0.9	-1.5	-2.3	-0.5	-1.1	-1.8	-2.6	-0.6	-1.3	-2.2	-3.3
CCNG	10.87	-0.1	-0.2	-0.3	-0.5	-0.4	-0.8	-1.4	-2.0	-0.4	-1.0	-1.6	-2.4
MINES	2.21	0.9	2.1	3.8	6.3	0.4	1.0	1.9	3.5	-0.4	-0.7	-0.9	-0.9
FDPR	34.79	-0.1	-0.3	-0.5	-0.8	-0.2	-0.4	-0.6	-1.0	-0.3	-0.7	-1.1	-1.8
TEXT	64.50	0.9	2.0	3.4	5.2	1.1	2.3	3.8	5.8	1.3	2.6	4.2	6.2
PAPER	11.37	-0.0	-0.0	-0.0	-0.0	0.0	0.0	0.1	0.1	0.1	0.3	0.5	0.9
CHEM	28.32	0.2	0.4	0.8	1.4	0.4	0.9	1.6	2.8	1.2	2.8	5.3	9.3
PETRO	19.54	-0.7	-1.6	-2.7	-4.3	-0.7	-1.5	-2.7	-4.2	-0.5	-1.3	-2.3	-3.7
FERT	7.31	4.6	8.3	11.5	14.2	4.4	7.8	10.6	12.9	4.2	7.4	9.9	11.8
CEMENT	10.80	1.5	3.2	5.6	8.9	1.6	3.4	5.9	9.2	1.6	3.3	5.4	8.1
METLS	21.45	-1.1	-2.3	-3.5	-4.8	-1.2	-2.3	-3.6	-4.9	-0.8	-1.6	-2.3	-2.7
MECHMC	13.57	1.3	2.7	4.3	6.2	1.8	3.8	6.1	9.0	3.0	6.5	10.9	16.8
ELECMC	16.87	0.9	1.8	2.8	4.0	1.2	2.6	4.1	6.0	2.0	4.3	7.1	10.8
VEHCL	16.18	0.9	1.7	2.7	3.8	1.1	2.3	3.7	5.3	1.6	3.5	5.7	8.4
OTHMFG	17.00	0.2	0.4	0.7	1.0	0.5	0.9	1.5	2.3	1.1	2.4	4.2	6.8
TRNSP	41.78	0.6	1.3	2.1	3.3	0.7	1.5	2.5	3.8	0.9	1.9	3.2	5.0
ELEC	21.52	0.3	0.5	0.7	0.9	0.3	0.7	1.0	1.4	0.5	1.0	1.6	2.4
CONSTR	56.20	-0.4	-0.6	-1.0	-1.7	-0.2	-0.3	-0.5	-0.8	-0.1	-0.0	-0.1	-0.2
SRVCE	183.18	0.1	0.1	0.2	0.3	0.0	0.0	0.0	-0.0	-0.1	-0.3	-0.5	-0.8

Source: Computed

The reason is the better terms of trade and lower depreciation which reduces volume of exports. As exports form a large share of output, there is a fall in output. METLS shows the opposite trend with smaller fall in output with low CET elasticity. This is on account of high import share and low export share in output.

The percentage change in share of imports in output with no CET is tabulated in Table 4.8. The table shows certain sectors CCNG, MINES, CHEM, FERT, METLS, MECHMC, ELECMC, VEHCL, OTHMFG that have a very high share of imports to domestic output. The share of imports in domestic output after trade liberalisation will depend on the demand elasticity, extent of tariff cuts, deterioration in the terms of trade and depreciation of the real exchange rate. If the terms of trade and real exchange rate deteriorate to such an extent that the post liberalisation cost of imports is higher than the base case tariff inclusive price of imports, there would be a fall in the level of imports and increase in consumption of domestic goods. For sectors in which the tariff has been very high in the base case,[2] trade liberalisation would lead to an increase in imports. The greater the liberalisation the larger would be the rise or fall in share of imports in output, depending on whether the base case tariffs were higher or lower than the post liberalisation scenario.

The impact on exports for various tariff cuts under the no CET case is tabulated in Table 4.9. The table shows an increase in the share of exports in output, which increases with higher tariff cuts. The increase or decrease in the share

---

[2]For details refer to Table 5.1.

Table 4.8: **Tariff Cuts without CET – Change in Share of Imports (%)**

Sector	M	$\eta = -1$				$\eta = -2$				$\eta = -5$			
		25	50	75	100	25	50	75	100	25	50	75	100
AGRI	0.9	-3.7	-8.4	-14.3	-21.9	-0.9	-2.4	-4.6	-7.8	0.9	1.7	2.2	2.5
CCNG	42.8	-2.3	-5.6	-9.7	-15.2	-0.4	-1.2	-2.6	-4.7	0.9	1.7	2.3	2.7
MINES	220.0	-1.8	-4.4	-8.0	-12.9	-0.7	-2.0	-4.0	-7.1	0.3	0.1	-0.5	-1.7
FDPR	1.5	4.2	8.0	11.2	13.3	7.2	15.4	24.5	34.5	9.2	20.2	33.5	49.9
TEXT	0.7	-3.8	-9.0	-15.7	-24.2	-1.1	-3.1	-6.3	-10.6	0.5	0.6	0.2	-1.0
PAPER	7.5	-0.9	-2.9	-6.4	-11.8	1.7	3.0	3.4	2.8	3.3	6.6	9.8	12.7
CHEM	15.4	5.6	11.7	18.8	26.8	7.8	17.1	28.6	43.4	9.0	20.0	34.0	52.4
PETRO	8.1	11.8	27.6	51.3	91.8	14.6	35.0	66.5	122.2	16.4	39.9	76.8	143.9
FERT	18.1	-31.6	-50.0	-62.2	-71.2	-30.0	-47.3	-58.7	-66.9	-29.0	-45.5	-56.3	-64.0
CEMENT	1.6	4.2	8.2	12.0	14.6	7.0	15.1	23.9	33.8	9.3	19.8	32.9	49.0
METLS	20.8	3.9	8.0	12.2	16.4	5.8	12.5	20.3	29.6	7.1	15.6	26.0	39.1
MECHMC	66.8	-1.1	-3.3	-7.0	-12.7	1.2	1.8	1.5	-0.1	2.3	4.2	5.8	6.3
ELECMC	19.9	3.6	6.8	9.5	11.0	6.1	12.8	20.3	28.3	7.5	16.2	26.5	38.6
VEHCL	13.2	-1.6	-4.4	-8.6	-14.8	0.8	0.9	0.3	-1.7	2.2	4.2	5.9	6.8
OTHMFG	16.9	8.5	19.0	33.0	53.1	11.1	25.6	45.9	76.6	12.5	29.3	53.1	90.0
TRNSP	9.4	-6.1	-13.2	-21.5	-31.2	-3.5	-7.7	-12.9	-19.3	-1.9	-4.3	-7.3	-11.2
ELEC	0.0	0.0	0.0	0.0	0.0	0.0	0.0	0.0	0.0	0.0	0.0	0.0	0.0
CONSTR	0.0	0.0	0.0	0.0	0.0	0.0	0.0	0.0	0.0	0.0	0.0	0.0	0.0
SRVCE	1.5	-5.8	-12.7	-20.6	-30.0	-3.0	-6.7	-11.2	-16.8	-1.2	-2.6	-4.6	-7.1

Source: Computed

of exports in output for the same tariff cut, differs with different foreign price elasticity of demand for Indian exports. The level of exports will depend on the terms of trade, real exchange rate, export taxes, elasticity of exports, the relative prices of export and domestic goods and the CET elasticity. Smaller the deterioration in the terms of trade and the real exchange rate, lower will be the level of exports. Greater the elasticity of exports, greater will be the exports. Higher the export taxes lower will be the exports. Lower domestic price of goods would lead to greater exports. If the domestic price rises with increased export elasticities, it would lead to a fall in the share of exports as a proportion of output.

The change in imports with *CET* is tabulated in Table 4.10. The objective of this table is to study the effect of CET elasticities on level of imports. A low CET elasticity as opposed to high value, leads to a smaller loss in the terms of trade and lesser depreciation of the real exchange rate. This leads to lower price of imports in the low CET case as compared to the high CET case. The result is a higher level of imports leading to an increased share of imports in output. The share increases with a greater extent of liberalisation and with higher foreign price elasticity of demand for domestic exports.

The impact on exports for various tariff cuts under the *CET* case is tabulated in Table 4.11. The exports reflect a behaviour opposite to the imports with low CET as opposed to high value of CET. The reason being smaller loss in terms of trade and lesser degree to which the real exchange rate depreciates. This leads to smaller volume of exports needed to maintain the trade deficit. As the price elasticity of exports increases a smaller fall in price of exports is required

Table 4.9: **Tariff Cuts without CET – Change in Share of Exports (%)**

Sector	X	$\eta = -1$				$\eta = -2$				$\eta = -5$			
		25	50	75	100	25	50	75	100	25	50	75	100
AGRI	1.6	5.8	13.7	24.5	40.2	5.2	12.2	22.0	36.3	2.6	6.8	12.8	22.0
CCNG	0.1	-0.4	10.0	20.1	29.6	0.1	11.3	22.6	33.8	0.4	12.1	12.7	24.8
MINES	22.2	3.6	8.2	13.7	21.2	3.9	9.0	15.2	23.7	2.8	6.8	11.7	18.6
FDPR	3.1	5.9	13.8	24.7	40.4	5.5	13.0	23.2	38.2	4.1	9.8	17.6	29.2
TEXT	11.3	5.1	11.9	21.0	33.8	5.2	12.1	21.2	34.1	5.4	12.5	21.7	34.4
PAPER	0.3	5.2	13.0	23.3	36.3	5.2	13.0	23.3	36.3	5.1	10.3	20.6	33.4
CHEM	8.3	6.3	14.6	25.6	41.2	7.7	17.7	31.1	49.9	11.1	25.6	44.9	72.3
PETRO	2.7	5.9	13.7	24.2	39.6	6.0	14.0	24.8	40.4	6.0	14.0	24.2	38.9
FERT	0.9	1.1	4.2	8.9	18.6	1.4	6.4	14.4	25.1	4.6	11.2	22.3	39.0
CEMENT	44.8	3.1	7.0	11.9	18.2	3.0	6.8	11.6	17.7	2.8	6.3	10.7	16.4
METLS	1.5	7.3	16.4	28.4	45.3	9.2	20.6	36.0	57.1	13.6	31.1	54.4	86.7
MECHMC	9.6	5.4	12.6	22.0	35.2	6.7	15.2	26.3	41.6	10.8	24.4	41.8	65.1
ELECMC	6.0	6.0	13.9	24.5	39.8	7.1	16.3	28.6	45.9	10.8	24.8	43.1	68.5
VEHCL	4.5	5.7	13.2	23.2	37.5	6.5	15.0	26.2	41.8	9.4	21.4	36.8	58.0
OTHMFG	5.0	6.6	15.3	26.9	43.6	8.2	19.0	33.2	53.5	13.1	30.0	52.7	84.9
TRNSP	7.4	5.4	12.7	22.4	36.4	5.8	13.6	24.0	39.0	6.8	15.8	27.9	45.5
ELEC	0.0	-0.2	14.0	13.9	28.0	-0.2	13.8	13.5	27.4	-0.4	13.5	13.1	26.7
CONSTR	0.0	0.0	0.0	0.0	0.0	0.0	0.0	0.0	0.0	0.0	0.0	0.0	0.0
SRVCE	5.4	5.5	13.0	23.2	37.9	5.2	12.2	21.7	35.5	3.7	8.8	15.8	26.1

Source: Computed

Table 4.10: **Tariff Cuts with CET – Change in Share of Imports (%)**

Sector	M	$\eta = -1$				$\eta = -2$				$\eta = -5$			
		25	50	75	100	25	50	75	100	25	50	75	100
AGRI	0.9	-1.1	-2.8	-5.2	-8.7	0.6	0.9	0.9	0.4	1.8	3.7	5.7	7.8
CCNG	42.8	-0.5	-1.5	-2.9	-5.2	0.6	1.1	1.3	1.2	1.3	2.8	4.3	5.8
MINES	220.0	-0.7	-1.7	-3.3	-5.7	0.0	-0.1	-0.7	-1.8	1.0	2.1	3.0	3.8
FDPR	1.5	6.8	14.6	23.0	32.3	8.7	19.0	31.1	45.9	10.0	22.1	37.3	56.5
TEXT	0.7	-1.6	-3.9	-7.1	-12.3	0.0	-0.5	-1.5	-4.0	0.9	1.7	2.1	1.8
PAPER	7.5	1.4	2.4	2.6	1.6	2.9	5.7	8.4	10.4	3.8	7.7	11.7	15.6
CHEM	15.4	7.1	15.7	26.3	39.5	8.2	18.3	31.0	47.4	8.1	18.0	30.1	44.9
PETRO	8.1	14.2	34.3	65.0	119.5	15.9	38.6	74.2	138.4	16.9	41.4	80.2	151.6
FERT	18.1	-30.3	-47.6	-59.2	-67.5	-29.3	-46.1	-57.1	-65.0	-28.8	-45.2	-55.9	-63.5
CEMENT	1.6	6.6	13.8	22.9	32.2	8.3	18.2	29.8	44.6	9.4	21.1	36.5	56.3
METLS	20.8	5.6	11.8	19.1	27.5	6.6	14.4	23.9	35.4	7.4	16.4	27.5	41.5
MECHMC	66.8	0.9	1.4	1.0	-0.8	2.1	4.0	5.4	5.9	2.0	3.8	5.1	5.3
ELECMC	19.9	5.9	12.4	19.5	27.1	7.2	15.6	25.5	37.0	7.6	16.5	27.0	39.5
VEHCL	13.2	0.5	0.5	-0.3	-2.6	1.9	3.5	4.7	5.1	2.4	4.9	7.0	8.7
OTHMFG	16.9	10.9	25.3	45.2	75.5	12.3	28.8	52.3	88.7	12.7	29.7	53.9	91.4
TRNSP	9.4	-3.6	-7.9	-13.1	-19.5	-2.1	-4.7	-8.0	-12.1	-1.3	-2.9	-4.9	-7.6
ELEC	0.0	0.0	0.0	0.0	0.0	0.0	0.0	0.0	0.0	0.0	0.0	0.0	0.0
CONSTR	0.0	0.0	0.0	0.0	0.0	0.0	0.0	0.0	0.0	0.0	0.0	0.0	0.0
SRVCE	1.5	-3.2	-7.0	-11.6	-17.5	-1.5	-3.4	-5.8	-8.9	-0.3	-0.8	-1.4	-2.2

Source: Computed

Table 4.11: **Tariff Cuts with CET – Change in Share of Exports (%)**

Sector	X	$\eta = -1$				$\eta = -2$				$\eta = -5$			
		25	50	75	100	25	50	75	100	25	50	75	100
AGRI	1.6	3.0	6.8	11.9	19.0	2.0	4.9	8.7	14.2	-1.1	-1.7	-2.1	-2.1
CCNG	0.1	0.1	0.2	11.5	22.8	0.4	0.8	12.6	13.3	0.4	1.0	1.7	13.9
MINES	22.2	1.8	4.2	6.8	10.2	1.7	3.9	6.3	9.6	0.4	0.7	1.3	1.9
FDPR	3.1	3.1	7.0	12.1	19.4	2.6	6.0	10.5	16.9	0.8	2.0	3.8	6.6
TEXT	11.3	2.5	5.6	9.7	15.2	2.6	5.9	10.0	15.6	2.9	6.4	10.5	15.8
PAPER	0.3	2.6	7.7	10.3	18.0	2.6	5.1	10.2	17.8	2.4	4.8	7.1	11.9
CHEM	8.3	4.0	9.1	15.5	23.9	5.3	11.9	20.0	30.8	9.2	20.2	33.9	51.4
PETRO	2.7	3.7	8.3	14.4	22.8	3.7	8.3	14.4	22.7	3.8	8.0	13.6	20.7
FERT	0.9	-0.1	-0.7	1.9	6.1	0.1	2.6	5.5	12.8	3.2	8.6	15.8	27.4
CEMENT	44.8	1.6	3.4	5.7	8.7	1.5	3.4	5.6	8.4	1.5	3.1	4.9	7.2
METLS	1.5	5.3	11.7	19.7	30.3	6.9	15.4	25.7	39.1	11.4	24.8	41.8	63.3
MECHMC	9.6	2.9	6.5	11.1	17.3	4.1	9.1	15.1	22.9	8.2	17.7	28.8	42.1
ELECMC	6.0	3.4	7.5	12.8	20.0	4.4	9.8	16.6	25.4	8.2	17.8	29.4	43.9
VEHCL	4.5	3.1	6.9	11.8	18.6	3.9	8.7	14.8	22.6	7.0	15.1	24.8	37.0
OTHMFG	5.0	4.1	9.5	16.1	25.0	5.7	12.6	21.3	32.6	10.2	22.5	37.5	56.1
TRNSP	7.4	2.9	6.6	11.4	17.9	3.2	7.2	12.4	19.5	4.1	9.0	15.2	23.5
ELEC	0.0	-0.3	-0.5	-0.7	13.3	-0.3	-0.7	-1.0	12.7	-0.5	-1.0	12.5	11.6
CONSTR	0.0	0.0	0.0	0.0	0.0	0.0	0.0	0.0	0.0	0.0	0.0	0.0	0.0
SRVCE	5.4	2.7	6.3	10.9	17.3	2.2	5.1	8.9	14.2	0.2	0.7	1.5	2.8

Source: Computed

to achieve a large change in exports. In other words the real exchange rate depreciates to a smaller extent with low elasticities in a CET function. Larger imports and domestic demand (obtained through Armington function) leads to greater output, causing a fall in the share of exports in output. The share of exports in output rises with greater degree of trade liberalisation. The reason is larger amount of exports are needed to match increased imports. Larger imports imply smaller domestic demand. Thus, the share of exports in output (sum of domestic and exports) rises with increased trade liberalisation.

The sensitivity of welfare estimates to the elasticity of the CET function is tabulated in Table 4.12. The table shows larger welfare gains with lower elasticities and lesser welfare gains or welfare losses with higher elasticities of the CET function. The gains or losses increase in magnitude with the extent of tariff cuts.

The terms of trade for the various simulations are tabulated in Table 4.13. The table shows an improvement in the terms of trade with increased foreign price elasticity of domestic exports and deterioration with increasing tariff cuts. There is a general deterioration in the terms of trade for all simulations, which do not necessarily translate into welfare loss. Welfare loss is correlated to the terms of trade with adverse terms leading to larger losses.

The impact on wage rate (w), rental price of capital (r) and exchange rate (er) is shown in Tables 4.14, 4.15 and 4.16 respectively. The elasticities in the CET function range from a low 0.25 to a high value of 50.

The factor prices, namely wage rate (w) and rental price of capital (r), are

Table 4.12: **Equivalent Variation (000s Crores) with different CET elasticities**

Cut (%)	η	0.25	0.50	1	2	5	10	50
25	-1	2.709	1.980	1.109	0.270	-0.540	-0.899	-1.232
	-2	3.202	2.637	1.981	1.354	0.747	0.477	0.226
	-5	3.821	3.211	2.625	2.100	1.604	1.385	1.182
50	-1	5.661	3.998	2.012	0.102	-1.74	-2.556	-3.312
	-2	6.738	5.446	3.943	2.507	1.118	0.501	-0.073
	-5	8.091	6.720	5.370	4.159	3.016	2.511	2.044
75	-1	8.887	6.016	2.587	-0.707	-3.879	-5.282	-6.580
	-2	10.670	8.436	5.828	3.334	0.925	-0.145	-1.139
	-5	12.751	10.558	8.218	6.102	4.104	3.223	2.407
100	-1	12.409	7.888	2.487	-2.696	-7.677	-9.875	-11.906
	-2	15.070	11.551	7.416	3.46	-0.358	-2.053	-3.626
	-5	17.651	14.675	11.026	7.653	4.463	3.055	1.752

Source: Computed

Table 4.13: **Terms of Trade with different CET elasticities**

Cut (%)	η	0.25	0.50	1	2	5	10	50
25	-1	0.984	0.977	0.968	0.960	0.952	0.949	0.945
	-2	0.992	0.988	0.984	0.979	0.975	0.973	0.971
	-5	0.997	0.995	0.993	0.991	0.990	0.989	0.988
50	-1	0.966	0.950	0.931	0.913	0.896	0.889	0.882
	-2	0.982	0.974	0.964	0.955	0.945	0.941	0.938
	-5	0.995	0.990	0.986	0.982	0.978	0.976	0.974
75	-1	0.945	0.918	0.888	0.859	0.832	0.820	0.809
	-2	0.971	0.958	0.941	0.925	0.910	0.903	0.897
	-5	0.995	0.985	0.977	0.970	0.963	0.960	0.957
100	-1	0.918	0.879	0.834	0.793	0.755	0.738	0.724
	-2	0.958	0.937	0.912	0.889	0.866	0.857	0.848
	-5	0.996	0.980	0.966	0.955	0.945	0.940	0.936

Source: Computed

Table 4.14: **Wage Rate with different CET elasticities**

Cut (%)	η	0.25	0.50	1	2	5	10	50
25	-1	1.010	1.009	1.007	1.005	1.003	1.002	1.001
	-2	1.011	1.010	1.008	1.007	1.005	1.005	1.004
	-5	1.013	1.011	1.009	1.008	1.007	1.006	1.006
50	-1	1.022	1.019	1.014	1.010	1.006	1.004	1.002
	-2	1.024	1.021	1.018	1.014	1.011	1.010	1.009
	-5	1.027	1.023	1.020	1.017	1.014	1.013	1.012
75	-1	1.037	1.031	1.023	1.016	1.009	1.006	1.003
	-2	1.040	1.035	1.029	1.023	1.018	1.015	1.013
	-5	1.043	1.038	1.033	1.028	1.023	1.021	1.019
100	-1	1.056	1.046	1.034	1.022	1.011	1.006	1.002
	-2	1.060	1.052	1.042	1.034	1.025	1.021	1.018
	-5	1.061	1.056	1.048	1.040	1.033	1.029	1.026

Source: Computed

Table 4.15: **Rental of Capital with different CET elasticities**

Cut (%)	η	0.25	0.50	1	2	5	10	50
25	-1	1.011	1.009	1.007	1.005	1.004	1.003	1.002
	-2	1.012	1.011	1.009	1.008	1.006	1.006	1.005
	-5	1.014	1.012	1.01	1.009	1.008	1.007	1.007
50	-1	1.024	1.020	1.015	1.011	1.007	1.006	1.004
	-2	1.026	1.023	1.019	1.016	1.013	1.011	1.010
	-5	1.030	1.026	1.022	1.019	1.016	1.015	1.014
75	-1	1.039	1.033	1.025	1.018	1.011	1.008	1.005
	-2	1.043	1.037	1.031	1.026	1.02	1.018	1.015
	-5	1.048	1.042	1.036	1.031	1.026	1.024	1.022
100	-1	1.059	1.049	1.037	1.026	1.015	1.01	1.006
	-2	1.064	1.056	1.046	1.037	1.029	1.025	1.021
	-5	1.069	1.062	1.053	1.045	1.037	1.034	1.031

Source: Computed

Table 4.16: **Real Exchange Rate with different CET elasticities**

Cut (%)	η	0.25	0.50	1	2	5	10	50
25	-1	1.016	1.023	1.032	1.041	1.049	1.053	1.057
	-2	1.008	1.012	1.016	1.02	1.024	1.026	1.028
	-5	1.003	1.004	1.006	1.007	1.009	1.010	1.010
50	-1	1.036	1.053	1.073	1.094	1.114	1.123	1.132
	-2	1.018	1.026	1.036	1.046	1.055	1.060	1.064
	-5	1.005	1.009	1.013	1.017	1.020	1.022	1.023
75	-1	1.061	1.090	1.127	1.164	1.200	1.217	1.232
	-2	1.031	1.045	1.062	1.079	1.095	1.103	1.110
	-5	1.005	1.015	1.022	1.029	1.034	1.037	1.039
100	-1	1.095	1.142	1.201	1.261	1.323	1.351	1.377
	-2	1.048	1.070	1.097	1.123	1.149	1.161	1.173
	-5	1.004	1.021	1.034	1.044	1.053	1.057	1.061

Source: Computed

higher for lower CET function elasticities and lower for higher elasticities of CET function. The real exchange rate (er) also depreciates to a lesser extent with lower elasticities of substitution in the CET function as opposed to a larger depreciation for higher elasticities.

The reason for larger (smaller) welfare gains (losses) with lower elasticities of CET function is as follows. The small country assumption is no longer valid and the country cannot export infinite amounts at a fixed world price. Based on foreign price elasticity of demand for Indian exports, lower world price of exports would imply larger export demand. The domestic producer being a profit maximiser would supply more of domestic good (non-tradable) or exports (tradable) depending on which fetches a higher price, thus altering the composition of output. The higher the CET elasticity the more homogeneous are the domestic and export commodities. On the demand side, tariff cuts would lead to lower domestic price of imports. The actual demand for imports would depend on exchange rate, Armington elasticities and price of domestic goods. The trade balance in units of foreign currency is the driving force to equilibrate the foreign market.

The higher the CET elasticity, a small change in the price of domestic (non-tradable) and export (tradable) goods will lead to a large change in their share in total output. Lower domestic price would imply an increased demand for imports, which has to be met from increased exports or greater depreciation of the exchange rate. Lower the world price of exports, higher the demand. On the production side, lower export price implies lower supply of exports and a higher supply of domestic goods. The Armington elasticities determine the substitution elasticities between demand for domestic and imported commodities. To bring about an equilibrium in the foreign market, the exchange rate depreciates higher for the high elasticity case as opposed to the low CET elasticity. Greater depreciation implies greater demand for exports, lower demand of imports and a corresponding increased demand for domestic goods. Larger the tariff cut, greater will be the demand for imports. This will lead to a greater depreciation of the exchange rate and a larger terms of trade loss. This is more acute at higher CET elasticities as compared to lower ones leading to larger (smaller) welfare loss (gain). From the demand side, the welfare gains (losses) can be explained as follows. Tariff cut implies larger demand for cheaper imports. A consumer will be better off, lower the price of the commodity. Larger depreciation of the exchange rate makes imports expensive, thus mitigating the welfare increasing effect of tariff cuts. Greater the tariff cut, greater would be the loss due to increased depreciation of the exchange rate.

At low CET elasticities, the change in composition of domestic and export goods is relatively smaller for the same change in their relative prices as compared to the high CET case. Or in other words, the low CET case will have a larger share of domestic goods as compared to the high CET case for the same output of export commodity. The consumer would prefer lower price of both domestic and imported commodities, and their shares in the consumption basket would depend on the relative prices and Armington elasticities. Larger tariff cuts would result in increased demand for imports, which would have to be met through higher exports. The consumer demand also determines the supply of domestic commodity. The same level of depreciation of the real exchange rate would lead to a smaller decrease in share of domestic good in output as compared to the higher CET case. This leads to greater imports (lesser depreciation) and welfare gains. It also puts a marginal upward pressure on factor prices, as domestic demand does not fall substantially with change in relative price of domestic and export goods. Larger the tariff cut, larger demand for cheaper imports. This is met by larger exports, with greater fall in price of exports. This however does not lead to large changes in composition of domestic and export goods on account of low CET elasticity. The exchange rate depreciates to reduce imports and increase exports. The terms of trade loss is lesser compared to the high CET case. Demand for domestic goods via Armington function is also met due higher production of domestic goods relative to the low CET case. This leads to welfare gains.

Exchange Rate Devaluation

This section deals with the welfare analysis of exchange rate devaluation coupled with various degrees of tariff cuts. As before, different export elasticities ranging from low (−1), medium (−2) and high (−5) are used. The producer behaviour is modelled with and without a CET function. The performance of top five exporting and importing sectors under various structures is analysed.

The Table 4.17 shows the effects of a 5% devaluation on the main indicators of the economy. The welfare effects exhibit a consistent pattern, which decrease with increased elasticity of exports for both the CET and the no CET case. Moreover there is an improvement in welfare with an increase in tariff cuts for both cases. The factor prices increase with larger cuts and are higher for the CET case as opposed to the no CET case. As expected the trade deficit falls with increased export elasticity and is lower for smaller tariff cuts. Also, the deficit in the CET case is lower than the no CET case, with a surplus in some cases. The income is correlated with the trade deficit with higher trade deficit implying higher incomes and corresponding higher welfare. The CET case exhibits higher incomes than the no CET case despite a lower trade deficit on account of higher factor prices.

A devaluation implies an increase in the price of tradable as compared to the non-tradable. This increase in price of tradable (exportable) leads to movement of resources from the production of non-tradable (domestic good) to the tradable (export) good. The devaluation also makes the imports more expensive. A tariff cut means fall in price of imports and increase in demand. At lower price elasticity of demand for exports, given the demand elasticities for Armington imports, the trade deficit adjusts to clear the external sector. A larger trade deficit implies transfers from the rest of the world. The higher the price elasticity of demand for exports, the lower the trade deficit, the lower is the welfare gain or higher the welfare loss. In the CET case the producers shift resources between production of goods for the export and domestic markets. The elasticity of the CET function will determine the relative composition of the two. For lower elasticities, any change in relative prices induced by tariff cuts and devaluation will not lead to large changes in the composition of output of domestic and export commodities. This leads to an appreciation of factor prices and incomes. At lower export elasticities, the trade deficit may also be large, implying transfers from the rest of the world. This income from higher factor prices and trade deficits leads to welfare gains besides the lower price of imports. In the no CET case the composition of output between domestic and export goods can change with small changes in their relative prices. With devaluation the prices received by exporters in domestic currency are higher resulting in increased output of exports. Tariff cuts lead to lower import prices and increased demand for imports, which to a certain extent is mitigated by the devaluation. This leads to a trade deficit which may be larger than the base case, resulting in welfare gains. The welfare gains increase with increased tariff cuts, primarily due to the increased trade deficit, which finances consumption of cheaper imports. Here the complementarity condition is in use. Either the exchange rate changes to clear the foreign market for a given

Table 4.17: **Tariff Cuts under 5% Devaluation**

Cut	η	Y	M	X	td	er	w	r	ev
0		456.174	48.903	37.011	11.892	1.000	1.000	1.000	0.000
				No CET					
25	−1	454.682	51.624	38.862	12.155	1.050	1.002	1.003	−0.617
	−2	452.614	51.549	40.845	10.194	1.050	1.002	1.003	−2.688
	−5	445.759	51.300	47.423	3.692	1.050	1.001	1.004	−9.552
50	−1	456.539	54.674	38.862	15.059	1.050	1.010	1.011	3.908
	−2	454.416	54.604	40.925	13.028	1.050	1.010	1.011	1.770
	−5	447.335	54.379	47.823	6.244	1.050	1.009	1.012	−5.361
75	−1	458.605	58.774	38.862	18.964	1.050	1.019	1.020	9.174
	−2	456.416	58.710	41.016	16.852	1.050	1.019	1.020	6.954
	−5	449.023	58.512	48.320	9.707	1.050	1.018	1.021	−0.542
100	−1	460.946	64.668	38.862	24.578	1.050	1.029	1.030	15.519
	−2	458.672	64.610	41.124	22.368	1.050	1.029	1.030	13.193
	−5	450.842	64.439	48.958	14.745	1.050	1.028	1.031	5.187
			CET [Elasticity $\eta_{cet} = 1$]						
25	−1	454.871	51.643	40.456	10.654	1.050	1.006	1.007	−0.463
	−2	453.028	51.604	44.053	7.192	1.050	1.010	1.012	−2.301
	−5	447.545	51.539	54.773	−3.081	1.050	1.022	1.026	−7.750
50	−1	456.714	54.688	40.475	13.537	1.050	1.014	1.015	4.065
	−2	454.840	54.665	44.235	9.933	1.050	1.019	1.021	2.177
	−5	449.168	54.670	55.732	−1.011	1.050	1.031	1.036	−3.528
75	−1	458.763	58.783	40.504	17.408	1.050	1.023	1.024	9.334
	−2	456.839	58.775	44.464	13.630	1.050	1.028	1.030	7.375
	−5	450.797	58.862	57.054	1.723	1.050	1.041	1.047	1.236
100	−1	461.081	64.667	40.547	22.972	1.050	1.034	1.035	15.679
	−2	459.077	64.677	44.759	18.969	1.050	1.038	1.040	13.616
	−5	452.382	64.860	58.913	5.664	1.050	1.053	1.060	6.762

For abbreviations refer to the glossary in Table 4.2

fixed level of trade deficit or the trade deficit adjusts for a given level of exchange rate.

Table 4.18 shows the export performance of the top five exporting sectors under various tariff cuts and producer behaviour. In the devaluation case since the trade deficit is allowed to adjust to clear the foreign market, the export behaviour of these sectors is not similar. Some sectors show increased exports with greater tariff cuts, while the others have reduced exports. The sectors with reduced exports are the ones which have an increase in their costs as reflected in the price of output. The sectors which had a fall in prices exhibited an increase in exports. The CET case does not show greater exports than the no CET case for some sectors. One reason is that the devaluation is only to the tune of 5%. So the producers find it more profitable to sell in the domestic market. Moreover there is no requirement of maintaining trade deficit, hence the exports need not increase to that extent.

Table 4.19 shows the change in imports for the top five importing sectors. The imports increase with an increase in export elasticity and with larger tariff cuts, attributed to the lower costs of imports. The other reason for increased

Table 4.18: **5% Devaluation – Change in Exports (%)**

Cut	Sector	base	$\eta = -1$ nc	c	$\eta = -2$ nc	c	$\eta = -5$ nc	c
25	AGRI	2.899	4.657	4.277	9.521	7.968	25.561	15.005
	TEXT	7.319	5.219	5.206	10.712	10.616	28.966	28.692
	CEMENT	4.837	4.631	4.652	9.469	9.427	25.326	24.375
	TRNSP	3.096	5.362	5.168	11.014	10.110	29.780	23.482
	SRVCE	9.893	4.913	4.559	10.068	8.612	27.140	17.154
50	AGRI	2.899	3.863	3.518	7.899	6.313	20.973	10.176
	TEXT	7.319	5.493	5.465	11.286	11.149	30.619	30.113
	CEMENT	4.837	4.672	4.693	9.531	9.489	25.491	24.333
	TRNSP	3.096	5.943	5.782	12.274	11.402	33.495	27.067
	SRVCE	9.893	4.468	4.124	9.148	7.672	24.482	14.263
75	AGRI	2.899	3.070	2.691	6.209	4.622	16.281	5.174
	TEXT	7.319	5.766	5.725	11.873	11.709	32.340	31.439
	CEMENT	4.837	4.693	4.734	9.572	9.551	25.594	24.168
	TRNSP	3.096	6.686	6.492	13.824	12.952	38.114	31.525
	SRVCE	9.893	3.993	3.649	8.147	6.651	21.652	11.089
100	AGRI	2.899	2.173	1.794	4.381	2.760	11.383	−0.138
	TEXT	7.319	6.053	6.012	12.474	12.269	34.158	32.614
	CEMENT	4.837	4.693	4.755	9.593	9.572	25.636	23.816
	TRNSP	3.096	7.623	7.461	15.859	14.987	44.380	37.403
	SRVCE	9.893	3.457	3.123	7.045	5.519	18.579	7.531

nc:no CET; c: CET; base in Rs. 000s Crores

imports is the increase in trade deficit.

Tariff Cuts with Increasing Returns and Imperfect Competition

Inclusion of ideas from industrial organisation in classical trade theory has given birth to the "new" trade theory. This is important as it identifies increasing returns, imperfect competition and product differentiation as a source of trade besides the traditional basis of comparative advantage. To find out the potential gains by incorporating scale economies the exposition by Rodrik (1988) is used. The income comprises of

1. pure profits given by the price (p_i) cost (c_i) margin times the output (X_i); $\sum_i^n [p_i - c_i] X_i$,

2. factor incomes given by factor price w_j times factor demand ν_j; $\sum_j^n w_j \nu_j$, and

3. tariff income given by the price difference between domestic (p_i) and imported price (p^*) times imports M_i; $\sum_i^n (p_i - p_i^*) M_i$.

Expenditure E equals income implying

$$E = \sum_i^n [p_i - c_i] X_i + \sum_j^n w_j \nu_j + \sum_i^n (p_i - p_i^*) M_i \qquad (4.1)$$

Table 4.19: **5% Devaluation – Change in Imports (%)**

			$\eta = -1$		$\eta = -2$		$\eta = -5$	
Cut	Sector	base	nc	c	nc	c	nc	c
25	CCNG	4.652	−1.612	−1.419	−1.505	−1.075	−1.118	0.086
	MINES	4.858	0.124	0.021	0.288	0.226	0.803	1.050
	CHEM	4.371	6.154	6.063	6.291	6.200	6.726	6.749
	METLS	4.468	3.290	3.469	3.469	3.872	4.051	5.327
	MECHMC	9.059	0.431	0.475	0.077	0.177	−1.115	−0.695
50	CCNG	4.652	−0.903	−0.666	−0.752	−0.279	−0.258	1.182
	MINES	4.858	0.659	0.576	0.844	0.803	1.379	1.750
	CHEM	4.371	18.325	18.097	18.508	18.211	19.149	18.760
	METLS	4.468	10.273	10.474	10.609	11.124	11.750	13.720
	MECHMC	9.059	6.579	6.623	6.204	6.325	4.990	5.486
75	CCNG	4.652	−0.322	−0.064	−0.150	0.408	0.494	2.193
	MINES	4.858	1.173	1.070	1.338	1.338	1.914	2.429
	CHEM	4.371	34.431	34.043	34.683	34.134	35.598	34.615
	METLS	4.468	18.800	19.002	19.315	19.987	21.173	24.194
	MECHMC	9.059	13.556	13.611	13.169	13.302	11.889	12.474
100	CCNG	4.652	0.043	0.344	0.258	0.881	1.032	3.095
	MINES	4.858	1.647	1.564	1.832	1.873	2.429	3.108
	CHEM	4.371	57.012	56.372	57.378	56.463	58.728	56.760
	METLS	4.468	29.521	29.722	30.260	31.132	33.124	37.645
	MECHMC	9.059	21.559	21.614	21.150	21.294	19.781	20.444

nc: no CET; c: CET; base in Rs. 000s Crores

for changes around the initial equilibrium, the welfare effects are obtained by total differentiation giving

$$E_w dW = \sum_{i}^{n}(p_i - p_i^*)dM_i + \sum_{i}^{n}[p_i - c_i]dX_i + \sum_{i}^{n}n_i c_i[1 - \frac{1}{\theta_i}]dx_i \qquad (4.2)$$

where x_i is the output of the ith firm with total output of n firms being $X_i = n_i x_i$ and θ_i is the ratio of the marginal to the average costs. The expression says that there will be welfare gains if imports are increased where the difference between domestic and imported prices is high. The second term captures the welfare gains due to pure profits earned by firms on the price cost margins. To improve welfare the output of such firms has to increase. Finally the last term captures the scale effects and to improve welfare the output of firms with scale economies should increase. The point of conflict arises with terms one and two. If import competing sectors have increasing returns term two calls for an expansion of output while term one implies reduction. The impact on welfare is ambiguous and should be determined empirically.

On the empirical front several studies exist which use numerical general equilibrium (GE) models to analyse trade liberalisation with increasing returns and imperfect competition using real-world data. The impetus to this literature was given by the seminal contribution of Harris (1984). Most of the studies have been restricted to developed countries with an exception of Devarajan and Rodrik (1989) for Cameroon.

Increasing Returns and Imperfect Competition

This part deals with the welfare effects of economies of scale in industries. The industries used to illustrate the impact of trade liberalisation with increasing returns and imperfect competition are CCNG, PETRO, FERT and METLS. The reason these industries were chosen is due to the absence of unorganised sector. A value of 5 firms in each industry was chosen for illustrative purposes. The objective is to find the qualitative impact of tariff cuts with market imperfections and increasing returns. As the conjectural variation approach is used by firms to determine output there are two options. One is to assume Cournot conjectures by each firm which implies that output of the industry changes fully by the amount of output of a firm or in other words each firm expects the output of other firms to remain constant when it changes its own output. After assuming Cournot conjectures one must then calibrate the number of firms in the benchmark such that there are zero profits. The other case is to read in number of firms and calibrate conjectures. Since the data on conjectures are not accurate, the second approach is adopted. Moreover a continuous function is used regarding entry and exit of firms.

The results tabulated in Table 4.20 show larger welfare loss in the increasing returns to scale (IRS) case (with average cost pricing) as compared to the long run (LR) (which has entry to drive profits to zero) and the short run (SR) (where profits or losses exist). The welfare losses are higher for higher tariff cuts and there is an improvement in welfare with higher export elasticities. The reason for the minor welfare gain in the LR case as compared to the SR case is the entry (exit) of firms in the long run which drive profits (losses) down to zero. The welfare effects in the long run can move in either direction. With losses in the short run exit of firms takes place and the existing firms move down their average cost curves resulting in efficiency gains. In the Indian case this is reflected in the smaller welfare loss in the long run with higher export elasticities and exit of firms. With profits in the short run, entry takes place and this might cause firms to travel up their average cost curves resulting in efficiency loss. In the Indian case, there is a larger welfare loss in the long run for low export elasticities caused due to entry of firms. In the short run, no entry enables firms to earn profits (losses) which imposes a cost due to restriction of output. This is clearly reflected in the results. The magnitude of welfare loss in the short run over long run is smaller when the amount of profits (losses) are larger (smaller). The results show lower welfare gain (higher) welfare loss in the contestable markets case with average cost pricing as compared to the imperfect markets case. The reason is the exit (entry) of firms in the long run which are making losses (profits) in the short run.

As shown in Table 4.21, there is an exit of firms from industry making losses in the short run. In the average cost pricing no firm makes losses and firms travel up their average cost curves due to a fall in output. This results in efficiency loss. In the short run despite the existence of losses, the fall in output is smaller, thus enabling firms to travel down their average cost curves and exploit scale economies. The existence of profits in the short run also results in smaller welfare

Table 4.20: Tariff Cut Under Various Market Structures

Cut	$\eta = -1$			$\eta = -2$			$\eta = -5$		
25	irs	lr	sr	irs	lr	sr	irs	lr	sr
Y	454.26	454.27	454.27	454.88	454.92	454.92	455.31	455.37	455.37
M	51.68	51.68	51.68	51.39	51.39	51.39	51.24	51.27	51.24
X	39.11	39.11	39.12	39.16	39.17	39.17	39.22	39.23	39.29
er	1.057	1.057	1.057	1.028	1.028	1.028	1.010	1.010	1.010
w	1.001	1.001	1.001	1.004	1.004	1.004	1.006	1.006	1.006
r	1.002	1.002	1.002	1.005	1.005	1.005	1.006	1.007	1.007
ev	−1.23	−1.23	−1.23	0.21	0.24	0.22	1.16	1.20	1.18
50									
Y	451.50	451.50	451.50	452.86	452.95	452.95	453.80	453.94	453.93
M	55.40	55.41	55.41	54.70	54.71	54.70	54.35	54.36	54.35
X	41.93	41.93	41.93	42.04	42.05	42.04	42.17	42.18	42.18
er	1.133	1.133	1.133	1.064	1.064	1.064	1.024	1.024	1.024
w	1.002	1.002	1.002	1.008	1.008	1.009	1.012	1.012	1.013
r	1.003	1.004	1.004	1.010	1.010	1.010	1.013	1.014	1.014
ev	−3.42	−3.41	−3.41	−0.18	−0.13	−0.15	1.94	2.03	1.98
75									
Y	447.57	447.58	447.59	449.85	450.00	450.00	451.40	451.62	451.61
M	60.43	60.43	60.43	59.13	59.14	59.13	58.50	58.52	58.51
X	45.73	45.73	45.73	45.91	45.92	45.91	46.13	46.15	46.14
er	1.236	1.236	1.236	1.111	1.112	1.111	1.040	1.040	1.040
w	1.002	1.002	1.002	1.012	1.013	1.013	1.018	1.019	1.019
r	1.005	1.005	1.005	1.015	1.015	1.016	1.021	1.022	1.022
ev	−6.82	−6.81	−6.81	−1.38	−1.28	−1.33	2.19	2.34	2.26
100									
Y	441.64	441.65	441.66	445.11	445.32	445.31	447.40	447.72	447.71
M	67.66	67.66	67.66	65.45	65.47	65.45	64.41	64.44	64.42
X	51.21	51.21	51.21	51.47	51.48	51.46	51.78	51.81	51.79
er	1.384	1.384	1.384	1.176	1.176	1.176	1.062	1.062	1.062
w	1.001	1.001	1.001	1.016	1.017	1.018	1.025	1.026	1.027
r	1.005	1.005	1.005	1.020	1.021	1.021	1.030	1.031	1.032
ev	−12.34	−12.33	−12.31	−4.04	−3.90	−3.96	1.38	1.60	1.50

For abbreviations refer to the glossary in Table 4.2
Increasing returns to scale(irs), Long run(lr) and Short run(sr).

Table 4.21: **Profits and Entry Under Various Market Structures**

25	Short Run-Profits			Long Run-Entry		
	−1	−2	−5	−1	−2	−5
CCNG	0.003	−0.003	−0.007	5.008	4.990	4.980
PETRO	−0.005	−0.015	−0.020	4.992	4.976	4.967
FERT	0.025	0.019	0.016	5.112	5.086	5.070
METLS	−0.027	−0.045	−0.052	4.962	4.936	4.925
50						
CCNG	0.007	−0.007	−0.014	5.020	4.980	4.958
PETRO	−0.009	−0.031	−0.043	4.985	4.950	4.930
FERT	0.047	0.033	0.025	5.207	5.148	5.112
METLS	−0.050	−0.090	−0.107	4.928	4.872	4.847
75						
CCNG	0.013	−0.010	−0.022	5.037	4.971	4.934
PETRO	−0.013	−0.050	−0.070	4.978	4.919	4.886
FERT	0.068	0.044	0.030	5.296	5.195	5.133
METLS	−0.071	−0.137	−0.164	4.898	4.804	4.766
100						
CCNG	0.022	−0.013	−0.032	5.064	4.962	4.906
PETRO	−0.017	−0.073	−0.103	4.971	4.881	4.833
FERT	0.090	0.053	0.031	5.390	5.232	5.138
METLS	−0.086	−0.185	−0.223	4.876	4.735	4.680

Profits in Rs. 000s Crores, Entry in number

loss in the short run over the average cost pricing case.

Table 4.22 depicts the price and output relationships for all scenarios after a 50% tariff cut. The implication of scale economies can be explained as follows. After liberalisation the subsidy on imported fertiliser is eliminated. This implies fall in imports of fertiliser and an increase in use of domestic fertiliser. With constant returns to scale (CRS) and marginal cost pricing there is a fall in marginal cost of fertiliser (FERT). With IRS an increase in domestic output leads to a fall in the average cost. This fall is more than the marginal cost (CRS) case since the average cost lies above the marginal cost. In the SR the fall in price is smaller as compared to the LR due to profits. In the case on iron and steel and other metals (METLS) increasing returns have the following impact. Liberalisation leads to increased imports of metals, resulting in a fall in domestic output. There is also a fall in the domestic price. In the SR, firms make losses which reduce to zero in the LR after exit of firms. This is reflected in the increased prices in the LR as compared to the SR. With IRS a fall in output leads to higher average costs. In the case of METLS the fall in average costs is lower than the fall in marginal costs in case of CRS. A similar phenomenon is observed in the case of petroleum products (PETRO).

A caveat needs to be added here. Only certain sectors of the economy have been assumed to have economies of scale. In reality any production process will have a minimum efficient scale of operation and corresponding returns to scale. In the remaining manufacturing sectors, there is a presence of small scale sector about which the data is difficult to obtain. This sector accounts for a large level

Table 4.22: **Various Market Structures – Change in Prices and Output (%)**

Sector	P	crs	irs	lr	sr	O/P	crs	irs	lr	sr
AGRI	1.0	1.0	1.0	1.0	1.0	180.981	-1.02	-1.00	-1.01	-1.03
CCNG	1.0	0.4	0.4	0.4	0.3	10.870	-0.21	-0.27	-0.21	-0.17
MINES	1.0	0.6	0.6	0.6	0.6	2.208	2.81	2.76	2.81	2.81
FDPR	1.0	0.5	0.4	0.5	0.5	34.793	-0.63	-0.63	-0.63	-0.65
TEXT	1.0	-0.5	-0.5	-0.5	-0.4	64.503	2.01	2.01	2.01	1.99
PAPER	1.0	0.2	0.2	0.2	0.2	11.367	-0.12	-0.13	-0.11	-0.12
CHEM	1.0	-2.0	-2.0	-2.0	-2.0	28.322	0.24	0.23	0.24	0.23
PETRO	1.0	0.4	0.6	0.5	0.4	19.540	-1.54	-1.61	-1.54	-1.50
FERT	1.0	-0.8	-1.4	-1.2	-0.9	7.306	8.19	8.32	8.28	8.20
CEMENT	1.0	0.4	0.5	0.5	0.4	10.800	5.14	5.11	5.14	5.15
METLS	1.0	-1.9	-1.6	-1.9	-2.2	21.449	-2.36	-2.48	-2.35	-2.22
MECHMC	1.0	-2.2	-2.1	-2.2	-2.2	13.570	2.76	2.70	2.76	2.81
ELECMC	1.0	-2.2	-2.2	-2.2	-2.2	16.868	1.78	1.75	1.79	1.81
VEHCL	1.0	-1.5	-1.5	-1.5	-1.6	16.182	1.70	1.66	1.71	1.72
OTHMFG	1.0	-2.7	-2.6	-2.7	-2.7	17.003	0.53	0.49	0.54	0.56
TRNSP	1.0	-0.9	-0.9	-0.9	-0.9	41.784	1.51	1.49	1.51	1.51
ELEC	1.0	-0.2	0.2	0.2	0.2	21.517	0.47	0.45	0.48	0.48
CONSTR	1.0	0.1	0.2	0.2	0.1	56.196	-0.70	-0.74	-0.70	-0.68
SRVCE	1.0	0.4	0.4	0.4	0.4	183.184	0.13	0.13	0.14	0.12

P: price (Rs.), O/P: output (Rs. 000s Crores)
crs: constant returns to scale, irs: increasing returns to scale,
lr: long run, sr: short run

of employment. If trade liberalisation leads to non competitiveness of small scale industries on account of their smaller minimum efficient scale, it would lead to exit of a large number of firms. Only a small number would be able to survive and supply the residual demand in the domestic market assuming all the demand is not met from imports. Unemployment would lead to fall in incomes and lower demand for domestic goods. This would imply a further worsening of the terms of trade and a greater depreciation of the real exchange rate, leading to a larger welfare loss than what the model exhibits. With the model, since all factors are assumed to be fully employed, the behaviour would be to lower factor incomes, domestic demand and increase welfare loss.

International Evidence

The results on welfare in the scale economies and imperfect competition case are quite similar to the CRS case. The international evidence is mixed for developed countries. Studies like Harris (1984) report welfare gain as a percentage of national income to the tune of 8.6% for a model with product differentiation with scale economies, 6.2% for a model without product differentiation and 2.4% for a model with constant returns to scale. The study for Spain by Roland-Holst, Polo, and Sancho (1995) show an increase in welfare by 1% due to incorporation of scale economies over the CRS case. The study by Harrison, Rutherford, and Tarr (1997) reports a marginal increase in welfare, for the world as a whole, in the IRS case of US$3 billion over the CRS case which stands at US$93 billion. For developing countries, the study by Devarajan and Rodrik (1989) for Cameroon shows, almost a doubling of welfare gains by incorporating IRS as opposed to the CRS case.

The theoretical reasoning behind the large welfare changes in general equilibrium models with increasing returns and imperfect competition can be attributed to the following reasons.

The cause of high welfare gains in the case of the Canadian model by Harris (1984) is the Eastman Stykolt Hypothesis (ESH) in which the domestic producers price their output equal to the tariff inclusive price of imports. As explained by Deardorff (1986) a tariff cut will lead to a fall in the domestic price. This in turn implies losses for some firms which exit. The remaining firms expand output and move down their average cost curves which results in efficiency gains despite a probable fall in total output. In the context of equation (4.2), there are welfare gains due to increased imports as mentioned in term 1. Also there are welfare gains due to increased output by each firm as they move down the average cost curves. In absence of this pricing rule, the welfare gains will depend on the elasticities of demand (the ratio of price minus marginal cost to price equals the reciprocal of the demand elasticity) provided there are no adverse terms of trade effects.

While modelling imperfect competition the other approach used is the conjectural variation approach as outlined in Chapter 7 of deMelo and Tarr (1992).

In this approach the ratio of price minus marginal cost to price equals that of exogenously calibrated conjectures to the number of firms times elasticity of market demand. While moving from the constant returns to scale or increasing returns to scale case with average cost pricing to imperfect competition there is a change in the demand elasticities. The price set by the firms and the subsequent profits (losses) are dependent on these elasticities and are often responsible for large welfare changes as shown by Harrison, Rutherford, and Tarr (1997). The importance of elasticities for welfare changes are also highlighted by Norman (1990).

Another cause for larger welfare changes is the inclusion of product differentiation. Harris (1984) allows for a change in the number of varieties available due to trade. The results show that there is a smaller welfare gain with product differentiation than without it. This is because any policy which leads to exit of firms will cause a reduction in the available varieties which results in smaller welfare gain. Harrison, Rutherford, and Tarr (1997) do not find large welfare gains by modelling product differentiation primarily because they do not allow for reduction in varieties.

The assumption used by many modellers is the perfect mobility of fixed capital across sectors. This has been relaxed by Mercenier and Schmitt (1996) who show less gain from trade liberalisation with economies of scale due to irreversibility of fixed costs. The main point is that sunk costs act as an entry as well as an exit barrier. Thus, efficiency gains are not realised to that extent, as observed in models without sunk costs.

Conclusion

The chapter analysed the impacts of trade liberalisation on welfare of the Indian economy. Simulations were performed under various market structures, regimes including economies of scale and incorporating devaluation of the real exchange rate. Each simulation was subjected to sensitivity analysis to see the robustness of the results and identify the parameters crucial for behaviour of the economy.

Consumers will be better of with lower prices of commodities. Trade liberalisation implies lowering/eliminating tariff barriers which would make consumers better off, by reducing prices. Hence every country should indulge in trade liberalisation. This argument will continue to hold provided the domestic country can increase exports to account for the increased imports. In the short run a trade deficit will not hamper welfare, but persistent trade deficits of a large magnitude would hamper welfare. The reason being the inability of exports to pay for imports. The trade deficit may persist on two counts. One, the inefficiency in domestic production, is either due to excessive domestic taxes or to inefficient scales of operation. Two, the adverse terms of trade that might arise after trade liberalisation. The study analysed trade liberalisation under all three effects of fixed terms of trade (small country), endogenous terms of trade (large country) and returns to scale to account for efficiencies of scale.

In the small country assumption, there are unambiguous gains from trade liberalisation. In the large country assumption, with endogenous terms of trade, what emerges is that tariff cuts may or may not lead to welfare loss depending on the capability of producers to effectively transfer resources between the domestic and export markets based on a CET function. The presence of a CET function may lead to welfare gains depending on the magnitude of the elasticity of transformation. The lower the elasticity of transformation larger the welfare gains. The higher the CET elasticities more homogeneous are the export and domestic goods. Normally export goods tend to be of high quality and also many firms operate for pure exports, implying a zero CET elasticity. If trade liberalisation leads to a fall in the exports, the model assumes that the factors would be absorbed to produce domestic commodities of lower quality. If this does not happen and factors remain under-utilised, then liberalisation would lead to welfare loss. If exports increase in sectors with low CET, then partial liberalisation would give smaller gains as opposed to full liberalisation. The magnitude of welfare estimates are sensitive to the export elasticities facing the domestic producers. Higher the export elasticity greater the welfare gains.

In dynamic model, change in the structure of production which accounts for larger share of imports, may eventually lead to welfare gains on account of lower price of commodities. However in a large country case, the terms of trade effects would persist. Adverse movement in the terms of trade would still lead to welfare loss despite a dynamic horizon.

Devaluation of the currency is also an important decision taken by the government. The welfare impacts are adverse for lower tariff cuts and become progressively better with larger levels of liberalisation captured by bigger tariff cuts.

Devaluation makes imports expensive and exports cheaper. This helps in reducing trade deficit while there is an increase in income due to transfers from the rest of the world. This free lunch is primarily responsible for increased welfare.

Increasing returns to scale and imperfect competition may not play an important role in trade liberalisation for the Indian economy. In theoretical as well as empirical literature the emphasis is on intra-industry trade rather than inter-industry trade, which enables firms within an industry to exploit economies of scale. In the Indian case the exports of industries with economies of scale are not large enough to gain from trade liberalisation. Traditionally these sectors were promoted for import substitution. The loss of terms of trade and decrease in revenue due to cut in import tariffs are primarily responsible for the large welfare loss due to trade liberalisation. The results in empirical literature which show large change in welfare due to increasing returns is mainly due to the different elasticities of demand in the increasing returns to scale case as opposed to the constant returns to scale case. The other point to note is that the scale economies were restricted only to organised sectors. Economies of scale persist in all sectors, whether organised or unorganised. The model did not account for the unorganised sector due to lack of data. If trade liberalisation leads to small inefficient firms in the unorganised sector to exit, the remaining firms may gain marginally from increasing output. The factors from firms which have exited may not be fully utilised. This would lead to welfare loss.

Though the model uses the latest data set available at the time of study, the technology coefficients in the Input–output table reflect the policy regime in the pre liberalisation era. As the result, the import coefficient matrix is sparse. This does not enable the producers to capture benefits accruing from lower input costs. Welfare effects could be adversely affected as a result of using old technology coefficients.

Chapter 5

Results from the Tax Model

Introduction

This chapter deals with the various tax policy simulations in the static and sequentially dynamic context. The government, since the initiation of the reforms process, has undertaken certain changes in the tax system. In addition, it has also proposed certain changes in the tax structure, which are yet to be implemented. The aim therefore is to analyse the welfare effects of the already implemented as well as proposed changes in the tax structure.

The chapter structure is as follows. The basic indirect tax structure existing before the changes were implemented is outlined to develop the basis for the various policy experiments. Later sections deal with the indirect tax reforms already implemented. This is followed by the analyses of a VAT in both the static and sequentially dynamic context. The last section concludes.

The inferences drawn from experiments are dependent on the model structure used and the structural characteristics of the data. These two determine the nature of the results, besides determining the range of feasible policy experiments. India had a serious balance of payments problem in the early 1990s and therefore any simulation would have to account for the trade deficit. The model does not have a transformation function between domestic sales and exports. The real exchange rate is responsible for clearing the external sector. The endogenously determined tax rates are such that revenue neutrality is maintained. An important factor that would influence the results is the sparse import matrix. The regime before liberalisation has followed an import substitution policy and hence the input–output table has an import matrix full of zeros. This limits the ability of the model to exploit the cost advantage of imports in the event of substitution of domestic intermediate goods by imported intermediates.

The value added functions are Cobb–Douglas, not by assumption. These functions were estimated using a Box-Cox procedure and were found to have unitary elasticities of substitution. From the demand side, the 19 sector disaggregation has made it difficult to estimate a demand system. As a result a Cobb–Douglas utility function is assumed. In simulations when the alternate tax systems are evaluated, essentials are given a favourable tax treatment as compared to the base case. The objective has been to ascertain the extent to which indirect taxes may affect welfare.

The fraction of the population paying direct taxes is very small and incorporating more than one income class is difficult. As a result, tax policies do not evaluate the impact on distribution.

The indirect tax structure is very complex and the government had restricted imports of many commodities. The result has been no imports for many commodities except essentials. From the model perspective, it implies a sparse import coefficient matrix. Therefore any functional form for substitution between domestic and imported intermediate inputs is not going to have a significant impact. Therefore the Leontief function is not a very strong assumption.

Description of Simulations and Tax Structure

The simulations performed are of two types. One termed as indirect tax reforms, which analyse the welfare effects of certain proposals already implemented by the government. The other are related to VAT, an issue which is actively investigated in policy circles. The indirect tax reforms are restricted only to reduction / elimination / substitution of agriculture and fertiliser subsidies, apart from analysing the impacts of MODVAT and its extensions to capital goods. The VAT simulations deal with the different structures which can possibly lead to higher welfare gains or lower welfare loss.

Table 5.1 shows the various tax rates imposed on different sectors. Only the major indirect taxes are shown in the table. The table also shows the Net Indirect Tax (NIT) collected by taxing inputs from various sectors. The agriculture sector gets subsidies in the form of irrigation, electricity, fertiliser. Of these, fertiliser is accounted separately from the others. The agriculture subsidy is reflected as a negative tax on input of agriculture. The sales tax is same for both domestic and imported commodities, but there is a substantial difference in the excise and tariff structure. The capital goods sectors, MECHMC, ELECMC, VEHCL and OTHMFG attract very high tariffs, as compared to excise. This was done to promote domestic capital goods. Other sectors such as CHEM and PETRO also have very high tariffs, primarily to raise revenues. T_{int}^{D} refers to the tax rate on domestic intermediate inputs paid by the producer. T_{final}^{D} refers to the tax rate on final domestic consumption paid by the consumer and may differ from that of the producer depending on subsidies and taxes levied to consumers. T_{int}^{M} depicts the tax rate on imported intermediate inputs paid by the producer.

The simulations would involve changing some or all of these taxes and endogenously determining new rates to maintain revenue neutrality. The precise change implemented will be described more accurately with the various scenarios.

Table 5.1: **Domestic and Imported Indirect Tax Structure**

Sector	Excise (%)	Sales (%)	T^D_{int} (%)	T^D_{final} (%)	Tariff (%)	T^M_{int} (%)	NIT
AGRI	0.1	0.5	-3.8	-5.9	4.8	5.3	-3.874
CCNG	27.4	10.0	37.4	37.4	0.0	10.0	0.331
MINES	1.1	0.0	1.1	0.0	4.5	4.5	0.054
FDPR	9.2	6.0	26.9	26.9	52.8	58.8	1.181
TEXT	1.8	2.0	3.8	3.8	8.9	10.9	2.577
PAPER	3.7	2.0	5.7	5.7	19.9	21.9	0.458
CHEM	15.7	7.0	22.7	22.7	84.6	91.6	3.150
PETRO	13.7	15.0	28.7	28.7	160.9	175.9	3.546
FERT	0.1	2.0	-49.5	0.0	0.0	-60.9	0.385
CEMENT	12.8	5.0	17.8	17.8	76.6	81.6	0.716
METLS	7.8	4.0	11.8	0.0	61.8	65.8	2.036
MECHMC	9.3	5.0	14.3	14.3	22.7	27.7	1.299
ELECMC	8.8	4.0	12.8	12.8	57.6	61.6	1.497
VEHCL	7.8	2.0	18.8	18.8	20.0	22.0	1.453
OTHMFG	2.4	0.0	2.4	2.4	128.9	128.9	1.670
TRNSP	0.0	0.0	2.3	2.3	0.0	0.0	3.123
ELEC	0.0	0.0	5.1	5.1	0.0	0.0	1.131
CONSTR	0.0	0.0	0.0	0.0	0.0	0.0	2.709
SRVCE	0.0	0.0	1.3	1.3	0.0	0.0	2.664

NIT (net indirect tax) in Rs. 000s Crores

Indirect Tax Reforms

The simulations are carried out to study the impact of indirect tax reforms. The purpose of carrying out reforms by the government was clarified in the introduction. What is not clear is the type of replacement tax structure required to maintain revenue neutrality. The government in its attempt to maintain revenue neutrality had increased the tax rates on goods not covered under MODVAT. Previous studies on impact of MODVAT have dealt with issues like cascading, impact on revenue, compliance and exports. Narayana, Bagchi, and Gupta (1991) have analysed these in a partial equilibrium framework which enables them to carry out the study at a much more disaggregated level. The present exercise is aimed at the welfare characteristics of the proposed or implemented policy change, simultaneously accounting for feedbacks in the economy.

The demand system is Cobb–Douglas which implies unitary elasticity of substitution. This might seem restrictive initially, but the scope of the analysis focusses on the relative efficiency of indirect taxes as compared to taxes on final consumption. Thus differential tax rates on basic and other goods is studied relative to elimination of indirect taxes and not on change in tax rates for final consumption.

Table 5.1: shows the composition of various taxes. Among them, sales tax is the only one amenable for change to raise revenue for the following reasons. Direct taxes have not been successful in the past in generating revenue. Customs duties are already quite high and further increase is difficult to justify and not possible in the light of the WTO agreements. MODVAT implies the reduction of union excise and counter-vailing duties. State excise is predominantly on liquor. Other indirect taxes are a number of taxes acting on specific commodities levied by the centre, but not a major source of revenue. When simulations are performed to eliminate subsidies, it implies reduction in tax rates for other commodities. In this case the reduction is applied across all commodities. If the sales tax rates for some commodities are zero, they are kept zero in the counterfactual and the reduction applies to other commodities.

To generate the added revenue either a uniform or differentiated rate is added to the existing sales tax structure. The resulting tax is then $\tau_{i/s} + \tau_s + \tau$, where $\tau_{i/s}$ are all the indirect taxes except sales tax, τ_s is the sales tax and τ is the new additive rate. This form of replacement is termed as additive. When this additive rate is same for all commodities it is termed as uniform as opposed to different rates for essentials and luxuries is termed as differentiated. When the existing sales tax is multiplied by a uniform or differentiated (2 rates),[1] the replacement is termed as multiplicative. In this case the resulting rate is $\tau_{i/s} + \tau_s \times \tau$. For some of the commodities (OTHMFG, TRNSP, ELEC, CONSTR and SRVCE.) the sales taxes are zero and this rate is maintained in counterfactual simulations. In case of reduction of tax rates, the reduction is applied across all commodities. In this case the additive case implies a tax rate of $\tau_{i/s} + \tau_s - \tau$, $\tau > 0$ and multiplicative implies $(\tau_{i/s} + \tau_s) \times \tau$, $\tau < 1$.

The sectors which comprise of essential commodities are agriculture (AGRI), food and food products (FDPR), textiles (TEXT), medicines, pharmaceuticals (CHEM) and subsidised diesel used in transport of food commodities (PETRO). As far as the petroleum[2] sector goes the government is involved in cross subsidisation of petroleum products. Commodities like petrol, aviation turbine fuel are priced very high while commodities like kerosene and diesel are heavily subsidised. As long as the revenues from high price commodities continue to subsidise the low price ones the government has no problems. Of late the revenues have not kept up with the subsidies and the deficit, termed as the oil pool deficit, is increasing. The above point is important from the simulation perspective. In the differentiated replacement the already highly taxed petroleum sector is given preferential treatment along with the above mentioned sectors by assigning them a replacement rate lower than that imposed on other commodities. The petroleum sector as such is not a major component of final consumption but it has an indirect impact on transportation that is relevant from the welfare point of view. The 6 sectors which account for more than 90% of the private final consumption expenditure are agriculture (AGRI): 102.334 (34.7%), service (SRVCE): 75.436 (25.6%), textiles (TEXT): 35.274 (12%), food and food products (FDPR): 34.466 (11.7%), transport services (TRNSP): 17.564 (6%) and chemicals and chemical products (CHEM): 10.241 (3.5%). Any change which affects the prices of these

---

[1]The lower rate is 50% of the higher in all scenarios.

[2]Petroleum is considered as one homogeneous commodity. The differential tax rates and subsidies prevalent on different petroleum commodities are not modelled. The arguments outlined below are only to highlight the relevance and importance of the pricing policy of the government.

goods is likely to have a major impact on welfare.

Depending on how this new tax is administered two possible cases arise. One is similar to VAT, with consumption of final commodities being taxed. The other being similar to the current structure in which taxes levied on commodities are not refunded. This leads to cascading. The simulations are performed to analyse the current state of tax administration as well as the potential case of VAT. Burgess and Stern (1993) discuss the various options and problems associated with VAT in India.

This section is arranged as follows. Elimination of subsidies is studied first followed by the impact of substitution of one subsidy for another. In conclusion implications of introduction of MODVAT and its extensions to the capital goods sector is studied.

Table 5.2 outlines the simulation particulars of indirect tax reforms undertaken in the study. The objective is to provide a brief formulation of the policy scenario. Each scenario is discussed as length during the discussion of the results.

The *scenario name* refers to the simulations performed. The *Change in Tax/Subsidy Rate* refers to the policy that is implemented. It depicts whether a tax or subsidy has been reduced, increased, imposed or eliminated and on which sector. The *Change in Sector* refers to the particular sector(s) on which the policy has its impact. The final column *Replacement Regime* deals with the structure and incidence of taxes and subsidies in the counter factual run.

Table 5.2: Simulation Particulars for Indirect Tax Reforms

Name of Scenario	Change in Tax/ Subsidy Rate	Change in Sector	Replacement Regime
1 Elimination of Agriculture Subsidy	Input Subsidy on AGRI eliminated	AGRI	Reduce indirect taxes (D and M) on remaining sectors
2 Elimination of Fertiliser Subsidy	Input Subsidy on FERT eliminated	FERT	Reduce indirect taxes (D and M) on remaining sectors
3 Substitution of FOOD with AGRI Subsidy	Final Subsidy on AGRI reduced	AGRI	Increase Intermediate subsidy (D) on AGRI sector
4 Substitution of FOOD with FERT Subsidy	Final Subsidy on AGRI eliminated	FERT	Increase Intermediate subsidy on FERT sector
5 Substitution of AGRI with FOOD Subsidy	Input Subsidy on AGRI eliminated	AGRI	Increase Final subsidy on AGRI sector
6 Substitution of FERT with FOOD Subsidy	Input Subsidy on FERT eliminated	FERT	Increase Final subsidy on AGRI sector
7 MODVAT	Excise eliminated on MODVAT sectors	MODVAT sectors	Increase Excise on non MODVAT sectors
8 MODVAT to Capital Goods	Excise Tax eliminated	ALL sectors	Increase Sales tax on sectors

Table 5.2 means the following.

- In the Elimination cases pertaining to AGRI and FERT, the subsidy rate on intermediate use is set to zero. The remaining sectors then face a reduction in their indirect tax rates on intermediate inputs.

- In the Substitution cases, FOOD (final) with AGRI and FERT (input) and vice a versa, the final (input) subsidy is set to zero and the corresponding input (final) subsidy on intermediate inputs (AGRI) is increased.

- In the **MODVAT** case and its extension to capital goods, excise tax is set to zero with a corresponding increase in sales tax, depending on the relevant sectors included in MODVAT.

Elimination of Subsidies

Fertiliser, food and agriculture are three major subsidies. The effects of elimination of each of these, either in isolation or in combination with one another will be analysed. This subsection deals with the removal of agriculture and fertiliser subsidies in isolation. This removal is compensated by the two types of sales tax regimes mentioned earlier.

As mentioned previously, the commodities with lower tax rates are specified exogenously with a tax rate half that of the remaining commodities.

Elimination of Agriculture Subsidy

The agriculture sector AGRI comprises of paddy, wheat, other cereals, pulses, sugarcane, jute, cotton, tea, coffee, rubber, other crops, animal husbandry, forestry and logging and fishing. Of these subsidy is given to crops in form of cheap electricity, irrigation etcetera. Farmers also gets fertilisers at a lower price, than the production price of fertilisers. This is accounted separately as fertiliser subsidy and is not included in the input subsidy to agriculture. This subsidy is termed as input subsidy for modelling purposes. The government also gives subsidy on final consumption of these crops through the public distribution system. For modelling purposes, this subsidy on final consumption is termed as food subsidy. In the model, there is a sector on manufacturing of food products called FDPR, which comprises of sugar, khandsari and boora, hydrogenated oil and other food and beverages. Commodities under this sector like sugar are also subsidised through the public distribution system. However from the simulation exercises, the subsidy is not extended to these commodities, but restricted only to those under the AGRI sector.

When agriculture subsidy is eliminated, the input subsidies to the AGRI sector are set to zero. Since subsidies are eliminated, the necessity to generate revenues reduces. This reduction is revenue requirements can be compensated by reducing tax rates either on final consumption only or extending them to the whole system including intermediate production. The simulations are performed using both these substitution regimes. The objective is to analyse the reasons for differential welfare gains in the two regimes. The FDPR, TEXT and CHEM sectors attract a tax rate that is half that of the other sectors. The reason is that these sectors comprise of essentials and expenditure on these commodities constitutes a large share of total expenditure.

Table 5.4 mentions the welfare effects and factor prices under various tax replacement structures for elimination of agriculture subsidy in isolation.

Table 5.3: Glossary of Abbreviations

imax	Maximum Income including value of leisure (Rs. 000 Crores)
pfce	Private Final Consumption Expenditure (Rs. 000 Crores)
inv	Investment Expenditure (Rs. 000 Crores)
cpi	Consumer Price Index
w	wage rate Rs
r	price of capital Rs
er	real exchange rate
leis	leisure consumption
lab	labour supply
ev	Equivalent Variation (Rs. 000 Crores)

Table 5.4: Removal of Agriculture Subsidies

	Base	Final				Intermediate			
		DA	DM	UA	UM	DA	DM	UA	UM
pfce	294.488	292.367	291.312	292.279	290.722	293.752	296.372	293.809	296.245
inv	108.396	107.718	106.640	107.729	106.496	108.251	108.630	108.310	109.187
cpi	1.000	0.994	0.991	0.995	0.997	1.000	0.999	1.001	1.017
w	1.000	0.992	0.985	0.992	0.980	0.997	1.007	0.997	1.003
r	1.000	0.993	0.987	0.992	0.983	0.997	1.007	0.998	1.005
er	1.000	1.008	1.073	1.014	1.111	1.008	0.994	1.010	1.052
leis	130.889	130.901	131.274	130.850	131.066	130.828	131.281	130.790	130.689
lab	174.519	174.507	174.134	174.557	174.342	174.579	174.126	174.618	174.718
ev	0.000	2.882	5.209	2.506	3.662	0.461	-0.123	0.063	-5.168

For abbreviations refer to the glossary in Table 5.3
U: uniform; D: differentiated; A: additive; M: multiplicative

The results show unambiguous welfare gains from the removal of agriculture subsidy, when the tax rates are reduced for final consumption only. When the tax rates are reduced for intermediate consumption as well, the corresponding welfare gains (losses) are lower (higher). The imposition of uniform tax rates on all commodities gives lower welfare gains as compared to differentiated case, where essentials are taxed at half the rate as other commodities. The multiplicative replacement scheme is more welfare enhancing as compared to the additive case with tax replacement on final consumption, as opposed to the replacement which includes intermediate consumption.

Table 5.5: **Removal of Agriculture Subsidy – Change in Prices (%)**

Sector	Base P_c	Final DA	DM	UA	UM	Intermediate DA	DM	UA	UM
AGRI	0.94	0.43	6.16	0.32	5.84	0.64	6.80	0.64	7.65
CCNG	1.37	-1.82	-5.09	-2.62	-11.79	-1.02	6.77	-1.31	-3.42
MINES	1.00	-2.40	-1.00	-3.40	-1.20	-1.20	-0.40	-1.50	-0.50
FDPR	1.26	-0.79	-10.47	-0.24	-6.90	0.71	-7.85	1.11	-0.63
TEXT	1.04	-3.08	-1.73	-2.41	-1.06	-1.54	-2.99	-1.06	-0.67
PAPER	1.06	-1.23	-0.28	-2.27	-1.51	-0.57	1.32	-1.04	-0.85
CHEM	1.23	-2.77	-10.11	-2.20	-6.44	-1.71	-11.25	-1.22	-3.02
PETRO	1.29	-3.03	-12.67	-2.41	-8.31	-2.02	-6.29	-1.79	-4.20
FERT	1.00	-2.00	0.60	-3.00	1.10	-1.70	-5.20	-2.00	-1.30
CEMENT	1.18	-1.78	-2.21	-2.63	-5.60	-1.19	3.65	-1.53	-2.38
METLS	1.00	0.00	0.00	0.00	0.00	0.00	0.00	0.00	0.00
MECHMC	1.14	-1.84	-1.05	-2.62	-3.41	-1.22	5.07	-1.66	-1.92
ELECMC	1.13	-1.86	-1.33	-2.75	-3.63	-1.24	4.70	-1.60	-1.77
VEHCL	1.19	-1.85	-2.02	-2.61	-5.47	-1.26	5.30	-1.60	-2.44
OTHMFG	1.02	-2.05	0.20	-2.93	0.20	-1.27	2.44	-1.66	-0.98
TRNSP	1.02	-0.49	-2.54	-0.49	-2.44	-0.59	-3.42	-0.59	-3.13
ELEC	1.05	-0.48	-4.57	-0.38	-4.09	-0.48	-5.71	-0.48	-6.37
CONSTR	1.00	-0.30	0.10	-0.20	0.30	-0.40	0.60	-0.50	-0.60
SRVCE	1.02	-0.49	-2.75	-0.49	-2.94	-0.20	-1.67	-0.20	-1.77

U: uniform; D: differentiated; A: additive; M: multiplicative

Table 5.5 depicts the percentage change in consumer prices for all scenarios under agriculture subsidy elimination. As seen from this table, there is an increase in price of agriculture, primarily due to reduced subsidy leading to an increase in the producer price. Higher producer price translates into a higher consumer price. As less revenue is now required to be generated there is a fall in the consumer price of other commodities. The sectors in which agriculture output is a large component exhibit an increase in their prices. As mentioned before, OTHMFG, TRNSP, ELEC, CONSTR and SRVCE sectors have no sales tax, which is maintained in the counterfactual simulation. So the consumer prices are dependent on producer price of these commodities. A rise in the producer price will lead to an increase in consumer price of these commodities. The producer price in turn depends on the technology and relative prices of inputs. The sectors in which there is a large share of agriculture input, either direct or indirect will lead to an appreciation of prices. As expected, the differential case leads to higher welfare on account of lower price of essentials. The additive and multiplicative replacement schemes show opposite welfare effects in the final and intermediate replacement scheme. The multiplicative scheme showing larger welfare loss than the additive scheme with replacement taxes on intermediate inputs as opposed to the case with final replacement only. Multiplicative case scales up the tax rates in the same proportion, thus maintaining the relative tax rates on commodities. The additive case, for the same rates across all commodities, results in a change in the relative tax rates, resulting in a fall in relative rates of the more expensive commodities as opposed to cheaper ones. When this tax structure is imposed on final consumption only, the additive case leads to less welfare gains for the reasons mentioned above. The implicit assumption, which is corroborated by data is that essentials attract lower taxes than non-essentials. Thus one expects and finds welfare effects to be ranked based on replacement structure to be $M > A$. Whether $UM > DA$ depends on the differential rates imposed on essentials and the original relative tax rates on these commodities. What can be said unambiguously is that $D > U$, as it makes essentials relatively cheaper.

With the replacement tax structure extended to include intermediate inputs, the ranking of welfare gains according to the different structure changes. The reasons are as follows. The fall in tax rate for final consumption is now much less as the cut in rates is extended to include intermediate inputs too. This leads to a decrease in the producer price of goods, but whether this translates to a lower consumer price as compared to the final consumption case, depends on the technology and relative prices of intermediate goods. As the essentials do not form a major component of intermediate inputs, even a small rise in the price of non-essentials intermediates relative to essential ones will lead to increased producer prices. Or in other words any tax structure that makes non-essentials more expensive in production process, will lead to higher producer prices. The other point is that final tax rates cannot be lower than the final consumption case as the reduction is spread over a larger base. The additive case leads to lower producer prices compared to the multiplicative case and corresponding higher welfare gains. The fixed coefficient technology restricts the substitution possibilities of more expensive inputs with cheaper ones, resulting in higher producer prices.

Table 5.6: **Removal of Agriculture Subsidy – Change in Output (%)**

Sector	base O/P	Final DA	DM	UA	UM	Intermediate DA	DM	UA	UM
AGRI	180.98	-0.74	-3.98	-0.79	-4.20	-0.74	-3.37	-0.76	-4.53
CCNG	10.87	0.76	3.42	0.70	2.77	0.65	1.93	0.65	2.24
MINES	2.21	1.00	2.76	1.54	3.94	0.82	0.23	1.04	2.85
FDPR	34.79	0.05	9.43	-0.45	5.63	-0.88	8.08	-1.20	1.16
TEXT	64.50	1.95	1.68	1.44	1.54	1.14	3.11	0.73	1.85
PAPER	11.37	0.44	1.17	0.67	1.32	0.41	1.21	0.54	1.98
CHEM	28.32	1.29	5.68	1.03	3.99	1.02	6.95	0.81	3.05
PETRO	19.54	0.85	4.14	0.72	2.80	0.74	2.40	0.73	2.30
FERT	7.31	-0.51	-4.35	-0.44	-5.27	-0.53	-1.04	-0.51	-4.41
CEMENT	10.80	0.63	3.22	0.97	5.18	0.88	-0.56	1.11	3.81
METLS	21.45	0.45	0.06	0.78	0.83	0.64	-1.19	0.88	2.13
MECHMC	13.57	0.97	0.44	1.58	2.25	0.93	-3.30	1.30	2.56
ELECMC	16.87	0.95	0.30	1.61	2.07	0.92	-3.02	1.30	2.57
VEHCL	16.18	0.88	1.12	1.46	3.57	0.90	-2.69	1.21	3.07
OTHMFG	17.00	0.94	0.81	1.44	1.06	0.78	-0.36	1.04	2.22
TRNSP	41.78	0.18	1.85	0.21	1.99	0.40	2.25	0.43	2.76
ELEC	21.52	0.46	1.57	0.42	1.45	0.44	2.12	0.42	2.48
CONSTR	56.20	-0.31	-1.34	-0.31	-1.53	0.25	-0.37	0.38	1.15
SRVCE	183.18	0.08	1.84	0.14	2.20	0.17	1.52	0.21	2.29

U: uniform; D: differentiated; A: additive; M: multiplicative

Table 5.6 depicts the percentage change in outputs for all scenarios under agriculture subsidy elimination. There is an unambiguous fall in output of agriculture and fertiliser sectors. Higher producer and consumer price of agricultural output leads to a fall in demand and output. Since fertiliser is a major input into agriculture, there is a corresponding fall in the demand and output of fertiliser sector. The larger the fall (rise) in price, the greater in the increase (decrease) in output. With replacement scheme extended to include intermediate goods, the fall (rise) in price is less (more) leading to a corresponding rise (fall) in output to a greater (smaller) extent.

Elimination of Fertiliser Subsidy

The elimination of fertiliser subsidy can take place by two methods. One by lowering the retention price offered to manufacturers. This price is based on a 12% return on investment and depends on capacity utilisation, type of input and differs from plant to plant. The other is by charging a higher price per tonne to farmers. The subsidy is modelled as ad valorem on the use of fertiliser, and for counterfactual simulations this ad valorem rate will be set to zero. From simulation purposes it does not matter whether the retention price offered to producers is lowered or price charged to farmers is higher. What matters is that fertiliser input in agriculture has become expensive on account of subsidy elimination on both domestic and imported fertilisers.

The impact on factor prices and welfare is given in Table 5.7. There are unambiguous welfare gains when the replacement tax structure is restricted to lowering tax rates on final consumption only. Moreover when there are lower tax rates on the essentials (differential scenario), there are more welfare gains as compared to the uniform case. The multiplicative scheme also has relatively higher welfare gains as opposed to the additive case. When the reduction in tax rates is extended to intermediate inputs the welfare gains reduce or in some cases lead to welfare loss when compared to the case where reduction is restricted to final consumption only. The relative rankings of the various scenarios however remains the same in both the cases.

A point to note is that the welfare gains in the fertiliser subsidy elimination are correspondingly higher than the agriculture subsidy elimination for each scenario. The implications are that fertiliser sector has limited impacts on producer price of commodities, with agricultural price bearing the brunt of subsidy elimination. Beyond the agriculture sector, there is hardly any impact of fertiliser use.

Table 5.7: Removal of Fertiliser Subsidies

	Base	Final DA	DM	UA	UM	Intermediate DA	DM	UA	UM
pfce	294.488	291.069	289.739	290.921	289.138	293.158	294.902	293.244	295.065
inv	108.396	107.320	105.949	107.332	105.775	108.129	108.247	108.218	108.800
cpi	1.000	0.990	0.989	0.992	0.995	0.999	1.003	1.001	1.019
w	1.000	0.987	0.978	0.986	0.974	0.995	0.999	0.995	0.997
r	1.000	0.989	0.981	0.988	0.977	0.996	1.001	0.996	1.000
er	1.000	1.014	1.096	1.022	1.132	1.013	1.030	1.017	1.077
leis	130.889	130.918	131.296	130.843	131.115	130.811	131.127	130.753	130.615
lab	174.519	174.489	174.111	174.565	174.292	174.596	174.280	174.654	174.792
ev	0.000	4.721	6.892	4.178	5.591	1.099	-0.005	0.503	-4.663

For abbreviations refer to the glossary in Table 5.3
U: uniform; D: differentiated; A: additive; M: multiplicative

The change in prices is given in Table 5.8. There is an increase in the price of agriculture output due to an increase in the cost of fertiliser input. The higher producer price of agriculture leads to a higher consumer price. The producer price of commodities will depend on the relative prices of inputs. The price rise in agriculture in this case is higher than in the elimination of agriculture subsidy. So all commodities using agriculture as inputs will experience an upward pressure on their producer price. However one finds larger welfare gains when fertiliser subsidy is eliminated. The reason is a fall in the price of SRVCE sector, which accounts for a large commodity in terms of consumption expenditure. The price of service sector falls mainly due to the negligible impact of fertiliser price on all other sectors except agriculture. As a result, prices of FDPR and CHEM sector fall to a larger extent in which SRVCE is a major input. The price of textiles rises mainly on account of higher price of agriculture despite a lower tax rate on TEXT. The other reason is the low consumer price in the base case for textiles.

The welfare is higher when the reduction in taxes is restricted to final consumption. When, reduction in taxes is extended to intermediate inputs, the reduction is much smaller as the base is increased to account for intermediate inputs. The fall in producer price will be higher than the case where reduction is restricted to final consumption, but may have higher consumer prices on account of smaller reduction in tax rates on final consumption. The multiplicative case shows larger variation in welfare across both the scenarios. The reason for this is the following. The multiplicative rate leads to larger distortion in rates, when the rate is > 1 and lesser distortion in rates when the factor is < 1. This is reflected in the smaller variation in prices in the *UM* case as opposed to the *DM* case. The cause for lower welfare loss in the *DM* case can be attributed only to the lower rates on essentials. The other reason for prices being higher is the fixed coefficient technology which prevents producers to substitute expensive inputs with cheaper inputs.

The change in output is given in Table 5.9. As expected there is a fall in the output of agriculture due to higher prices. There is a corresponding fall in the output of fertiliser on account of lesser demand for fertiliser in agriculture

Table 5.8: **Removal of Fertiliser Subsidy – Change in Prices (%)**

Sector	Base P_c	Final DA	DM	UA	UM	Intermediate DA	DM	UA	UM
AGRI	0.94	1.81	7.55	1.70	7.33	2.23	9.67	2.23	9.78
CCNG	1.37	-2.84	-8.22	-4.00	-14.19	-1.60	1.89	-2.04	-6.19
MINES	1.00	-3.60	-1.50	-5.30	-1.70	-1.90	-1.30	-2.40	-1.30
FDPR	1.26	-3.81	-13.01	-3.01	-9.99	-1.59	-8.80	-0.95	-1.90
TEXT	1.04	-5.49	-2.70	-4.53	-2.12	-3.28	-3.66	-2.41	-1.35
PAPER	1.06	-2.84	-1.51	-4.26	-2.55	-1.80	0.00	-2.46	-1.70
CHEM	1.23	-4.65	-11.25	-3.75	-8.07	-3.10	-13.53	-2.36	-5.46
PETRO	1.29	-4.66	-13.83	-3.81	-10.10	-3.11	-10.49	-2.80	-7.54
FERT	1.00	2.80	6.70	1.20	7.20	3.30	0.40	2.80	2.80
CEMENT	1.18	-2.89	-3.90	-4.16	-6.96	-1.95	0.34	-2.46	-4.24
METLS	1.00	-3.10	1.10	-4.50	1.80	-2.20	-0.60	-2.90	-2.10
MECHMC	1.14	-2.80	-2.19	-4.02	-4.29	-1.92	1.84	-2.54	-3.76
ELECMC	1.13	-2.93	-2.48	-4.17	-4.52	-1.86	1.60	-2.48	-3.55
VEHCL	1.19	-2.78	-3.70	-4.04	-6.73	-2.02	1.52	-2.53	-4.55
OTHMFG	1.02	-3.12	0.00	-4.49	0.00	-1.95	0.59	-2.54	-2.15
TRNSP	1.02	-0.88	-2.83	-0.88	-2.74	-1.08	-4.79	-1.08	-4.30
ELEC	1.05	-0.67	-4.66	-0.57	-4.28	-0.76	-6.47	-0.76	-6.95
CONSTR	1.00	-0.60	-0.20	-0.60	0.00	-0.90	-0.40	-1.00	-1.30
SRVCE	1.02	-0.98	-3.34	-1.08	-3.53	-0.59	-2.36	-0.59	-2.36

U: uniform; D: differentiated; A: additive; M: multiplicative

production. The output for the uniform case is higher for non-essentials and lower for essentials than the differentiated case. The reason for this is the lower price of commodities in the differential case.

Substitution of Subsidies

The final simulation deals with the analysis of interchanging one subsidy for another. The first part deals with substitution of two major input subsidies with a subsidy on final consumption. Agriculture and fertiliser subsidies are each in turn substituted by food subsidy keeping revenue neutral. In the second part food subsidy on final consumption is substituted by subsidies on inputs. The rationale for carrying out this simulation is as follows. The government's objective is to make food and other basic commodities available to a large populace at prices that are affordable. That is the reason it gives subsidies in the first place. The question posed is the following. Whether inputs subsidies with smaller subsidies on final consumption are better than lower input subsidies with higher subsidies on final consumption? The implicit assumption made here is that the increased food subsidy would reach the populace. The other point to be noted is that the part of production of agriculture output that is retained by agriculture households for personal consumption would become more expensive on account of removal of this subsidy. This would lead to a welfare loss. Whether this would eventually lead to welfare gains or losses depends on the fraction of food grains accessible from fair price shops as proportion of total consumption. The fraction of the

Table 5.9: **Removal of Fertiliser Subsidy – Change in Output (%)**

	Base	Final				Intermediate			
Sector	O/P	DA	DM	UA	UM	DA	DM	UA	UM
AGRI	180.98	-1.79	-4.98	-1.87	-5.20	-1.76	-5.44	-1.80	-6.04
CCNG	10.87	1.32	3.97	1.23	3.41	1.14	3.55	1.14	3.45
MINES	2.21	1.77	3.76	2.58	4.89	1.49	2.36	1.81	4.35
FDPR	34.79	2.45	11.84	1.68	8.40	1.02	8.71	0.53	2.06
TEXT	64.50	3.83	2.51	3.08	2.41	2.58	3.99	1.97	2.62
PAPER	11.37	1.16	1.71	1.53	1.84	1.12	2.29	1.31	2.73
CHEM	28.32	2.37	6.50	1.98	5.01	1.93	8.92	1.63	4.73
PETRO	19.54	1.39	4.60	1.19	3.40	1.21	4.21	1.18	3.66
FERT	7.31	-1.72	-5.87	-1.63	-6.61	-1.74	-4.34	-1.72	-6.27
CEMENT	10.80	1.17	4.54	1.70	6.38	1.54	2.40	1.89	5.83
METLS	21.45	0.83	0.34	1.34	1.02	1.11	0.44	1.47	3.15
MECHMC	13.57	1.55	1.06	2.48	2.67	1.48	-0.86	2.04	4.07
ELECMC	16.87	1.52	0.85	2.54	2.43	1.48	-0.65	2.05	4.02
VEHCL	16.18	1.41	2.00	2.31	4.22	1.44	-0.02	1.92	4.76
OTHMFG	17.00	1.64	1.15	2.41	1.37	1.39	1.27	1.77	3.32
TRNSP	41.78	0.46	2.18	0.50	2.31	0.78	3.49	0.83	3.66
ELEC	21.52	0.92	1.81	0.86	1.71	0.88	2.89	0.86	3.04
CONSTR	56.20	-0.33	-1.60	-0.33	-1.81	0.51	0.28	0.71	1.49
SRVCE	183.18	0.36	2.27	0.46	2.61	0.50	2.31	0.55	2.86

U: uniform; D: differentiated; A: additive; M: multiplicative

population who comprise of landless agriculture labourers and who may have access to the public distribution system may stand to gain by increasing subsidy on final consumption. The model does not account for any of the above mentioned items, and thus would overestimate the welfare gains or losses. The assumption made is that the government does not run buffer stock operations and does not procure a part of the agriculture output at below market prices. All commodities are traded at market prices. The objective is to evaluate the efficacy of distortion effects of subsidy on production and consumption behaviour.

Substitution of Fertiliser and Agriculture Subsidy with Food Subsidy

This exercise is undertaken to evaluate the welfare effects of substituting subsidies in production by subsidies in final consumption. In this simulation fertiliser and agriculture subsidy was reduced by 25, 50 and 75% before being finally eliminated. At each reduction the food subsidy was increased to keep revenue the same. The effect on factor prices and welfare is shown in Table 5.10. There are small welfare gains of the tune of 0.2% for 25% reduction to 0.7% of income for elimination of agriculture subsidy. The corresponding figures for fertiliser are higher ranging from 0.27% to 1.2% of income.

The reduction of input subsidies leads to an increase in price of agriculture and fertilisers. This increased price would lead to an appreciation of producer prices of commodities that use these two goods intensively. One expects the price of manufactured food and beverages to rise on account of the elimination of agriculture and fertiliser subsidy. However the increased food subsidy compensates for the rise in output price and is reflected in a marginal fall in the price index.

The table shows larger welfare gains with reduction/elimination of fertiliser subsidy as compared to agriculture subsidy. The reason is the limited effect of fertiliser as an input into the production process. Though both would lead to an increase in producer price of some commodities, the increase would be lower with fertiliser subsidy elimination.

Table 5.10: **Replacement of Subsidies by Food Subsidy**

	Agriculture				Fertiliser				
	25%	50%	75%	100%	25%	50%	75%	100%	*base*
pfce	294.099	293.712	293.325	292.938	293.869	293.238	292.594	291.937	294.488
inv	108.227	108.057	107.888	107.717	108.153	107.905	107.652	107.393	108.396
cpi	0.998	0.997	0.996	0.994	0.997	0.995	0.992	0.990	1.000
w	0.998	0.996	0.994	0.992	0.997	0.994	0.990	0.987	1.000
r	0.999	0.998	0.996	0.995	0.998	0.996	0.995	0.993	1.000
ev	0.709	1.412	2.113	2.813	1.151	2.324	3.521	4.743	0.000

For abbreviations refer to the glossary in Table 5.3

Substitution of Food Subsidy with Fertiliser and Agriculture Subsidy

Table 5.11 shows welfare effects of substituting food subsidy with input subsidies on agriculture and fertiliser. In this simulation, the food subsidy was reduced in the same way as in the earlier case. Increasing agriculture subsidy at the cost of food subsidy leads to a welfare loss of 0.41% for 25% reduction to 1.6% of income for full reduction of food subsidy. The corresponding figures for fertiliser subsidy are 0.45% and 1.75% respectively. An agriculture subsidy increase shows lower welfare losses as its output price directly affects food commodities. In the fertiliser case, the effect is secondary due to its initial interaction with the agriculture sector. There is a welfare loss because the reduction in food subsidy is not adequately compensated by a fall in output price.

Table 5.11: **Food Subsidy Replacement by Agriculture and Fertiliser Subsidy**

	Agriculture				Fertiliser				
	25%	50%	75%	100%	25%	50%	75%	100%	*base*
pfce	295.400	296.288	297.152	297.994	295.468	296.429	297.371	298.295	294.488
inv	108.789	109.168	109.534	109.887	108.777	109.15	109.514	109.871	108.396
cpi	1.004	1.007	1.011	1.015	1.004	1.008	1.012	1.016	1.000
w	1.005	1.009	1.014	1.018	1.005	1.01	1.014	1.019	1.000
r	1.003	1.005	1.008	1.01	1.003	1.006	1.008	1.011	1.000
ev	−1.668	−3.306	−4.914	−6.493	−1.817	−3.597	−5.342	−7.054	0.000

For abbreviations refer to the glossary in Table 5.3

The model uses a fixed coefficient Leontief production function. A commodity which has a larger share (agriculture) in the production function will affect the output price more than a commodity with a smaller share (fertiliser). Any subsidy will imply a larger demand for that commodity, but the actual use of the commodity is determined by the output, which is a function of final demand. The intermediate use of commodities is determined by the technology. Any policy, like giving a subsidy, which distorts producer behaviour will have effects on relative use of inputs. Any subsidy on input commodities will result in greater use of that commodity. With a fixed coefficient technology, the possibility of substitution of expensive inputs with cheaper ones is eliminated. When subsidies are eliminated, the commodities which were subsidised become expensive. The fixed coefficient technology prevents a substitution of these commodities, by other commodities, leading to higher producer prices.

In the simulations performed, substituting subsidies on final consumption with those on intermediate inputs lead to welfare loss and vice versa. The welfare loss is higher (lower) depending on lower (higher) intensity of use of the commodity which is subsidised. Lowering the price of fertiliser will result in lowering of price of agriculture output. This will lead to an indirect effect on prices of other sectors, using agriculture output intensively (larger share in input). When subsidy on agriculture is increased, it not only reduces its own price but also has a larger impact on lowering price in other sectors, which use agriculture. Since agriculture output is more widely used in intermediate and final consumption as opposed to fertiliser, there is a smaller welfare loss. The welfare loss arises on account of higher consumer prices of agriculture, which forms the single largest item for consumption in terms of consumer expenditure. The welfare effects are reversed when input subsidies are substituted with subsidies on final consumption.

In the model used, there is only one representative consumer. As a result the welfare effects are aggregated. With many consumer classes, based on income/expenditure or occupation, the welfare effects would be different. Those consumers who spend a larger fraction of their income on agriculture output would gain with elimination of input subsidies being substituted with a subsidy on final consumption. From consumer classes based on occupation the welfare effects are a little ambiguous. Elimination of input subsidies make agriculture produce expensive, but reduce price of final consumption. That class of consumers who are classified under agriculture producers, who consume a part of their produce, would lose on account of higher input costs. If however the share of consumption from the public distribution system is higher than from home output, they would also stand to gain on account of lower consumer price. All the above is without taking into account the buffer stock operations of the government. If subsidy on final consumption is increased at the cost on intermediate inputs, it would imply a greater demand for food grains. This would mean a larger procurement of food grains, which can be possible at higher procurement prices or restricting trade of food grains to a larger extent. The welfare effects cannot be identified a priori, and require an agriculture model to analyse, an issue beyond the scope of the study.

The other important point is the allocative efficiency of capital in the various sectors. The model assumes the capital is freely mobile between sectors. If capital was more efficient in non agriculture sectors, there would be welfare gains from eliminating agriculture and fertiliser subsidy. The reason being lower returns to capital on account of higher costs.

MODVAT and Extensions

To reduce cascading and make export prices more competitive the government introduced a MODVAT. Under this scheme the central government gave refunds on excise duties on certain commodities used as inputs in production process. However goods like petroleum and textiles were clubbed along with capital goods and not brought under the purview of MODVAT. The following commodities are not a part of MODVAT: MECHMC, ELECMC, VEHCL, PETRO and TEXT. The government realised the potential loss of revenue from MODVAT and levied higher duties on commodities not under the scheme. The other rationale for not extending MODVAT to capital goods is the impression that producers would substitute labour by capital resulting in adverse impacts on employment and wages.

Application of MODVAT with Excise Tax Replacement

The welfare impacts of MODVAT with substitution of excise duties by higher rates on commodities not covered under MODVAT are shown in Table 5.12. There are minor welfare gains with the introduction of MODVAT which fall with the increased elasticity of savings. The reason for analysing the sensitivity of the elasticity of savings (η_{sav}) is that capital goods are not a part of MODVAT. Higher excise taxes on capital goods to compensate for the refund of excise taxes on other commodities, result in higher prices for commodities exempted from MODVAT. The capital accumulation and growth depend on the price of capital goods. Lower the price elasticity of savings, the smaller is the extent to which investment in capital goods will be affected.

Table 5.12: **MODVAT with Substitution of Excise Duties**

	base	$\eta_{sav} = 0.2$	$\eta_{sav} = 0.25$	$\eta_{sav} = 0.3$	$\eta_{sav} = 0.35$	$\eta_{sav} = 0.4$	$\eta_{sav} = 0.45$
imax	528.913	534.439	534.432	534.424	534.417	534.409	534.401
pfce	294.488	296.056	296.166	296.281	296.397	296.518	296.636
inv	108.397	108.239	108.070	107.894	107.716	107.531	107.349
cpi	1.000	0.997	0.997	0.997	0.997	0.997	0.997
w	1.000	1.007	1.007	1.007	1.007	1.007	1.007
r	1.000	1.004	1.004	1.004	1.004	1.004	1.004
er	1.000	0.995	0.995	0.994	0.994	0.993	0.993
ev	0.000	0.272	0.263	0.254	0.245	0.235	0.226

For abbreviations refer to the glossary in Table 5.3

The impact on prices and output along with the base case excise tax rates is shown in Table 5.13. MODVAT would imply a reduction in excise on all commodities except those to which MODVAT does not apply. The prices of commodities not under MODVAT have increased, with a corresponding fall in their output. The price fall due to MODVAT has been offset by the rise in prices of essentials due to higher excise rates on commodities used in the manufacture of these essentials. The only exception being the petroleum (PETRO) sector, which shows a fall in the price despite being out of the MODVAT scheme. The reason for it is as follows. Crude oil is the major input into producing petroleum, and attracts the highest excise tax. When MODVAT is implemented, the excise tax on crude reduces. Though crude oil production is capital intensive, and that the capital goods under MODVAT attract still higher rates, the fall in tax rate of crude compensates for the price rise. The net effect is to lower the price of petroleum. Petroleum is an important input in industry. If the demand for industrial commodities falls on account of higher prices, it leads to lower output. Given the fixed coefficient technology, the producers cannot use more petroleum which has become cheaper. Consequently there is a fall in the output of petroleum.

The welfare gains are very negligible, mainly on the account of a minor fall in the price index and a small appreciation of the exchange rate. It is necessary to reiterate the fact that the exchange rate and terms of trade will adjust to clear the foreign market. For the simulations a medium value of export elasticity of -2 has been used. The gains may primarily be due to higher export elasticities of -2 as compared to low elasticity of -1.

Table 5.13: **MODVAT – Change in Prices and Output (%)**

Sector	Base O/P	% Change in Output	Price	% Change in Price	Excise Tax Base rate
AGRI	180.980	0.65	1	0.7	0.00
CCNG	10.870	-0.67	1	1.7	0.27
MINES	2.208	-0.50	1	1.2	0.01
FDPR	34.793	8.71	1	-1.1	0.09
TEXT *	64.503	-3.26	1	1.0	0.02
PAPER	11.367	2.31	1	-2.2	0.04
CHEM	28.322	9.01	1	-3.7	0.16
PETRO *	19.540	-2.33	1	-7.9	0.14
FERT	7.306	0.70	1	-1.0	0.00
CEMENT	10.800	2.89	1	-1.3	0.13
METLS	21.449	-2.04	1	-0.9	0.08
MECHMC*	13.571	-10.75	1	0.7	0.09
ELECMC*	16.869	-11.18	1	1.8	0.09
VEHCL *	16.182	-9.08	1	1.1	0.08
OTHMFG	17.003	0.93	1	-0.9	0.02
TRNSP	41.784	-1.37	1	2.9	0.00
ELEC	21.517	-0.24	1	0.2	0.00
CONSTR	56.197	0.59	1	-0.9	0.00
SRVCE	183.184	0.01	1	0.2	0.00

Output (O/P) in Rs. 000s Crores, Price in Rs.
* commodities **not** under MODVAT

Application of MODVAT with Sales Tax Replacement

The simulations carried out use the sales taxes as instruments of generating the revenues to achieve neutrality. The model does not distinguish between levels of government (centre and state) and accrual and reduction of revenues takes place for a single government. The welfare impacts are outlined in Table 5.14. There are welfare gains for all the cases except the UA case. As expected, the scenarios ranked on basis of welfare are $DM > DA > UM > UA$. The reason is quite straightforward. Implementation of MODVAT means less revenue. To generate additional revenue, additive or multiplicative sales taxes are imposed. Since revenue has to be generated there is a positive rate of tax for the additive case and larger than unity rate for the multiplicative case. Both cases imply rise in rates. The reason for lesser welfare loss in the differentiated case compared to the uniform case is that it favours the essentials with lower tax rates. In the additive case the relative structure of sales tax changes as opposed to the multiplicative case where it remains the same. The structure in this context implies the ratios of tax rates on various goods. The structure of tax rates after the replacement is shown in Table 5.16.

Table 5.14: **MODVAT and its Extensions to Capital Goods**

	MODVAT				MODVAT to Capital Goods				
	UA	DA	UM	DM	UA	DA	UM	DM	base
pfce	296.209	295.906	294.953	294.398	296.017	295.595	294.278	293.689	294.488
inv	108.819	108.463	108.348	107.667	109.142	108.629	108.551	107.756	108.396
cpi	1.002	0.997	0.999	0.989	1.005	0.997	1.001	0.988	1.000
w	1.008	1.006	1.003	0.999	1.007	1.005	1.000	0.996	1.000
r	1.006	1.005	1.001	1.001	1.006	1.005	1.000	0.999	1.000
ev	-1.583	0.285	0.049	3.533	-2.286	0.481	-0.207	4.028	0.000

For abbreviations refer to the glossary in Table 5.3
U: uniform; D: differentiated   A: additive; M: multiplicative

Table 5.15 shows the changes in prices and output due to MODVAT using sales tax as replacement under different schemes.

Table 5.15: **MODVAT**

Sector	P	% change in Price				O/P	% change in Output			
		UA	DA	UM	DM		UA	DA	UM	DM
AGRI	1	0.7	0.6	0.3	0.1	180.981	0.2	0.3	0.5	0.8
CCNG	1	0.3	0.5	0.5	0.8	10.87	2.0	2.0	-0.9	-0.8
MINES	1	0.1	0.1	0.6	0.4	2.208	-0.9	-1.8	-0.5	-1.4
FDPR	1	-0.5	-0.7	-0.6	-1.3	34.793	4.1	5.6	2.5	6.0
TEXT*	1	1.4	0.7	0.7	-0.2	64.503	-4.5	-2.8	-2.4	-1.1
PAPER	1	-0.2	0.3	-1.1	-0.7	11.367	0.3	-0.1	0.9	0.5
CHEM	1	-2.6	-3.1	-1.5	-3.1	28.322	6.0	7.0	3.7	6.5
PETRO*	1	-8.4	-7.8	-3.7	-0.3	19.54	2.2	2.2	-1.9	-1.4
FERT	1	-2.0	-2.1	0.2	-0.8	7.306	-0.1	-0.1	0.2	0.4
CEMENT	1	-1.4	-1.2	-0.7	-0.4	10.8	2.1	1.0	0.9	-1.2
METLS	1	-0.2	0.3	0.3	1.2	21.449	-0.5	-1.5	-0.4	-2.2
MECHMC*	1	0.5	1.2	0.5	1.8	13.57	-3.1	-4.6	-3.8	-7.6
ELECMC*	1	0.8	1.3	0.4	1.4	16.868	-3.3	-4.8	-3.1	-6.3
VEHCL *	1	0.4	0.8	0.0	0.6	16.182	-2.6	-3.9	-1.5	-3.2
OTHMFG	1	0.0	0.4	-0.4	0.3	17.003	-0.9	-1.9	0.9	0.2
TRNSP	1	0.1	0.1	1.2	0.8	41.784	0.1	-0.0	-0.8	-0.7
ELEC	1	-0.1	0.2	1.0	2.4	21.517	-0.3	-0.1	-0.4	-0.5
CONSTR	1	-0.4	0.0	-0.6	0.1	56.196	0.7	0.1	0.4	-0.5
SRVCE	1	0.4	0.3	0.0	-0.2	183.184	-0.2	-0.1	-0.1	-0.1

U: uniform; D: differentiated; A: additive; M: multiplicative
* commodities **not** under MODVAT

Now, a priori, there is no reason to believe the superiority of one replacement scheme over the other in terms of its impact on welfare. What can be stated unambiguously is that any scheme which makes essentials more expensive will lead to welfare reduction. Since the additive case changes the relative structure it has a larger potential to affect welfare. If the structure becomes adverse due to large revenue requirements then potential welfare loss is higher in the additive case than in the multiplicative one. The adverse structure implies that essentials become more expensive after the policy change.

There is a general price rise barring a few commodities. The reason why prices of certain commodities have fallen is the following. The tax burden of replacement sales tax is less than the burden due to the eliminated excise tax rate. The exception is petroleum products which show a fall in prices. This sector is not under MODVAT and attracts the highest sales tax. After the replacement the tax burden further increases. As mentioned earlier, crude oil, a major input to producing petroleum, attracts the highest excise. As crude is under MODVAT it results in a decline in excise rates. The corresponding increase in sales tax rates does not lead to higher input cost of crude, despite a marginal increase in crude prices. The repercussion of this price fall is noticed in the marginal fall in price of transportation sector. However the general price fall leads to a marginal decrease in the consumer price index relative to the base case as shown in Table 5.14. Only in the case of UA, there is an increase in the price level and a corresponding welfare loss.

Table 5.16 shows the percentage change from the base case in tax rates in various replacement scenarios for MODVAT and its extension to capital goods.

Table 5.16: **Change in Tax Rates (τ%)**

Sector	τ	τ_s	MODVAT				MODVAT to Capital Goods			
	%	%	UA	DA	UM	DM	UA	DA	UM	DM
AGRI	- 3.78	0.5	-1.7	-1.7	-14.9	-14.9	-1.7	-1.7	-14.9	-14.9
CCNG	37.42	10.0	-60.2	-56.4	-43.7	-21.1	-53.8	-48.1	-29.9	-1.9
MINES	1.06	0.0	357.6	493.0	-100.0	-100.0	585.1	785.4	-100.0	-100.0
FDPR	26.88	6.0	-16.1	-22.5	-9.5	-23.6	-7.1	-16.7	1.9	-15.6
TEXT	3.75	2.0	129.7	84.0	59.0	25.3	147.4	78.7	39.7	-2.2
PAPER	5.72	1.5	20.0	45.1	-26.3	3.1	62.3	99.5	-8.3	28.2
CHEM	22.69	7.0	-47.7	-55.2	-35.0	-54.4	-37.0	-48.4	-19.1	-43.4
PETRO	28.73	15.0	16.9	10.9	57.8	24.8	-22.4	-31.4	36.9	-4.2
FERT	-49.47	2.0	9.5	12.4	4.2	7.6	14.4	18.7	6.2	10.5
CEMENT	17.83	5.0	-44.6	-36.5	-40.9	-17.2	-31.1	-19.1	-26.4	2.8
METLS	11.80	4.0	-24.8	-12.6	-28.6	0.0	-4.3	13.6	-11.1	24.2
MECHMC	14.25	5.0	34.1	44.2	38.8	68.4	-13.8	1.1	-8.0	28.6
ELECMC	12.81	4.5	37.9	49.2	34.5	60.9	-11.9	4.6	-18.1	14.4
VEHCL	18.78	2.0	25.9	33.5	11.7	20.7	-2.7	8.6	-24.2	-13.0
OTHMFG	2.39	0.0	103.1	163.3	-100.0	-100.0	204.1	293.1	-100.0	-100.0
TRNSP	2.25	0.0	0.0	0.0	0.0	0.0	0.0	0.0	0.0	0.0
ELEC	5.05	0.0	0.0	0.0	0.0	0.0	0.0	0.0	0.0	0.0
CONSTR	0.00	0.0	0.0	0.0	0.0	0.0	0.0	0.0	0.0	0.0
SRVCE	1.29	0.0	0.0	0.0	0.0	0.0	0.0	0.0	0.0	0.0

U: uniform; D: differentiated; A: additive; M: multiplicative

The tax rates for commodities not covered under the MODVAT scheme increase after a sales tax replacement scheme. The reason being an additional burden of sales tax along with excise tax which is not refunded. By extending MODVAT to capital goods sectors, the tax rates fall relative to the base case.

Extension of MODVAT to Capital Goods

Extension of MODVAT to capital goods shows larger welfare losses or gains for each of the scenarios as compared to MODVAT. This is shown in Table 5.14. There is a welfare gain with differential rates for essentials and luxury items and a welfare loss under uniform rates. The increase in factor prices in the UA case leads to higher incomes, but results in welfare loss due to increase in price index of consumption. Table 5.17 shows the percentage change of prices and quantities from benchmark for this scenario. In the cases where there is welfare gain there is a fall in the price index, which is mainly on account of lower final prices of essentials. The price of petroleum falls for two reasons. One as mentioned above in the MODVAT case. The second being the replacement sales tax is less than the earlier tax levied on this sector. However there is not much difference in the prices due to the production structure. Fall in petroleum prices lead to fall in transportation prices. This fall in petroleum prices is for the aggregate output. Whether this will lead to an increase in the prices of agriculture and other essentials will depend on the pricing policy adopted by the government.

If the subsidy on diesel and natural gas which form a component of petroleum products is lowered, the prices of agriculture and other commodities will increase more than shown due to increased transport costs. The prices of commodities which were not under the MODVAT scheme earlier, now show a fall in price.

Table 5.17: **Extending MODVAT to Capital Goods**

Sector	P	UA	DA	UM	DM	O/P	UA	DA	UM	DM
		% change in Price					% change in Output			
AGRI	1	0.6	0.6	0.1	-0.1	180.981	-0.1	0.1	0.2	0.6
CCNG	1	-0.3	-0.1	-0.1	0.3	10.87	3.6	3.7	-0.8	-0.5
MINES	1	-0.4	-0.5	0.3	0.0	2.208	-1.0	-2.3	-0.2	-1.3
FDPR	1	-0.1	-0.6	-0.2	-1.2	34.793	1.9	4.1	-0.3	3.9
TEXT	1	1.6	0.5	0.5	-0.5	64.503	-5.3	-2.7	-2.0	-0.3
PAPER	1	0.9	1.6	-0.6	0.0	11.367	-0.6	-1.1	0.4	-0.1
CHEM	1	-1.9	-2.7	-0.4	-2.4	28.322	4.5	6.1	1.6	4.9
PETRO	1	-8.5	-7.7	-1.8	2.3	19.54	4.8	5.0	-1.5	-0.6
FERT	1	-2.3	-2.6	0.6	-0.7	7.306	-0.5	-0.5	-0.2	0.1
CEMENT	1	-1.4	-1.1	-0.5	-0.2	10.8	1.7	0.2	0.2	-2.3
METLS	1	0.2	1.0	0.8	1.9	21.449	0.4	-1.1	0.7	-1.5
MECHMC	1	0.5	1.5	0.3	2.0	13.57	1.1	-1.4	0.2	-4.8
ELECMC	1	0.4	1.2	-0.2	1.0	16.868	1.0	-1.5	1.6	-2.8
VEHCL	1	0.1	0.7	-0.5	0.2	16.182	0.7	-1.3	2.8	0.5
OTHMFG	1	0.5	1.1	-0.1	0.7	17.003	-1.7	-3.1	1.1	0.2
TRNSP	1	-1.2	-1.2	0.3	-0.2	41.784	0.7	0.6	-0.4	-0.3
ELEC	1	-0.2	0.2	1.4	3.0	21.517	-0.3	-0.1	-0.4	-0.5
CONSTR	1	-0.2	0.4	-0.5	0.4	56.196	0.7	-0.1	0.5	-0.7
SRVCE	1	0.5	0.3	-0.1	-0.4	183.184	-0.2	-0.2	-0.1	-0.1

U: uniform; D: differentiated; A: additive; M: multiplicative

Implementation of Value Added Tax

Before proceeding with the analysis of a value added tax, the principles of value added taxation will be dealt with in brief. For further details the reader is referred to Fehr, Rosenberg, and Wiegard (1995) for a computable general equilibrium approach and Tait (1988) for an exposition on value added taxation.[3] The following choices have to be considered while implementing a VAT.

- Type of tax, namely consumption, income or gross product type.

- Rate structure, namely uniform or differentiated.

- Accounting methods to calculate tax liabilities.

- International taxation principles, namely destination or origin principle.

- Other issues like zero rating versus exemption and tax treatment of special industries.

---

[3]The description closely follows Fehr, Rosenberg, and Wiegard (1995).

Types of Value Added Taxes

Value added tax need not be a tax on value added either at the firm level or the aggregate industry level. The different types of VAT arise due to the different treatment of capital goods and depreciation allowances. There are three types namely consumption, income and product type VAT.

Consumption Type VAT

The consumption type allows for deduction of capital goods and depreciation along with the input of goods from total sales to arrive at the tax base. This is equivalent to a single retail sales tax to final consumers.

Income Type VAT

The income type tax allows for the deduction of intermediate inputs and depreciation allowances from the total sales, but not investment expenditure. Hence the base for income type VAT exceeds that of consumption type VAT by the amount of investment expenditure. Here the aggregate tax base is equal to the net value added.

Product Type VAT

The product type VAT allows only for deduction of intermediate inputs from the total value of sales. Thus the aggregate tax base corresponds to the gross national product.

In the simulation exercises the VAT implemented is the product type VAT. This allows for capital goods to be treated in a similar manner as intermediate inputs.

Rate Structure of a VAT

A VAT may be operated with a uniform rate or a differentiated rate. From the viewpoint of equity the differentiated rate structure is preferred with low rates on essentials and higher rates on luxuries. From the administrative point of view a uniform rate is desirable. Sometimes a zero rate is also used on essentials.

Methods to Calculate Tax Liabilities

Value added is the value that a producer adds the raw material purchases before selling the product or service. In other words, inputs are bought, workers are paid wages to work, the finished goods are sold and some profit may be left. So value added from the additive side is wages plus profits or from the subtractive side is output minus inputs. To impose a tax on value added leads to the following methods of calculating tax liabilities.

    1. $t(wages + profits)$: the additive-direct accounts method.

2. $t(wages) + t(profits)$: the additive-indirect method, where the total tax liability is the sum of taxes on individual components of value added.

3. $t(output - input)$: the subtractive-direct method.

4. $t(output) - t(input)$: the subtractive-indirect or invoice or credit method.

Of the methods listed above, only the invoice or credit method has been popular. This method never calculates the value added but the tax on components of value added and the resultant tax liabilities are subtracted to get the final tax payable. This method is very popular due to the tax liability associated with the transaction and the invoice is an evidence for the transaction and tax liability.

International Taxation Principles

This distinction arises in case of open economies which are a part of a trade block. With a single country, which is not a part of any trade block, the exports are free of any VAT and imports are subjected to the same rates as domestic commodities. For countries in a trade block, in the destination principle (DP), the commodities are taxed in the country they are consumed. Thus VAT revenues accrue to the country where they are consumed regardless of the country they are produced.

The alternative principle is the origin principle (OP). Here there are no rebates for exports and commodities are taxed in the country of production, regardless of the country of destination.

Other Issues: Zero Rating versus Exemption

Under the consumption type VAT administered under the credit method, the tax base is the domestic consumption. However, the government may wish to treat different industries differently on the basis of distributive or administrative reasons. For both these cases the industries are excluded from VAT.

However, there arise two cases of exclusion from VAT. One case is the zero rating of certain sectors. In this case the firms are expected to file returns and are imposed a zero rate on their output. As a result these firms can claim refund on the tax paid on inputs. Thus they are *in the system*. In the other case termed as exemption, the industry or sector is not a part of the system. They are not required to file returns and do not get refund on the tax paid on inputs. This results in double taxation if exempted goods enter as inputs for other sectors. Thus consumption type VAT with exemption is not a consumption tax. In this case the sectors are termed as *outside the system*.

Implementation of VAT: A Case for India

This subsection deals with the application of the above theory of VAT in a general equilibrium framework to the Indian economy. The simulations are performed using the static model in which the economy shifts from the existing indirect taxation structure to a VAT.

Two types of simulations are undertaken. One deals with the implementation of a product type VAT, in which the tax is similar to a single retail sales tax. The other case incorporates the exemption of certain sectors. With exemption, the exempted sectors pay tax/receive subsidies on inputs and are not accounted for in the system. This does not mean that there is no tax rate on consumption of these goods. This rate can be positive, negative or zero depending on the government. In the simulations undertaken, this rate on consumption of goods produced by exempt sectors is set to zero. Note that this is different from zero rating, in which the zero rated sectors do collect a refund on their taxes paid. In other words, the tax base in the exempt case exceeds that in the zero rated case by the amount of indirect taxes generated in the production process, everything else remaining the same.

It needs to be emphasised here that the VAT scenarios not only involve tax reform, but also trade liberalisation. Furthermore in all the scenarios, trade deficit is maintained in units of foreign currency along with revenue neutrality. This specification prevents hidden transfers. To maintain uniformity, a counter-vailing duty is imposed on imports, which equals the endogenously determined VAT rate. On the trade front a large country assumption is used with an export elasticity of -1. The producers are assumed to have high flexibility of resource shifts between domestic and export goods. In terms of the trade model this implies the no CET case. Lower elasticity of exports implies larger changes in the terms of trade for the same cut in tariffs, as compared to higher elasticities.

The simulation particulars are given in the Table 5.18

Table 5.18: **Simulation Particulars for VAT**			
Name of Scenario	Indirect Tax/Subsidy to Sector	Zero VAT rate on Sector	Subsidy by Sector Final Consumption
Full VAT	*no sector*	AGRI, SRVCE	*no sector*
Exemption	AGRI, TEXT, FDPR	AGRI, TEXT, FDPR, SRVCE	*no sector*
VAT with AGRI Subsidy	AGRI	TEXT, FDPR, SRVCE	AGRI

Table 5.18 means the following.

- In the **full VAT** case, indirect taxes/subsidies are fully eliminated from the production structure for all sectors. Therefore *no sectors* have indirect taxes. The AGRI, SRVCE sectors have a **zero** VAT rate on consumption. *No sector* gets subsidy on final consumption. Agriculture was the only sector that received food subsidy due to reduced prices of food grains.

- In the **Exemption** case, indirect taxes/subsidies are fully eliminated from the production structure for all sectors except TEXT and FDPR. Therefore these sectors have indirect taxes. The AGRI, TEXT, FDPR and SRVCE sectors have a **zero** VAT rate on consumption. *No sector* gets subsidy on final consumption.

- In the **VAT with AGRI subsidy** case, indirect taxes/subsidies are fully eliminated from the production structure for all sectors except AGRI. Therefore agriculture sector continues to get irrigation, fertiliser, electricity subsidy. The TEXT, FDPR and SRVCE sectors have a **zero** VAT rate on consumption. AGRI gets subsidy on final consumption. This subsidy is the food grain subsidy given to consumers through the ration shops.

A general consensus is that VAT reduces distortions introduced by taxation. It also leads to efficiency gains and more tax compliance. The reason for compliance increasing is that evasion becomes difficult. Whether it is possible to capture these aspects of VAT in simulations remains to be seen. The compliance aspect cannot be modelled with the current framework and therefore, the accrual of gains from higher compliance or lower VAT rates due to increased tax collection is understated. To capture efficiency from the domestic perspective, the domestic income valued at world prices is used. Welfare gains or losses depend on incomes and relative prices and shares of commodities in the consumption basket. There might be a fall in welfare on account of higher prices, but efficiency gains by elimination of distortions in the domestic production process.

There are two simulations carried out from a policy perspective. One in which the VAT rates on all commodities is the same, and the other where essentials are given preferential treatment. This preferential system can again be implemented using *exemption* or *zero rating* of these preferential sectors. From India's perspective, the agriculture (AGRI) and service (SRVCE) sectors are not imposed with a VAT. The former is not considered for political reasons and the latter for administrative reasons. The other aspect of simulations is that subsidy on final consumption of AGRI (food grains) is also eliminated. The essential commodities are *food products* (FDPR) and *textiles* (TEXT). The preferential treatment is simulated by *exempting* these sectors. Exemption results in the old tax rates still prevailing on inputs of these sectors, consequently making production expensive. On the final consumption side, the tax rates on final consumption is set to zero. Thus the VAT rates are calculated endogenously for the remaining sectors.

The welfare effects of both these regimes are compared in Table 5.19. There is a substantial welfare loss after the implementation of a VAT. The reasons are the following. The major sources of revenue for the government were the indirect taxes. A VAT leads to the loss of these revenues, which are compensated by taxes on final consumption. The resulting tax rates on final consumption are higher than the benchmark rates. Moreover subsidies on agriculture are removed which lead to a higher price of agriculture. Also difficult to tax sector like services is given a zero rate. The combined effect is the increase in prices of final consumption, despite the fall in production prices. To meet the higher prices of final consumption there is an increase in the factor prices. The rise however is inadequate leading to a fall in welfare. The impact of elasticity of savings with respect to the real rate of return (η_s) is very insignificant. There is a marginal fall in welfare with higher elasticities. Due to the VAT, there is an increase in the final price of investment goods. Thus the rate of return falls resulting in lower investment with increased elasticities.

Table 5.19: **Implementation of a Full VAT**

η_{sav}	0.20	0.25	0.30	0.35	0.40	0.45	base
	Full VAT						
pfce	311.670	312.040	312.410	312.780	313.160	313.520	294.490
inv	112.200	111.770	111.330	110.900	110.460	110.040	108.400
leisure	128.039	128.148	128.259	128.369	128.480	128.587	130.889
w	1.081	1.082	1.082	1.083	1.083	1.084	1.000
r	1.054	1.054	1.054	1.054	1.054	1.054	1.000
er	1.175	1.172	1.168	1.165	1.162	1.158	1.000
ev	-34.244	-34.364	-34.486	-34.606	-34.728	-34.846	0.000
	Exemption of Agriculture, Food and Textiles						
pfce	309.690	310.100	310.510	310.920	311.340	311.740	294.490
inv	111.240	110.750	110.250	109.750	109.240	108.750	108.400
leisure	132.453	132.581	132.711	132.840	132.972	133.098	130.889
w	1.040	1.041	1.041	1.042	1.043	1.043	1.000
r	1.051	1.051	1.051	1.051	1.051	1.051	1.000
er	1.142	1.138	1.134	1.130	1.126	1.122	1.000
ev	-16.338	-16.435	-16.533	-16.631	-16.731	-16.827	0.000

For abbreviations refer to the glossary in Table 5.3

The welfare loss with exemption of agriculture, food and textile sectors is much lower compared to the full VAT case. The reason is that the exempt sectors have no VAT rate on them, but also pay the indirect taxes or VAT on inputs. This leads to higher production prices but lower consumption prices as compared to the full VAT case. Moreover, agriculture, food and textiles form a major part of the consumption expenditure. With lower final consumption prices, the impact on welfare is adverse but mitigated. As earlier there is an increase in the factor prices to account for the higher consumption prices, but this is inadequate. The elasticity of savings plays a minor role here too, with a marginal fall in welfare with increased elasticities.

The other point to be noted is the depreciation in the real exchange rate is higher in the full VAT case than the exempt case. In both the simulations the original structure is substituted by a new set of tax rates. This implies changing the import tariff structure too. The exempt case has higher tax rates on account of some sectors having a zero VAT rate. This makes imports more expensive where VAT is imposed and cheaper where this rate is zero. The main imports were capital goods, which are subjected to higher tariffs in the exempt case as opposed to the full VAT case. Since the demand for imports is less, the exchange rate depreciates to a lesser extent as compared to the full VAT case, to maintain trade balance.

Table 5.20 tabulates the percentage change in output and price in the full VAT case and the case where agriculture, food and textiles sectors are exempted from the system. As expected, the producer price of commodities under VAT falls, while that of the exempted sectors rises. This is due to the refund of indirect taxes on use of commodities in sectors under VAT, which is not available for exempt sectors. The simulation uses a uniform VAT rate for all commodities in both cases. The tax rate on final consumption is higher for the exempt case as certain commodities are levied with zero rates.

Table 5.20: Full VAT and Exemption – Tax Rates, Change in Price and Output

Sector	Output	VAT	Ex	P_p	VAT	Ex	P_c	VAT	Ex	τ (%)	
		% Change			% Change			% Change		VAT	Ex
AGRI	180.98	-5.77	-4.83	1	7.9	9.6	0.94	14.67	16.47	0.0	0.0
CCNG	10.87	4.78	5.33	1	-0.6	-2.1	1.37	-7.26	-5.15	28.0	33.0
MINES	2.21	-1.27	-1.72	1	0.9	-0.6	1.00	29.34	32.31	28.0	33.0
FDPR	34.79	3.53	23.64	1	0.7	4.8	1.26	2.37	-16.89	28.0	0.0
TEXT	64.50	-6.91	5.37	1	-1.7	4.0	1.04	21.40	0.19	28.0	0.0
PAPER	11.37	-3.91	-3.57	1	-1.8	-3.0	1.06	19.10	22.16	28.0	33.0
CHEM	28.32	8.61	8.10	1	-11.4	-12.4	1.23	-7.43	-4.97	28.0	33.0
PETRO	19.54	7.04	6.75	1	-18.0	-19.3	1.29	-18.32	-16.53	28.0	33.0
FERT	7.31	-7.98	-7.21	1	-7.3	-8.7	1.00	18.83	21.53	28.0	33.0
CEMENT	10.80	6.54	5.06	1	-4.7	-6.1	1.18	3.71	6.11	28.0	33.0
METLS	21.45	-4.09	-5.32	1	-9.6	-11.3	1.00	15.88	18.07	28.0	33.0
MECHMC	13.57	3.27	1.89	1	-8.4	-10.2	1.14	2.73	4.58	28.0	33.0
ELECMC	16.87	-0.94	-3.04	1	-7.5	-9.1	1.13	5.12	7.27	28.0	33.0
VEHCL	16.18	3.64	1.92	1	-7.9	-9.8	1.19	-0.62	1.07	28.0	33.0
OTHMFG	17.00	-1.69	-2.06	1	-8.1	-9.7	1.02	15.05	17.38	28.0	33.0
TRNSP	41.78	-2.53	-2.42	1	-6.3	-7.9	1.02	17.41	19.84	28.0	33.0
ELEC	21.52	-3.78	-1.91	1	-2.5	-4.4	1.05	18.92	21.08	28.0	33.0
CONSTR	56.20	-13.79	-15.28	1	-2.7	-5.0	1.00	24.73	26.46	28.0	33.0
SRVCE	183.18	3.23	4.09	1	3.5	1.8	1.02	1.57	-0.10	0.0	0.0

Output in Rs. 000s Crores, Price in Rs., Ex: Exemption of Agri, Food, Textiles

Sequential Dynamics

Tax policy has implications which go beyond a single period. So the welfare calculations can be misleading. A policy which results in more savings today will imply lower consumption. Thus any welfare measure based on current consumption will exhibit welfare loss. However, the added saving will imply a higher consumption in the future periods. Similarly any welfare measure based on the expected present and expected future consumption is also biased for the following reasons. Any tax policy which induces higher savings implies higher consumption. This is based on the myopic expectations that the current prices continue to prevail in the future. Capital deepening due to added savings implies a lower rate of return to capital thus lowering expected future consumption.

The use of present consumption as a welfare measure is correct as long as the economy is on a balanced growth path where myopic expectations hold. The equilibria are connected over time through a series of capital stocks which are augmented on the basis of a balanced growth path. The savings in the economy are augmented to the existing capital stock leading to a flow of capital services in the future. The capital stock grows at the same rate of growth as the labour force and hence the economy is on a balanced growth path.

For simulation purposes the economy is assumed to grow at a steady state balanced growth path in the base case. The counterfactual simulations are performed by incorporating the new tax policy. This results in a different growth path depending on the consumption and savings choice. These two paths are then compared for analysing the welfare implications of a tax policy in a sequentially dynamic context.

From policy perspective, the government can shift to a full VAT in one particular year or can gradually phase out indirect taxes and move to the full VAT regime after a specified period. The welfare impacts are studied for both the cases. The government can also decide to opt for a *consumption* or *income* or *product* type VAT. From modelling perspectives to implement consumption and income type VAT requires the information on the investment by destination and the corresponding figures for depreciation and capital stock. Most modellers assume a fixed coefficient matrix for investment by destination. Since this model does not make use of such a matrix, only product type VAT is considered which accounts for refund of taxes on intermediate goods only. The other assumption the modeller has to make is about the sources of financing additional investment. This requires information on the debt-equity ratios of firms and explicit modelling of investment behaviour of firms, which is beyond the scope of the study.

The other options the government has, include imposing VAT rates on commodities either at uniform rate or differentiated rates depending on whether the goods are luxuries or necessities. It can also *zero rate* or *exempt* certain sectors. Having done that it has to accept the deficit or surplus in its budget. From the modelling perspective, to make meaningful welfare comparisons, the modeller can impose exogenously VAT rates for certain sectors, or can impose a differentiated regime, or can zero rate and exempt certain sectors, but cannot exogenously specify all VAT rates. The reason being that revenues generated in counter-factual simulations, weighted by a price index, have to be equal to the base case. This implies an endogenous determination of some or all VAT rates.

The following simulations are performed. Exogenously, a type of VAT structure is chosen. This implies deciding a priori whether sectors are to be exempted or not. If sectors are to be exempted, the choice of exempt sectors and sectors liable for VAT are chosen. Exogenous VAT rates are chosen for certain sectors based on their importance in consumption. Necessities have lower rates than luxuries. Having chosen the VAT structure, the choice of instant versus gradual implementation is analysed. In the gradual case, the rates on final consumption are endogenously determined. These rates are different from those existing in the base case. On the production side, the tax burden of intermediate taxes is reduced over time, with the regime moving to a full VAT at the end of the time period. Thus instant and gradual implementation regimes become the same at the end of the specified time period.

Table 5.21: Base Case						
	1990	1995	2000	2005	2010	2015
pfce	294.49	326.28	361.50	400.53	443.77	491.68
gov	53.29	59.04	65.42	72.48	80.30	88.97
inv	108.40	120.10	133.06	147.43	163.35	180.98
w	1.000	1.000	1.000	1.000	1.000	1.000
r	1.000	1.000	1.000	1.000	1.000	1.000
ev	0.000	0.000	0.000	0.000	0.000	0.000
imax	531.86	589.28	652.90	723.38	801.48	888.00
leisure	130.889	145.019	160.675	178.021	197.240	218.533
labour	174.519	193.359	214.234	237.362	262.987	291.378
capital	209.307	231.903	256.939	284.677	315.410	349.461
Output (Rs. 000 Crores)						
AGRI	180.981	200.519	222.166	246.151	272.725	302.167
CCNG	10.870	12.043	13.343	14.784	16.380	18.148
MINES	2.208	2.446	2.710	3.003	3.327	3.686
FDPR	34.793	38.549	42.711	47.322	52.430	58.091
TEXT	64.503	71.466	79.182	87.730	97.201	107.694
PAPER	11.367	12.594	13.954	15.460	17.130	18.979
CHEM	28.322	31.380	34.768	38.521	42.680	47.287
PETRO	19.540	21.650	23.987	26.576	29.446	32.624
FERT	7.306	8.095	8.969	9.937	11.010	12.199
CEMENT	10.800	11.966	13.258	14.689	16.275	18.032
METLS	21.449	23.765	26.330	29.173	32.322	35.812
MECHMC	13.570	15.036	16.659	18.457	20.450	22.657
ELECMC	16.868	18.690	20.707	22.943	25.420	28.164
VEHCL	16.182	17.929	19.864	22.009	24.385	27.017
OTHMFG	17.003	18.838	20.872	23.126	25.622	28.388
TRNSP	41.784	46.294	51.292	56.830	62.965	69.762
ELEC	21.517	23.840	26.414	29.265	32.425	35.925
CONSTR	56.196	62.263	68.985	76.432	84.684	93.826
SRVCE	183.185	202.961	224.872	249.148	276.046	305.847

For abbreviations refer to the glossary in Table 5.3

The growth of income, consumption, leisure, labour, capital and factor prices along with output of various sectors in the base case is outlined in Table 5.21. As the economy is assumed to be on the balanced growth path, all prices are equal to unity in all sectors in all time periods. The reason is that expectations are myopic, and consumers expect the price prevailing in period t to prevail in period $t + 1$. The labour force or effective labour units grow at the same rate as the growth rate of capital.

Instantaneous and Gradual Implementation of VAT

Table 5.22 compares the sequence of equilibria for the full VAT case. In this simulation the same rate is imposed on final consumption across all sectors except agriculture and services that have zero rates, the former for distributive reasons and the latter for administrative reasons. The zero rate on agriculture implies the removal of subsidy through the public distribution system.

The simulations show a substantial welfare loss with the implementation of a full VAT in the instantaneous case. Welfare is based on the consumption of current goods and leisure. A fall in current consumption due to increased savings and larger capital stock will lead to welfare gains in the future. However the simulations reveal welfare losses to continue. On the balanced growth path the factor prices remain constant due to myopic expectations. Despite the rise in factor prices, the high VAT rates on final consumption negate the effect of lower producer prices which continues in the future. The higher factor prices also do not translate into higher leisure.

The impact on welfare, output, factor prices, income and consumption for the gradual implementation of a full VAT is depicted in Table 5.22.

The gradual implementation of VAT also shows a welfare loss, which is small in the initial years and increases progressively. When the system approaches a full VAT the welfare loss is of the same magnitude as the instantaneous case. In the gradual implementation case, the following is done. The base case indirect tax/subsidy structure is maintained. Only it is reduced in magnitude by a fifth every five years. At the end of the 25th year, the indirect taxes/subsidies are completely eliminated. The factor prices increase monotonically with time while the exchange rate appreciates.

Table 5.22: **Implementation of a Full VAT**

	1990	1995	2000	2005	2010	2015
Instant Implementation						
pfce	311.67	346.55	385.33	428.45	476.40	529.72
gov	58.03	64.52	71.74	79.77	88.70	98.63
inv	112.20	124.76	138.72	154.25	171.51	190.71
w	1.08	1.08	1.08	1.08	1.08	1.08
r	1.05	1.05	1.05	1.05	1.05	1.05
er	1.18	1.18	1.18	1.18	1.18	1.18
tot	0.84	0.84	0.84	0.84	0.84	0.84
leisure	128.04	142.37	158.30	176.02	195.72	217.62
labour	177.37	197.22	219.29	243.83	271.12	301.46
capital	209.31	232.73	258.78	287.74	319.94	355.75
ev	-34.24	-38.08	-42.34	-47.08	-52.34	-58.20
Gradual Implementation						
pfce	294.49	327.65	366.78	412.89	465.74	526.35
gov	53.29	59.82	67.31	76.14	86.30	98.00
inv	108.40	117.86	131.99	148.63	167.67	189.49
w	1.00	0.99	1.02	1.04	1.06	1.08
r	1.00	1.00	1.01	1.03	1.04	1.05
er	1.00	1.24	1.22	1.21	1.19	1.18
tot	1.00	0.81	0.81	0.82	0.83	0.84
leisure	130.89	146.05	159.90	176.28	194.95	216.24
labour	174.52	192.33	213.59	238.57	267.05	299.55
capital	209.31	231.90	255.97	284.31	316.62	353.48
ev	0.00	-1.69	-12.54	-25.25	-40.21	-57.83

For abbreviations refer to the glossary in Table 5.3

From the modelling perspective the welfare loss due to VAT can be explained as follows. The VAT imposed is a product type VAT for reasons explained earlier. This implies no refund of taxes on investment goods. The ability of the government to widen the direct tax base is assumed to be the same. As a result there is no increase in the direct tax rate on the representative consumer. The switch to a full VAT implies the base for taxation depends only on final consumption and investment. The burden of raising taxes is mitigated to the extent that subsidies are eliminated. The endogenous tax rates on final consumption and investment will determine the cost of present and future consumption. As the tax base reduces, the cost of final consumption and investment rises, despite a perceptible fall in the producer price. Investment would have been cheaper in the consumption and income type VAT. This would have led to increased saving at the cost of current consumption and increased capital stock. However, the high VAT rates on both consumption and investment goods, lead to a higher price of final consumption leading to more labour and less leisure. This results in a welfare loss, on account of lower leisure and higher cost of final consumption due to reduction in tax base.

In the gradual case, the indirect taxes and subsidies are reduced by 20% each period and finally are eliminated. This allows the economy to move to a VAT over a period of time. The reduction in welfare loss over the instantaneous case can be explained from the model as follows. The exogenously specified tax rates on final consumption and investment are substituted by endogenously determined rates. The relative rate structure is similar to the instantaneous case. However the structure of indirect taxes is similar to the old regime. This introduces distortions in the production process implying higher producer prices than the instantaneous case. The difference in the two arises on account of the larger tax base in the gradual case, which leads to lower tax rates on final consumption. Lower tax rates on final consumption imply lower tariff rates on imports, since imports and domestic goods are subjected to the same VAT rate. Lower price of imports leads to an increased demand for imports. To restore trade balance the exchange rate depreciates to a larger extent in the initial years. As imports become progressively expensive with passage of time, on account of higher rates on final consumption, the exchange rate appreciates. With the instantaneous case, once the regime is changed, the economy in absence of any other shocks/ policy decisions continues on the new growth path. As expectations are myopic there is no change in the prices of commodities over time.

The impact on output in both the instantaneous and gradual case is depicted in Table 5.23.

Table 5.23: Full VAT – Change in Output (%)

	Instant Implementation						Gradual Implementation					
	1990	1995	2000	2005	2010	2015	1990	1995	2000	2005	2010	2015
AGRI	-5.8	-5.4	-5.1	-4.8	-4.4	-4.1	0.0	-2.8	-4.0	-4.5	-4.7	-4.7
CCNG	4.8	5.2	5.5	5.9	6.3	6.7	0.0	3.5	3.3	3.9	4.7	6.0
MINES	-1.3	-0.9	-0.5	-0.2	0.2	0.5	0.0	2.9	1.4	0.6	0.1	-0.1
FDPR	3.5	3.9	4.3	4.6	5.0	5.4	0.0	12.1	9.4	7.5	5.9	4.7
TEXT	-6.9	-6.6	-6.2	-5.9	-5.6	-5.2	0.0	-2.2	-3.8	-4.8	-5.4	-5.8
PAPER	-3.9	-3.6	-3.2	-2.9	-2.5	-2.2	0.0	-2.0	-2.9	-3.1	-3.1	-2.8
CHEM	8.6	9.0	9.4	9.8	10.2	10.6	0.0	6.2	6.3	7.2	8.4	9.9
PETRO	7.0	7.4	7.8	8.2	8.6	9.0	0.0	4.0	4.2	5.1	6.5	8.3
FERT	-8.0	-7.7	-7.3	-7.0	-6.7	-6.3	0.0	-5.3	-6.4	-6.8	-7.0	-6.9
CEMENT	6.5	6.9	7.3	7.7	8.1	8.5	0.0	7.7	7.0	6.9	7.2	7.8
METLS	-4.1	-3.8	-3.4	-3.1	-2.7	-2.4	0.0	-4.1	-4.5	-4.3	-3.8	-3.0
MECHMC	3.3	3.6	4.0	4.4	4.7	5.1	0.0	0.3	0.7	1.6	2.9	4.5
ELECMC	-0.9	-0.6	-0.2	0.1	0.5	0.8	0.0	-2.0	-2.1	-1.6	-0.8	0.2
VEHCL	3.6	4.0	4.4	4.8	5.1	5.5	0.0	2.4	2.3	2.9	3.7	4.8
OTHMFG	-1.7	-1.3	-1.0	-0.6	-0.3	0.1	0.0	-2.8	-2.9	-2.4	-1.6	-0.6
TRNSP	-2.5	-2.2	-1.8	-1.5	-1.1	-0.8	0.0	-1.4	-2.1	-2.1	-1.9	-1.4
ELEC	-3.8	-3.4	-3.1	-2.7	-2.4	-2.1	0.0	-2.1	-2.9	-3.1	-3.0	-2.7
CONSTR	-13.8	-13.5	-13.2	-12.9	-12.6	-12.2	0.0	-10.9	-12.0	-12.5	-12.7	-12.8
SRVCE	3.2	3.6	4.0	4.3	4.7	5.1	0.0	3.1	2.7	3.0	3.6	4.4

The impact on producer and consumer prices in both cases is shown in Table 5.24.

The simulation shows reduction in producer prices with passage of time. The fall in producer price is the largest at the final period after the complete elimination of indirect taxes. The consumer prices however portray the opposite picture. There is a progressive increase in the consumer prices with the elimination of indirect taxes. The effect of moving to a VAT can be seen in the variation in consumer prices. In the base case, the tax rates on final consumption had a higher degree of variability, which is reduced with the onset of VAT. This variability in the base rates is reflected in larger variation in consumer prices as the time progresses to a full VAT.

The output figures also reinforce the impact of VAT on consumer prices. Output rises in those sectors in which there is a fall in consumer price and falls in those where there is a rise. As there is a gradual movement towards VAT, the variation in output is greater.

Table 5.24: **Full VAT – Change in Prices (%)**

Sector	Gradual Implementation of VAT					Instant
	1990	1995	2000	2005	2010	2015
Producer Prices						
AGRI	0	0.1	2.1	4.1	6.0	7.9	7.9
CCNG	0	-0.8	-0.7	-0.7	-0.6	-0.6	-0.6
MINES	0	-0.9	-0.4	0.1	0.5	0.9	0.9
FDPR	0	-0.7	-0.4	0.0	0.4	0.7	0.7
TEXT	0	-0.2	-0.6	-1.0	-1.3	-1.7	-1.7
PAPER	0	0.3	-0.3	-0.8	-1.3	-1.8	-1.8
CHEM	0	-0.3	-3.3	-6.1	-8.8	-11.4	-11.4
PETRO	0	-1.5	-5.7	-9.9	-14.0	-18.0	-18
FERT	0	1.1	-1.1	-3.3	-5.3	-7.3	-7.3
CEMENT	0	0.7	-0.7	-2.1	-3.4	-4.7	-4.7
METLS	0	1.8	-1.3	-4.2	-6.9	-9.6	-9.6
MECHMC	0	2.1	-0.7	-3.4	-6.0	-8.4	-8.4
ELECMC	0	1.0	-1.2	-3.4	-5.5	-7.5	-7.5
VEHCL	0	0.8	-1.5	-3.7	-5.8	-7.9	-7.9
OTHMFG	0	1.2	-1.3	-3.6	-5.9	-8.1	-8.1
TRNSP	0	-0.8	-2.2	-3.7	-5.0	-6.3	-6.3
ELEC	0	1.8	0.7	-0.4	-1.4	-2.5	-2.5
CONSTR	0	0.4	-0.4	-1.2	-1.9	-2.7	-2.7
SRVCE	0	-0.5	0.6	1.6	2.6	3.5	3.5
Consumer Prices						
AGRI	0	6.4	8.5	10.6	12.6	14.7	14.7
CCNG	0	-18.3	-15.5	-12.8	-10.0	-7.3	-7.3
MINES	0	12.2	16.5	20.8	25.1	29.3	29.3
FDPR	0	-10.8	-7.6	-4.3	-0.9	2.4	2.4
TEXT	0	8.9	12.0	15.1	18.3	21.4	21.4
PAPER	0	7.4	10.3	13.3	16.2	19.1	19.1
CHEM	0	-8.0	-7.8	-7.6	-7.5	-7.4	-7.4
PETRO	0	-13.3	-14.3	-15.5	-16.8	-18.3	-18.3
FERT	0	14.5	15.7	16.7	17.9	18.8	18.8
CEMENT	0	-3.2	-1.4	0.3	2.1	3.7	3.7
METLS	0	15.3	15.5	15.6	15.9	15.9	15.9
MECHMC	0	1.1	1.6	2.0	2.4	2.7	2.7
ELECMC	0	1.4	2.5	3.4	4.3	5.1	5.1
VEHCL	0	-3.9	-3.0	-2.1	-1.3	-0.6	-0.6
OTHMFG	0	11.9	12.7	13.6	14.4	15.0	15.0
TRNSP	0	9.8	11.8	13.6	15.6	17.4	17.4
ELEC	0	9.7	12.1	14.4	16.8	18.9	18.9
CONSTR	0	13.7	16.5	19.3	22.1	24.7	24.7
SRVCE	0	-2.4	-1.3	-0.3	0.7	1.6	1.6

Instantaneous and Gradual Implementation of VAT with Exemption

In the earlier simulations, the full VAT case was analysed. In the full VAT case, essentials were not given a preferential treatment. As essentials form a major component of consumer expenditure, any increase in prices is going to affect welfare adversely. This can be simulated in two ways. One is to implement a full VAT and put a zero rate on the consumption of these essentials. In fact the industries receive a refund on the taxes paid on inputs. The other is to keep the existing indirect tax structure the same and putting a zero tax rate on final consumption of these commodities. The reason why the second approach is adopted is as follows. From the earlier scenario on full VAT, one finds that the VAT rates are quite high, due to the smaller base of final consumption. To this if certain commodities were zero rated, this rate on other sectors would rise further. If these sectors were exempted, then the subsidies/tax would still remain in place. May be it would lead to an increased producer price, but as the base is now increased, the VAT rates would be lower. The welfare effect though remains to be seen. Table 5.25 depicts the welfare impacts when agriculture, food and textiles sectors are exempt from VAT.

Table 5.25: **Implementation of a VAT with Exemption**

	1990	1995	2000	2005	2010	2015
Instant Implementation						
pfce	309.69	344.04	382.20	424.59	471.68	524.00
gov	55.71	61.89	68.75	76.38	84.85	94.26
inv	111.24	123.58	137.29	152.52	169.43	188.23
w	1.04	1.04	1.04	1.04	1.04	1.04
r	1.05	1.05	1.05	1.05	1.05	1.05
er	1.14	1.14	1.14	1.14	1.14	1.14
tot	0.86	0.86	0.86	0.86	0.86	0.86
leisure	132.45	147.14	163.46	181.59	201.74	224.11
labour	172.96	192.14	213.45	237.12	263.42	292.64
capital	209.31	232.52	258.31	286.96	318.79	354.15
ev	-16.34	-18.15	-20.16	-22.40	-24.88	-27.64
Gradual Implementation						
pfce	294.49	329.08	369.77	417.92	473.33	524.72
gov	53.29	58.78	65.79	74.10	83.66	94.39
inv	108.40	117.93	132.38	149.45	169.05	188.48
w	1.00	1.00	1.02	1.04	1.05	1.04
r	1.00	1.00	1.02	1.04	1.06	1.05
er	1.00	1.16	1.13	1.11	1.08	1.14
tot	1.00	0.86	0.88	0.90	0.91	0.86
leisure	130.89	147.00	162.40	180.66	201.58	224.42
labour	174.52	191.38	211.13	234.54	261.31	293.04
capital	209.31	231.90	256.00	284.55	317.23	354.64
ev	0.00	3.81	-3.65	-12.46	-22.90	-27.68

For abbreviations refer to the glossary in Table 5.3

There is a welfare loss when there is an instantaneous implementation of a VAT. However, this loss is smaller when compared to the full VAT case with no exemption. The exempt sectors are not a part of the system and have no tax on outputs. At the same time they have to pay taxes on inputs for which they get no refund. The first causes the final price of consumption to fall due to absence of consumption taxes. The latter results in an increase in producer prices. However the first effect outweighs the latter. This results in a welfare gain as compared to the full VAT case only because a major share of expenditure is on these exempted commodities. The results persist in the future due to myopic expectations and the instantaneous adjustment of the economy to a new balanced growth path.

Gradual movement to a VAT shows welfare gains in the initial years which reduce in a monotonic fashion leading to the same magnitude of welfare loss as in the instantaneous case. The real exchange rate depreciates initially. The exchange rate tends to appreciate as the structure resembles the VAT, finally depreciating to the same level as in the instantaneous case.

The impact on prices (producer and consumer) is depicted in Table 5.26. As expected the consumer (producer) prices of textiles and food are lower (higher) in the exempt case as compared to the no exempt case. The only exception being the consumer price of agriculture, which is higher on account of higher producer price, there being no subsidy or tax on final consumption of agriculture. Comparing the producer prices between the full VAT and VAT with exemption case, one finds that the prices of most of the non-exempt goods have fallen in the exempt case. The reason is the following. With the new structure, the tariff structure is also changed. With certain sectors exempt and with a zero rate on their final consumption, the VAT rate and tariff rate on the remaining sectors will be higher as compared to the full VAT case. This leads to a higher domestic price of imports in the exempt case, provided the foreign price of imports is same in both cases. To maintain trade balance, the value of exports has to be equal to the value of imports minus the trade deficit. As imports are cheaper in the full VAT case, the real exchange rate depreciates more to achieve trade balance as compared to the exempt case. This makes imports cheaper in domestic prices in the exempt case despite a higher VAT rate. As imports are a major input into capital goods and petroleum sector, cheaper imports leads to a fall in producer price. The consumer prices show the opposite trend on account of higher VAT rates on final consumption in the exempt case.

Table 5.26: **VAT with Exemption – Change in Prices (%)**

Sector	Gradual Implementation of VAT						Instant
	1990	1995	2000	2005	2010	2015	
Producer Prices							
AGRI	0.0	0.7	2.7	4.7	6.6	9.6	9.6
CCNG	0.0	-0.5	-0.3	-0.2	-0.1	-2.1	-2.1
MINES	0.0	-0.4	0.2	0.7	1.3	-0.6	-0.6
FDPR	0.0	-0.4	0.0	0.4	0.8	4.8	4.8
TEXT	0.0	-0.2	-0.6	-1.0	-1.3	4.0	4.0
PAPER	0.0	0.0	-0.6	-1.1	-1.6	-3.0	-3.0
CHEM	0.0	-1.1	-4.0	-6.7	-9.3	-12.4	-12.4
PETRO	0.0	-2.3	-6.6	-10.7	-14.8	-19.3	-19.3
FERT	0.0	0.1	-2.2	-4.3	-6.3	-8.7	-8.7
CEMENT	0.0	0.0	-1.4	-2.7	-4.1	-6.1	-6.1
METLS	0.0	0.3	-2.7	-5.6	-8.3	-11.3	-11.3
MECHMC	0.0	0.6	-2.2	-4.9	-7.4	-10.2	-10.2
ELECMC	0.0	0.1	-2.1	-4.2	-6.2	-9.1	-9.1
VEHCL	0.0	-0.1	-2.5	-4.7	-6.9	-9.8	-9.8
OTHMFG	0.0	0.1	-2.3	-4.6	-6.7	-9.7	-9.7
TRNSP	0.0	-1.0	-2.4	-3.7	-5.0	-7.9	-7.9
ELEC	0.0	0.9	-0.3	-1.4	-2.5	-4.4	-4.4
CONSTR	0.0	-0.1	-1.1	-2.0	-2.9	-5.0	-5.0
SRVCE	0.0	0.0	1.1	2.1	3.1	1.8	1.8
Consumer Prices							
AGRI	0.0	7.0	9.1	11.3	13.3	16.5	16.5
CCNG	0.0	-12.7	-8.3	-4.1	0.3	-5.2	-5.2
MINES	0.0	20.1	26.6	33.0	39.7	32.3	32.3
FDPR	0.0	-21.0	-20.7	-20.4	-20.1	-16.9	-16.9
TEXT	0.0	-3.9	-4.2	-4.6	-4.9	0.2	0.2
PAPER	0.0	14.1	18.8	23.6	28.4	22.2	22.2
CHEM	0.0	-2.8	-1.2	0.4	2.0	-5.0	-5.0
PETRO	0.0	-8.4	-8.3	-8.3	-8.7	-16.5	-16.5
FERT	0.0	20.7	23.5	26.4	29.3	21.5	21.5
CEMENT	0.0	2.4	5.7	9.1	12.3	6.1	6.1
METLS	0.0	21.0	22.9	24.7	26.5	18.1	18.1
MECHMC	0.0	6.2	8.1	9.9	11.8	4.6	4.6
ELECMC	0.0	7.0	9.6	12.2	14.7	7.3	7.3
VEHCL	0.0	1.4	3.7	6.0	8.1	1.1	1.1
OTHMFG	0.0	17.9	20.5	23.1	25.7	17.4	17.4
TRNSP	0.0	16.7	20.5	24.4	28.1	19.8	19.8
ELEC	0.0	15.8	19.8	23.9	28.0	21.1	21.1
CONSTR	0.0	20.5	24.9	29.5	34.0	26.5	26.5
SRVCE	0.0	-1.9	-0.8	0.2	1.2	-0.1	-0.1

The impact on output is depicted in Table 5.27.

Table 5.27: VAT with Exemption – Change in Output (%)

	Instant Implementation						Gradual Implementation					
	1990	1995	2000	2005	2010	2015	1990	1995	2000	2005	2010	2015
AGRI	-4.8	-4.6	-4.3	-4.1	-3.8	-3.6	0.0	-1.5	-2.0	-1.7	-1.2	-3.4
CCNG	5.3	5.6	5.9	6.2	6.5	6.7	0.0	1.6	1.3	1.7	2.6	6.9
MINES	-1.7	-1.4	-1.2	-0.9	-0.7	-0.4	0.0	-1.6	-3.6	-4.9	-5.8	-0.2
FDPR	23.6	24.0	24.3	24.6	25.0	25.3	0.0	24.9	25.9	27.6	29.7	25.5
TEXT	5.4	5.7	5.9	6.2	6.5	6.8	0.0	6.2	7.2	8.9	10.8	6.9
PAPER	-3.6	-3.3	-3.1	-2.8	-2.5	-2.3	0.0	-4.2	-5.2	-5.5	-5.5	-2.1
CHEM	8.1	8.4	8.7	9.0	9.3	9.5	0.0	3.2	3.0	3.4	4.2	9.7
PETRO	6.8	7.0	7.3	7.6	7.9	8.2	0.0	1.4	1.3	2.0	3.1	8.3
FERT	-7.2	-7.0	-6.7	-6.5	-6.2	-6.0	0.0	-4.4	-4.8	-4.6	-4.1	-5.8
CEMENT	5.1	5.3	5.6	5.9	6.2	6.5	0.0	2.1	0.6	-0.1	-0.6	6.6
METLS	-5.3	-5.1	-4.8	-4.6	-4.3	-4.1	0.0	-7.9	-8.9	-9.2	-9.2	-3.9
MECHMC	1.9	2.2	2.4	2.7	3.0	3.2	0.0	-3.4	-3.7	-3.4	-2.8	3.4
ELECMC	-3.0	-2.8	-2.5	-2.3	-2.0	-1.7	0.0	-6.6	-7.6	-8.0	-8.1	-1.6
VEHCL	1.9	2.2	2.5	2.7	3.0	3.3	0.0	-2.1	-3.0	-3.1	-3.0	3.4
OTHMFG	-2.1	-1.8	-1.5	-1.3	-1.0	-0.7	0.0	-5.6	-6.1	-6.0	-5.6	-0.6
TRNSP	-2.4	-2.2	-1.9	-1.6	-1.4	-1.1	0.0	-4.1	-5.0	-5.2	-5.2	-1.0
ELEC	-1.9	-1.6	-1.4	-1.1	-0.9	-0.6	0.0	-2.6	-3.2	-3.1	-2.7	-0.5
CONSTR	-15.3	-15.1	-14.8	-14.6	-14.4	-14.1	0.0	-15.1	-16.7	-17.7	-18.4	-14.0
SRVCE	4.1	4.4	4.7	4.9	5.2	5.5	0.0	2.3	2.1	2.6	3.4	5.6

The output for the exempt sectors increases and is more in the gradual case as opposed to the instantaneous case. In the gradual case the VAT rates on final consumption are lower than in the instantaneous case. This makes imports cheaper in the exempt case. Cheaper imports leads to decrease in demand for domestic goods and a corresponding fall in output. A fall in the producer price of exempt sectors makes them competitive on the world market. Moreover, increased imports have to be matched with increased exports. The increase in exports leads to greater output for the exempt sectors apart from increased domestic demand.

Instantaneous and Gradual Implementation of VAT with Agriculture Subsidy

In all the earlier simulation with VAT, what was not considered was the favourable treatment of agriculture sector from the demand side. In other words the subsidy on food grains was eliminated. This simulation attempts to capture the impact of eliminating the distortions in the production process in the non-agriculture sectors and subsidising food grains in final consumption. The reason being the political difficulty in eliminating agriculture subsidy, and its importance to the production of agriculture output. Here the remaining sectors are under VAT, so the existing indirect tax and subsidy structure is completely replaced.

Table 5.28 depicts the welfare implications of a VAT with agriculture subsidy in a dynamic context with instant and gradual implementation.

Table 5.28: **Instant Implementation of a VAT with Agriculture Subsidy**

	1990	1995	2000	2005	2010	2015
Instant Implementation						
pfce	320.80	357.07	397.45	442.38	492.40	548.07
gov	55.17	61.41	68.36	76.08	84.69	94.26
inv	113.31	126.12	140.38	156.25	173.92	193.58
w	1.09	1.09	1.09	1.09	1.09	1.09
r	1.09	1.09	1.09	1.09	1.09	1.09
er	0.95	0.95	0.95	0.95	0.95	0.95
tot	1.03	1.03	1.03	1.03	1.03	1.03
leisure	133.82	148.96	165.80	184.54	205.41	228.63
labour	171.58	190.98	212.58	236.61	263.36	293.14
capital	209.31	232.97	259.31	288.63	321.27	357.59
ev	-19.63	-21.85	-24.32	-27.07	-30.13	-33.53
Gradual Implementation						
pfce	294.49	334.46	375.97	424.25	479.70	544.71
gov	53.29	58.59	65.61	73.76	83.12	93.68
inv	108.40	119.62	134.11	150.93	170.21	192.39
w	1.00	1.03	1.04	1.06	1.07	1.09
r	1.00	1.02	1.04	1.06	1.08	1.09
er	1.00	0.95	0.96	0.97	0.98	0.95
tot	1.00	1.05	1.04	1.02	1.01	1.03
leisure	130.89	146.40	162.63	181.44	202.93	227.23
labour	174.52	191.98	211.97	235.04	261.25	291.34
capital	209.31	231.90	256.73	285.43	318.12	355.39
ev	0.00	-0.41	-6.54	-13.94	-22.87	-33.33

For abbreviations refer to the glossary in Table 5.3

The results show a welfare loss by moving to a full VAT despite a subsidy on agriculture. This welfare loss is much less than the case of full VAT with no subsidy to agriculture. The agriculture sector is exempt from the system. It receives subsidies and at the same time does not get refunded for the taxes paid on other inputs. Similar to the earlier cases the welfare loss is much less in the gradual case, which progressively increases in magnitude to the same level of a full VAT, at the end of the horizon. The factor prices show a gradual appreciation over time in the gradual case. The exchange rate in the gradual case, appreciates as compared to the base case. The extent of appreciation decreases with time before finally increasing at the end of the simulation period. The welfare losses are smaller compared to the full VAT case on account of the lower producer and consumer prices.

Table 5.29: **Agriculture Subsidy and VAT – Change in Prices (%)**

Sector	1990	1995	2000	2005	2010	2015	Instant
			Gradual Implementation of VAT				Instant
Producer Prices							
AGRI	0.0	1.8	3.1	4.4	5.7	7.1	7.1
CCNG	0.0	0.3	0.4	0.6	0.9	1.1	1.1
MINES	0.0	0.7	1.3	1.8	2.4	3.0	3.0
FDPR	0.0	0.4	0.5	0.7	0.8	1.0	1.0
TEXT	0.0	-0.3	-0.5	-0.8	-1.0	-1.2	-1.2
PAPER	0.0	-0.6	-1.0	-1.3	-1.7	-2.2	-2.2
CHEM	0.0	-3.0	-5.2	-7.4	-9.6	-11.9	-11.9
PETRO	0.0	-4.5	-8.2	-11.8	-15.4	-19.4	-19.4
FERT	0.0	-2.5	-4.0	-5.5	-6.9	-8.8	-8.8
CEMENT	0.0	-1.6	-2.5	-3.4	-4.3	-5.6	-5.6
METLS	0.0	-3.3	-5.3	-7.3	-9.3	-11.8	-11.8
MECHMC	0.0	-3.0	-4.8	-6.6	-8.3	-10.6	-10.6
ELECMC	0.0	-2.3	-3.7	-5.1	-6.5	-8.2	-8.2
VEHCL	0.0	-2.4	-4.1	-5.7	-7.3	-9.2	-9.2
OTHMFG	0.0	-2.5	-4.0	-5.6	-7.1	-9.0	-9.0
TRNSP	0.0	-1.4	-2.5	-3.5	-4.6	-5.6	-5.6
ELEC	0.0	-1.3	-1.9	-2.5	-3.0	-4.0	-4.0
CONSTR	0.0	-0.8	-1.6	-2.3	-3.0	-3.7	-3.7
SRVCE	0.0	1.4	2.3	3.3	4.2	5.3	5.3
Consumer Prices							
AGRI	0.0	1.8	3.1	4.4	5.7	7.1	7.1
CCNG	0.0	-4.4	0.2	5.0	10.1	15.8	15.8
MINES	0.0	31.8	38.8	46.0	53.5	62.1	62.1
FDPR	0.0	-20.4	-20.3	-20.1	-20.1	-19.9	-19.9
TEXT	0.0	-3.9	-4.1	-4.4	-4.6	-4.8	-4.8
PAPER	0.0	23.1	28.4	33.9	39.4	45.7	45.7
CHEM	0.0	3.5	5.9	8.2	10.5	13.0	13.0
PETRO	0.0	-2.9	-2.2	-1.7	-1.4	-1.4	-1.4
FERT	0.0	27.6	31.6	35.5	39.6	43.6	43.6
CEMENT	0.0	9.3	13.4	17.6	21.8	26.2	26.2
METLS	0.0	26.6	29.8	32.9	36.0	38.8	38.8
MECHMC	0.0	11.1	14.2	17.2	20.3	23.1	23.1
ELECMC	0.0	13.4	17.0	20.7	24.3	28.1	28.1
VEHCL	0.0	7.5	10.6	13.8	17.0	20.3	20.3
OTHMFG	0.0	24.6	28.5	32.2	36.0	39.9	39.9
TRNSP	0.0	26.2	30.6	35.3	39.8	45.3	45.3
ELEC	0.0	22.9	27.9	33.0	38.4	43.8	43.8
CONSTR	0.0	29.8	34.9	40.1	45.4	51.6	51.6
SRVCE	0.0	-0.5	0.4	1.4	2.3	3.3	3.3

The effect on prices (producer and consumer) is shown in Table 5.29. The producer prices show a monotonic behaviour with time. Some increase with time while some decrease with time. The prices are determined by the technology, composition of imports and domestic goods in production, the real exchange rate and tariffs. With a VAT on all sectors except agriculture, tariffs do not account for cost escalation. The cost of most of the capital goods falls. One also observes an improvement in the terms of trade accompanied with an appreciation of the real exchange rate across scenarios. The reason is the following. The model imposes trade balance in units of foreign currency. Giving a subsidy to final consumption of food grains along with imposing a zero rate on essentials like textiles and food products, leaves very few sectors to impose taxes on. To add to it the tax structure for agriculture production is not changed. It implies subsidies for agriculture and fertilisers. The net effect of all this is a very high VAT rate that has to be imposed to maintain revenue neutrality. If this rate exceeds the existing tariff rates, then the net effect is to impose extra tariffs, leading to terms of trade appreciation, using large country assumption. The terms of trade appreciation, coupled with high domestic costs of imports, leads to an exchange rate appreciation. The reason being to reduce exports and or increase imports to maintain trade balance. Unfortunately, the terms of trade gains coupled with exchange rate appreciation do not lead to welfare gains on account of high consumption prices. As opposed to the full VAT case the welfare losses are low on account of lower consumer prices of essential commodities which constitute a large share of consumption expenditure.

The effect on output is shown in Table 5.30.

Table 5.30: **Agriculture Subsidy and VAT – Change in Output (%)**

	Instant Implementation						Gradual Implementation					
	1990	1995	2000	2005	2010	2015	1990	1995	2000	2005	2010	2015
AGRI	4.1	4.6	5.0	5.5	6.0	6.5	0.0	2.6	2.9	3.7	4.7	5.9
CCNG	-2.0	-1.5	-1.1	-0.6	-0.2	0.3	0.0	-2.5	-2.4	-1.8	-1.0	-0.3
MINES	-14.9	-14.5	-14.1	-13.7	-13.3	-12.9	0.0	-10.9	-11.7	-12.1	-12.2	-13.5
FDPR	31.5	32.1	32.7	33.3	33.9	34.5	0.0	25.1	26.6	28.7	31.1	33.7
TEXT	10.2	10.7	11.3	11.8	12.3	12.8	0.0	4.1	5.7	7.7	10.0	12.1
PAPER	-11.0	-10.6	-10.2	-9.8	-9.4	-8.9	0.0	-8.2	-8.9	-9.2	-9.3	-9.5
CHEM	-2.1	-1.7	-1.2	-0.8	-0.3	0.2	0.0	-2.1	-2.1	-1.6	-0.8	-0.5
PETRO	-1.4	-0.9	-0.5	-0.0	0.4	0.9	0.0	-2.5	-2.3	-1.6	-0.6	0.3
FERT	0.3	0.7	1.2	1.7	2.1	2.6	0.0	-1.0	-0.7	0.0	1.0	2.0
CEMENT	-10.4	-9.9	-9.5	-9.1	-8.7	-8.3	0.0	-9.4	-9.2	-8.7	-7.8	-8.8
METLS	-16.2	-15.8	-15.4	-15.0	-14.6	-14.2	0.0	-12.4	-13.4	-14.0	-14.3	-14.8
MECHMC	-9.6	-9.1	-8.7	-8.3	-7.9	-7.5	0.0	-7.4	-8.0	-8.2	-8.0	-8.0
ELECMC	-16.3	-15.9	-15.5	-15.1	-14.7	-14.3	0.0	-11.6	-12.8	-13.6	-14.1	-14.8
VEHCL	-10.9	-10.5	-10.0	-9.6	-9.2	-8.8	0.0	-7.1	-8.1	-8.6	-8.9	-9.4
OTHMFG	-11.8	-11.4	-11.0	-10.6	-10.2	-9.8	0.0	-9.9	-10.4	-10.5	-10.3	-10.3
TRNSP	-11.0	-10.6	-10.2	-9.8	-9.4	-9.0	0.0	-9.1	-9.5	-9.5	-9.3	-9.5
ELEC	-6.6	-6.2	-5.8	-5.3	-4.9	-4.5	0.0	-5.6	-5.9	-5.7	-5.3	-5.0
CONSTR	-25.5	-25.1	-24.8	-24.4	-24.1	-23.7	0.0	-19.2	-20.8	-22.1	-23.1	-24.2
SRVCE	1.1	1.6	2.0	2.5	3.0	3.4	0.0	0.1	0.3	1.1	2.0	2.8

The output changes follow from the price changes. The level of output depends on domestic and export demand. An appreciation of the exchange rate and improvement in the terms of trade will lead to lower exports. To compensate if domestic demand increases then the net effect on output is ambiguous. However, appreciation of the exchange rate leads to lower landed cost of imports, which is not compensated with the fall in producer price. The net result being domestic output is relatively more expensive for certain commodities. This leads to an unambiguous fall in output. An example is the CEMENT sector, which is a large sector in terms of exports. Even here the output falls. The output for sectors comprising essentials rises, due to increased domestic demand, a natural consequence of lower consumer prices.

A caveat is due here. The methodology used to analyse the questions posed relating to VAT is not capable of incorporating the added tax compliance due to a VAT. This causes the endogenous VAT rates to be over estimated, leading to higher final price of final consumption and lower welfare. The other point is that simulations have incorporated trade reforms along with a VAT primarily to account for accurate welfare impacts. Had the trade balance constraint not been imposed in addition to the revenue neutrality, there could have been welfare gains due to free lunch from the rest of the world in the form of increased trade deficit. One thing could however have been done. That is to keep the tariff structure as per the base case and modify the tax rates on domestic consumption. This would have limited the impact of trade on welfare.

A comparison of VAT rates that emerged from the simulations with the rates that persisted in the base case (Table 5.1) would help to clarify the results obtained. Table 5.31 compares the tax structure of VAT rates across the scenarios. In the simulations only a subset of the sectors were imposed a VAT. The remaining had either zero rates on their output, or a subsidy (negative rate) on final consumption. As is seen from the table, the number of sectors which have VAT, zero rate and subsidy vary across scenarios. This would imply different levels of endogenous VAT rates being generated from the model. Based on the rates that emerge, the domestic producer price, the real exchange rate coupled with the landed price of imports and taxes on imports will determine the consumption decision of domestic and imported goods for final consumption. It has to be pointed out that the tariff structure is also changed in all these simulations and the same VAT is applied for consumption of imports. Implicitly it means complete trade liberalisation accompanied with counter vailing duties.

Table 5.31: **Structure of VAT rates on Sectors by Simulation**

Name of Scenario	Sector with VAT	Sector with Zero Rate	Sector with Final Subsidy
Full VAT	*all sectors except* AGRI, SRVCE	AGRI, SRVCE	*no sector*
Exemption	*all sectors except* AGRI, TEXT, FDPR	AGRI, TEXT, FDPR, SRVCE	*no sector*
VAT with AGRI Subsidy	*all sectors except* AGRI, FDPR, TEXT, SRVCE	TEXT, FDPR, SRVCE	AGRI

Table 5.32 depicts the various rates in the simulations in the gradual and instantaneous case. Across all scenarios except *exemption*, the rates increase gradually with time before being equal to the rates from the instantaneous case. The rates are lowest for the full VAT and highest for VAT with agriculture subsidy. The reason is as follows. In the full VAT case, the base is spread over a larger number of sectors (includes FDPR and TEXT). This reduces the final tax

rate as compared to the other cases where these commodities attract no VAT. The largest rates are encountered when VAT is coupled with agriculture subsidy. The reason is the revenue required is much higher on account of increased subsidy.

Table 5.32: **VAT rates by Simulation (%)**

Name of Scenario	1990	1995	2000	2005	2010	2015	Instant
Full VAT	0.0	13.2	17.0	20.7	24.5	28.2	· 28.2
Exemption	0.0	20.6	26.3	32.1	38.0	33.1	33.1
VAT with AGRI subsidy	0.0	30.9	37.1	43.4	49.9	57.4	57.4

This leads to welfare losses than the base case on account of high VAT rates. Higher the VAT rates greater is the welfare loss.

Conclusion

In this chapter the impacts of various indirect tax reforms are analysed. What emerges is the following. The reforms process did not generate large welfare gains as hoped. On the contrary some policy decisions lead to a welfare loss. The impacts of policy are essentially dynamic in nature and the results are obtained using a static modelling framework. In all the simulations the neutrality of government revenues was emphasised. In reality governments run deficits and the policy questions should be analysed incorporating government deficits in a dynamic context.

The salient points of the study are the following. Eliminating subsidies do have welfare gains, which are further accentuated with combination of food subsidy. Food subsidy via fair price shops has been an effective instrument to target the poor and an increase will be beneficial is the implicit assumption made. On the indirect tax front MODVAT and its extensions lead to welfare losses. This is primarily due to the narrow tax base on which the economy is operating. Any change in structure without increasing the base does not yield benefits, but increases the burden on a few commodities without alleviating the problem of cascading. Any reform which distorts the structure against essential commodities is welfare reducing as is exhibited by the additive replacement case. And finally food subsidy emerges as a major welfare improving instrument provided it can be effectively used to target the masses. For indirect tax reform the structure of indirect tax rates also affect the outcome on welfare and prices.

The results from the prospective implementation of VAT are also welfare reducing. This is mainly due to the fact that government has relied excessively on indirect tax revenues because it was not successful in raising revenues through direct taxes. After a VAT the only source of revenues is taxes on final consumption and direct taxes. The pressure to generate revenues is somewhat mitigated by the removal of subsidies due to the implementation of a VAT. Exemption of certain important sectors leads to a lower welfare loss on account of the major expenditure as a fraction of total expenditure on these sectors. The other reason for a welfare loss is the administrative problems faced while taxing service sectors. In the simulations the service sector has been zero rated to account for the administrative difficulties arising in collecting VAT.

The instant implementation of a VAT is more welfare reducing than a gradual one. The main cause being the lower rates on final consumption in the initial years of gradually moving to a VAT. The cause for lower rates is the larger tax base which includes intermediate and final consumption. As the economy moves more close to a VAT the base reduces, the tax rates on final consumption increase and welfare falls.

The main conclusions that emerge from a VAT implementation are

1. Replacing the old indirect tax structure with a VAT is welfare worsening. The increase in final consumer prices on account of reduced tax base lead to higher price of essentials, which causes welfare loss.

2. When Agriculture, food and food products and textiles are exempted the welfare loss is reduced by half, on account of lower final tax rates on consumption.

3. Even a change in tax/subsidy policy of one sector (agriculture) produces a dramatic change in welfare.

The results reiterate the complex interaction of the tax/subsidy structure, enforcing the need for computable general equilibrium models to analyse complex issues. It also highlights the importance of multi sector models which are crucial to analyse tax/subsidy issues in a meaningful way.

The nature of results reflects the modelling methodology used and may change with different modelling assumptions. The models are of a relatively old vintage, where producer behaviour is crudely modelled. Fully dynamic behaviour of producers based on q theory of investment, may lead to more richer results. Given the inability of various governments to substantially increase the direct tax base, the move to a VAT would imply lowering the tax base further leading to very high VAT rates. As the model does not account for the leakages currently prevailing in the tax collection system, the welfare gains that might have accrued due to larger compliance, from moving to a VAT are not captured. To that extent, the welfare losses (gains) are higher (lower).

However, one fact emerges unambiguously from the simulations. Favourable treatment of essential commodities as opposed to luxuries leads to welfare gains or smaller welfare losses.

Chapter 6

Summary and Conclusion

Overview

Any attempt to model national economic policies engenders a host of problems. The first being the subset of policies to be addressed and their relative importance, as importance of issues varies with time. The second, a selection of appropriate tools used to analyse the issues and the costs incurred to validate the exercise empirically.

The study focussed on the tax and trade policies. The magnitude of change envisaged by the policy determines the efficacy of the policy and the tool to analyse it. Thus, analysing impact of sales tax on a commodity can be effectively tackled in a partial equilibrium framework, but to analyse across the board tariff cuts requires a general equilibrium approach.

The study used a structure similar to two existing general equilibrium models to analyse a host of issues relating to tax and trade policies. The salient points of these models are the incorporation of all the major taxes in the Indian economy and the large level of disaggregation of sectors. What is missing is the disaggregation of consumers to analyse the important issues of income distribution. This aspect was omitted not because of the mathematical or programming complexity but due to the lack of data on the consumption side at this level of disaggregation. The results of various simulations using the two models are also documented.

Structure of Models

This section briefly summarises the model structures used to address the policy questions raised. The explanation of the trade model structure precedes that of the tax model. Both the models are built using the latest data set at the time of the study (1989-90) and are at the 19 sector level of disaggregation.

Trade Models

The model is a static model following deMelo and Tarr (1992). The production follows a fixed coefficient Leontief technology, with each intermediate input being an Armington composite. The composite is a Cobb–Douglas between domestic and imported good. Initially the model assumes constant returns to scale. This assumption is relaxed for certain sectors which are then modelled with increasing returns to scale.

There is only one representative consumer with Cobb–Douglas preferences over 19 commodities of consumption. Each commodity is an Armington composite of domestic and imported goods.

Tax Models

The model is a static model following Ballard, Fullerton, Shoven, and Whalley (1985). The production follows a fixed coefficient Leontief technology, with each intermediate input being an Armington composite of domestic and imported good. The domestic and imported intermediate goods are also combined in fixed proportions. The technology exhibits constant returns to scale. Initially the model is static and later limited dynamics are modelled. The dynamic extension assumes the economy to be on a balanced growth path and that there are no adjustment costs.

There is only one representative consumer who maximises utility over present and future consumption. Present consumption comprises of leisure and 19 commodities of consumption. Each commodity is an Armington composite of domestic and imported goods. In the dynamic extension the savings are used to buy capital stock, which augments the existing capital stock.

Results from the Models

The section highlights the main findings to the policy questions raised in the study, which analysed trade and tax policy. Keeping this distinction in mind it is only natural to classify the results according to the policy issues and model structure. The results from the tax model follow those from the trade model. A caveat is due here. It has to be noted that the data set used at the time of the study, though being the latest, reflects the technology coefficients of an earlier policy regime. Just as a chain is as strong as its weakest link, model results are as robust as its weakest assumption.

Trade Models

The model analysed the impacts of trade liberalisation on welfare of the Indian economy. Various market structures, regimes incorporating devaluation and economies of scale were simulated. Each simulation was subjected to sensitivity analysis to ascertain the robustness of the results and identify the parameters crucial for behaviour of the economy.

- *Tariff Cuts*

  The model structure and parameter values will determine the impact on welfare. Two types of models to simulate tariff cuts used in literature are

  1. Multi-country models implying endogenous terms of trade. A unilateral trade liberalisation in a two-country set-up implies tariff cuts may lead to deterioration in terms of trade and welfare loss. A multilateral trade liberalisation may lead to welfare gains due to the increase in the volume of trade.

  2. Single-country models with and without a constant elasticity of transformation (CET) function between exports and domestic markets. A

structure without a CET function implies parametric modelling of export demand. Thus, the country faces endogenous terms of trade despite the fact that import prices may be fixed. In such a case, unilateral trade liberalisation may lead to welfare loss.

A structure with a CET function can incorporate a small-country assumption with both export and import prices fixed or can have export prices determined by the home country. In the former case, tariff cuts may lead to welfare gains due to the increase in the volume of trade and the elasticity of the CET function. In the latter case tariff cuts may lead to welfare losses depending on the elasticity of the CET function.

The small-country assumption leads to an unambiguous gain from trade liberalisation. In the large-country case, the study uses two types of model structures to simulate tariff cuts. One uses a CET function while the other does not. In both cases the export prices are not fixed exogenously, implying endogenous terms of trade. The findings are mixed, with lower (higher) welfare losses (gains) at higher export elasticities. In the presence of a CET function there are higher (lower) welfare gains (losses) with low (high) values of elasticity of CET function. What emerges is that tariff cuts may or may not lead to welfare loss depending on the capability of producers to effectively transfer resources between the domestic and export markets. Moreover, the magnitude of welfare estimates are sensitive to the export elasticities facing the domestic producers. The export elasticities and absolute values of welfare estimates are positively correlated.

- *The Impact of Real Exchange Rate Devaluation on Welfare, Trade Deficit and Export Performance.*
  The welfare results are mixed with welfare losses for lower tariff cuts and higher price elasticity of foreign demand for exports. Higher export elasticities leads to smaller trade deficit or less transfers from the rest of the world. Loss of revenue coupled with lower trade deficit leads to welfare loss. At larger tariff cuts, the trade deficit is higher, which more than compensates for revenue loss from tariffs leading to welfare gains. As far as the modelling goes, either the exchange rate can be fixed with trade deficit and corresponding transfers adjusting to clear the external sector, or exchange rate adjusts to clear the market for a fixed trade deficit. Greater tariff cuts imply higher imports, which are compensated with transfers from the rest of the world at lower price elasticity of domestic exports. At higher price elasticities, these transfers are less and the welfare loss is higher.

- *Increasing Returns to Scale and Imperfect Competition*
  This may not play an important role in trade liberalisation for the Indian economy. In theoretical as well as empirical literature the emphasis is on intra-industry trade rather than inter-industry trade, which enables firms within an industry to exploit economies of scale. In the Indian case, the

exports of industries with economies of scale are not large enough to gain from trade liberalisation. Traditionally, these sectors were promoted for import substitution. The sectors with increasing returns happen to be import competing, and then cheaper imports reduce output of domestic firms pushing them up their average cost curves. This results in higher price of domestic goods. The loss of terms of trade and the decrease in revenue due to the cut in import tariffs are primarily responsible for the large welfare loss due to trade liberalisation.

International evidence on the welfare implications of increasing returns to scale and imperfect competition is mixed. Some of it points to large changes in magnitude of welfare compared to the constant returns to scale case. Other studies support the view that there is a marginal difference in welfare magnitudes between these two cases. This study with Indian data supports the latter view. The probable reason for no significant welfare change from the constant returns to scale case is that the demand elasticities are the same in both the IRS and CRS cases.

Tax Models

In this study, the impacts of various indirect tax reforms are analysed. What emerges is the following. The tax reforms process does not seem to have generated large welfare gains by itself. On the contrary some tax policy decisions may have lead to a welfare loss. However, the expected impacts of tax reform are essentially dynamic in nature while the results are obtained using a static modelling framework. Also, in all the simulations the neutrality of government revenues was emphasised. In reality governments run deficits and the reform process was also motivated by dealing with deficits. Ideally policy questions should be analysed incorporating government deficits in a dynamic context, yet the analysis provides some insight.

- *What is the impact of removal of input subsidies, namely agriculture and fertiliser in the agriculture sector?*
  The input subsidies on agriculture and fertiliser are reduced to zero. To maintain revenue neutrality there is a reduction in the indirect tax rates across all commodities either in a uniform or differentiated manner.

  The effects for elimination of agriculture subsidy are mixed with minor welfare losses in some cases and minor welfare gains in the other. The main point to note however is that the magnitude of welfare changes is very small. A similar result is obtained for fertiliser subsidy elimination. The magnitude of welfare change in small, except that there is an unambiguous welfare gain in all cases.

  The causes for minor welfare changes are as follows. Elimination of subsidies raises input price and therefore output price. A mitigating effect is the lower requirement of generating revenues. However, since the tax rates are cut across all commodities (essentials and luxury items), the welfare changes are not of a high magnitude. The reason is the fall in final consumption price of essentials is not large enough to generate large welfare gains.

- *Is it welfare improving to remove these input subsidies and give a corresponding food subsidy? Or is it beneficial to replace food subsidy with corresponding increase in input subsidies?*
These input subsidies are reduced to zero and only food subsidy is increased with other tax rates untouched. Food subsidy via fair price shops is an instrument to transfer income to the consumers and an increase in subsidy will be beneficial to the consumer.

The results show an unambiguous welfare gain for all cases with larger magnitude of welfare gains than the case where tax rates are cut for all commodities. The reason is the fall in the consumer price of agriculture commodities distributed via the public distribution system. This has a larger impact on consumer welfare than a small reduction in the price of all commodities.

The welfare gains with fertiliser subsidy elimination are larger than with agriculture subsidy elimination. The reason is the larger level of distortion introduced by fertiliser subsidy. Though fertiliser subsidy contributes to lower agriculture prices, it also distorts production of fertiliser.

The opposite effect is seen with the substitution of food subsidy with input subsidies. There is an unambiguous welfare loss in all cases with fertiliser subsidy being increased at the cost of food subsidy. The comparative figures for an increase in agriculture subsidy at the cost of food subsidy are lower though negative.

- *Does MODVAT and its extension to capital goods improve welfare?*
MODVAT falls under the jurisdiction of the central government which imposes central excise. MODVAT enables firms to claim refund on excise duties and countervailing duties only while other indirect taxes still remain. Here the excise duties on sectors under MODVAT are reduced to zero.

This is simulated in two ways. One is the way it currently operates in India with elimination of excise duties for MODVAT sectors and an increase in excise duties for non-MODVAT sectors. The non-MODVAT sectors are essentially capital goods sectors. The results show a marginal welfare gain with the introduction of MODVAT. Though MODVAT results in a fall in prices of commodities covered by it, there is an increase in prices of goods not covered by MODVAT. Since the model accounts for utility from current and future consumption, the fall in price of current consumption is negated by the rise in price of future consumption via savings or capital goods, not covered under MODVAT.

The other is to substitute by a sales tax structure. Conceptually there is no difference from the earlier regime without MODVAT as both sales taxes and excise are distortional. This is carried out only to compare with the case of extension of MODVAT to capital goods, where the only degree of freedom left to meet revenue neutrality are the sales taxes. The point of the exercise is to compare the relative levels of distortions of sales and excise taxes. If the sales taxes were levied only on final consumption it would be similar to a VAT.

Using sales tax to replace excise taxes in MODVAT has mixed welfare effects. The sales tax regime has lesser variation in tax rates across commodities and also lesser rates for many goods as compared to excise duties. This results in lower cascading and a fall in prices for commodities under MODVAT. As a result, there are welfare gains in cases where the tax rates on essentials is less. In the case where rates are same across all commodities, there is a welfare loss. A similar result is observed in the simulations performed on MODVAT extensions to capital goods. The only difference being the magnitude of welfare effects. In this case the effects are larger than the previous case where MODVAT was not extended to capital goods. The reasons being the fall in prices of goods now covered under MODVAT.

- *Will the introduction of a full VAT be welfare improving?*
  A full VAT implies complete elimination of indirect taxes on intermediate goods with taxes on final consumption. The indirect tax rates are reduced to zero and VAT rates computed such that revenue neutrality is maintained. One set of simulations is carried out with total elimination of indirect taxes and subsidies as in the case of a consumption type VAT. In the other case the subsidies are maintained while the taxes are eliminated.

  There are large welfare losses with the full implementation of a VAT. The reason being elimination of input and final subsidies making the consumption of essentials expensive. In addition, the burden of raising the required revenues falls on certain subset of commodities as it is difficult to generate revenues from sectors like service. This results in a narrow tax base, higher tax rates for final consumption and higher prices. The VAT with subsidies is welfare improving only due to the presence of subsidies which reduce price of final consumption of agriculture. VAT eliminates cascading.

- *Is it beneficial to go to a full VAT at one go or gradually implement a VAT by cutting indirect taxes over a period of time?*
  To implement VAT reform one can change the structure at one go or gradually move to a VAT at the end of a certain time period. The gradual implementation involves uniform reduction in indirect taxes with compensating taxes on final consumption, whose structure is different from the existing one. This includes elimination of tariffs on consumption of imports and substituting it with a counter-vailing duty which equals the endogenously determined VAT rate to maintain revenue neutrality. Indirect taxes are completely eliminated at the end of the period. The gradual implementation of VAT means that in the intermediate years cascading prevails but to

a lower extent due to reduction of indirect taxes. This also generate revenues from the production process and therefore reduces the requirement of generating revenues from final consumption. The resultant tax rates on final consumption, which affect welfare are lower, leading to a lower welfare loss than the instantaneous case. Also, the existence of subsidies helps in improving welfare. As time progresses, the tax burden on final consumption increases due to a fall in revenues from production, leading to progressively higher welfare losses. At the end of the period the magnitude of welfare loss is similar to the instantaneous case.

- *What will be the impact of exempting certain sectors while implementing a VAT?*
  Exempted sectors are not a part of the VAT and have to pay taxes on inputs with zero taxes on their outputs. Zero rated sectors get a refund on their inputs and have zero tax rate on final consumption. In the exempt case the indirect tax rates on these sectors is maintained while putting rates of final consumption to zero. To implement these simulations the taxes on final consumption for the exempt sectors are set to zero while for the non-exempt sectors they are calculated endogenously.

  Exempted sectors imply higher producer prices in these sectors as taxes on inputs are not refunded. As they do not form a part of the system, there are no taxes on these sectors. The consumer prices would be therefore be the same as producer prices. However, exempting certain sectors, means higher rates on other sectors. The extent to which the relative prices are affected between consumption and investment and essentials and luxuries will determine the overall welfare level. Exempting of essential sectors resulted in welfare losses which are smaller than the case when there was no exemption. The reason being the lower consumption prices for these sectors.

Strengths and Limitations of the Study

The major advantage of the computable general equilibrium approach is its ability to incorporate interactions which are important in a complex economy. Apart from this, large and simultaneous changes in a number of policies can be analysed and the studies need not be limited to small changes around the equilibrium.

The problem with this approach is the non-transparency associated with model building. The models are generally perceived as black boxes and get increasingly difficult to decipher as the complexity increases. Models of large disaggregation involve high costs for data collection and computer resources. The availability of software is another hurdle in implementing models, since solving models generally requires sophisticated algorithmic tools. On the economics front, the models are selected before the analysis can begin and hence the analysis is affected by a selection bias. The choice of a model is often in the jurisdiction of the modeller and depends on the resources available. The models, despite having very sound micro-economic behavioural foundations, lack statistical rigour as they are calibrated to a particular year which is the base year for which the economy is assumed to be in equilibrium. The solution to this problem is mitigated to a certain extent by subjecting the model to a sensitivity analysis by varying the elasticity and other parameters over a range of values.

The study can be criticised on the grounds that the vintage of models selected for analysis is not recent and incapable of tackling important issues of lifetime behaviour of individuals, financial and investment decision of firms, buffer stock operations and deficits of the government in a more realistic manner. The point to be noted is that the models built are a precursor and form the foundation to the state of the art dynamic models. In order to implement these models for India, substantial resources have to be invested in collecting the requisite data.

The study has exclusively focussed on neoclassical modelling of wages across all sectors in the economy and not focussed on real wage rigidity. Real wage rigidity can be modelled using the complementarity condition. Either wages adjust to keep full employment or the labour market clears to maintain exogenously specified real wage. Real wage rigidity would give rise to two cases.

1. Exogenously fixed real wage at benchmark level is higher than endogenously determined wage under neoclassical case with wage flexibility.

2. Real wage fixed at benchmark level is lower than endogenously determined wage under neoclassical case with wage flexibility.

The first case would witness a movement of labour into sectors with wage rigidity, subject to the price elasticity of labour for the specific sectors tending to reduce labour input. In the latter case, labour would tend to move out while lower price would lead to producers increasing the demand for labour. The market can clear in two ways. Wage rates adjusting in the residual sectors to achieve full employment or endogenous unemployment coupled with a minimum wage rigidity on the residual sectors at a level lower than that set for other sectors. From the perspective of welfare it is not important what fraction is unemployed, but how is the unemployed fraction consuming? If their consumption basket is derived from support of the employed, it would imply an increase in income of the employed. If the support was through government transfers, it would imply an increase in taxes, leading to increased income of employed. One fact that can be inferred unambiguously is that the price of capital will rise to account for higher income to compensate the unemployed.

Agenda for Future Research

The value of modelling depends on how efficiently the real world is approximated by equations and its use for policy analysis. Economic theory gives tremendous insights but in general terms. In today's environment, one is forced to make decisions for which an analytical approach is indispensable. Moreover, an analytical approach helps empirically validate the underlying economic theory. From the study the use of models for policy analysis is quite evident.

In India, agriculture and agricultural policy have a major role in politics and economics. At the same time, the country is liberalising and it becomes imperative to achieve a harmonious balance between agriculture and industry. The study did not disaggregate the agriculture sector and agricultural production was crudely modelled. On the production side, investment decisions of the firms have to be incorporated using the optimal control approach, which mathematically translates into the solution of a two-point boundary value problem. On the consumption side, there have to be more income classes or an overlapping generations approach. Energy and environment are also crucial and a KLEM production function would be helpful to address these issues. These are some of the potential areas where research can be carried out immediately and it is hoped that computable general equilibrium becomes an important tool for policy analysis and research in India.

Appendix A
Mathematical Appendix

Utility Functions

The closed form solutions of the agents optimization problems are derived below
for various utility functions.

Cobb–Douglas (CD)

It takes the form as shown below. The αs are the coefficients of consumption
(known), thus goods are consumed in fixed proportion of the income.

$$U = \prod_{i=1}^{n} X_i^{\alpha_i} \qquad \sum_{i=1}^{n} \alpha_i = 1 \tag{A.1}$$

The two good case is illustrated below and the general result for the n good case
is stated without derivation as it is readily extended from the two good case. The
consumer solves the following optimisation problem.
Maximise

$$U = X_1^{\alpha} X_2^{(1-\alpha)} \tag{A.2}$$

subject to

$$I = p_1 X_1 + p_2 X_2 \tag{A.3}$$

The lagrangian is as follows

$$\pounds = X_1^{\alpha} X_2^{(1-\alpha)} + \lambda(I - p_1 X_1 - p_2 X_2) \tag{A.4}$$

The first order conditions are

$$\frac{\partial \pounds}{\partial X_1} = 0 \Rightarrow \alpha \left(\frac{X_2}{X_1}\right)^{(1-\alpha)} = \lambda p_1 \tag{A.5}$$

$$\frac{\partial \pounds}{\partial X_2} = 0 \Rightarrow (1-\alpha) \left(\frac{X_1}{X_2}\right)^{\alpha} = \lambda p_2 \tag{A.6}$$

dividing equation (A.5) by equation (A.6) results in

$$\frac{\alpha}{(1-\alpha)} \frac{X_2}{X_1} = \frac{p_1}{p_2} \tag{A.7}$$

equation (A.7) $\Rightarrow$

$$X_2 = \frac{(1-\alpha)p_1}{\alpha p_2} X_1 \tag{A.8}$$

Substituting equation (A.8) in the expression for income

$$I = p_1 X_1 + p_2 \left[\frac{(1-\alpha)p_1}{\alpha p_2} \right] X_1 \tag{A.9}$$

From equation (A.9), it follows

$$\alpha I = p_1 X_1 \tag{A.10}$$

The demand functions for X_1 and X_2 are given below

$$X_1 = \frac{\alpha I}{p_1} \qquad X_2 = \frac{(1-\alpha)I}{p_2} \tag{A.11}$$

In the general n goods case the demand equations are as mentioned below

$$X_i = \frac{\alpha_i I}{p_i} \tag{A.12}$$

Let p_U be the price index corresponding to utility U, i.e. $p_U U = I$; then the price index for the above Cobb–Douglas function is as follows

$$U = \left(\frac{\alpha I}{p_1} \right)^{\alpha} \left(\frac{(1-\alpha)I}{p_2} \right)^{(1-\alpha)} \tag{A.13}$$

$$U = I \prod_{i=1}^{n} \left(\frac{\alpha_i}{p_i} \right)^{\alpha_i} \tag{A.14}$$

$$I = U \prod_{i=1}^{n} \left(\frac{p_i}{\alpha_i} \right)^{\alpha_i} \tag{A.15}$$

Hence once the consumer prices are known the price index can be calculated as the shares (coefficients) of consumption αs are known already.

$$I = p_U U \Rightarrow p_U = \prod_{i=1}^{n} \left(\frac{p_i}{\alpha_i} \right)^{\alpha_i} \tag{A.16}$$

Constant Elasticity of Substitution (CES)

It takes the form as shown below. The αs are the coefficients of consumption (known) and σ is the constant elasticity of substitution between various goods. As before the results for the two goods case are derived and those for the n good case follow.

$$U = \left(\sum_{i=1}^{n} \alpha_i^{(\frac{1}{\sigma})} X_i^{\{\frac{(\sigma-1)}{\sigma}\}} \right)^{\{\frac{\sigma}{(\sigma-1)}\}} \qquad \sum_{i=1}^{n} \alpha_i^{(\frac{1}{\sigma})} = 1 \tag{A.17}$$

The consumer maximises the above *CES* utility function subject to the following budget constraint

$$I = p_1 X_1 + p_2 X_2 \tag{A.18}$$

The lagrangian is as follows

$$
\mathcal{L} = \left(\alpha^{(\frac{1}{\sigma})} X_1^{\{\frac{(\sigma-1)}{\sigma}\}} + (1-\alpha)^{(\frac{1}{\sigma})} X_2^{\{\frac{(\sigma-1)}{\sigma}\}} \right)^{\{\frac{\sigma}{(\sigma-1)}\}}
$$
$$
+ \; \lambda(I - p_1 X_1 - p_2 X_2) \tag{A.19}
$$

The first order conditions are

$$\frac{\partial \mathcal{L}}{\partial X_1} = 0 \Rightarrow A^{\{\frac{1}{(\sigma-1)}\}} X_1^{(\frac{-1}{\sigma})} \alpha^{(\frac{1}{\sigma})} = \lambda p_1 \tag{A.20}$$

$$\frac{\partial \mathcal{L}}{\partial X_2} = 0 \Rightarrow A^{\{\frac{1}{(\sigma-1)}\}} X_2^{(\frac{-1}{\sigma})} (1-\alpha)^{(\frac{1}{\sigma})} = \lambda p_2 \tag{A.21}$$

where

$$A = \left(\alpha^{(\frac{1}{\sigma})} X_1^{\{\frac{(\sigma-1)}{\sigma}\}} + (1-\alpha)^{(\frac{1}{\sigma})} X_2^{\{\frac{(\sigma-1)}{\sigma}\}} \right) \tag{A.22}$$

dividing equation (A.20) by equation (A.21) results in

$$\left(\frac{\alpha X_2}{(1-\alpha) X_1} \right)^{(\frac{1}{\sigma})} = \frac{p_1}{p_2} \tag{A.23}$$

expressing X_2 in terms of other variables

$$X_2 = \left(\frac{p_1}{p_2} \right)^{\sigma} \left(\frac{(1-\alpha)}{\alpha} \right) X_1 \tag{A.24}$$

substituting the above expression in the income equation

$$p_1 X_1 + p_2 \left(\frac{p_1}{p_2} \right)^{\sigma} \left(\frac{(1-\alpha)}{\alpha} \right) X_1 = I \tag{A.25}$$

$$\left(\frac{p_1 X_1}{\alpha p_1^{(1-\sigma)}} \right) \left[\alpha p_1^{(1-\sigma)} + (1-\alpha) p_2^{(1-\sigma)} \right] = I \tag{A.26}$$

the demand functions for X_1 and X_2 follow from equations (A.25) and (A.26)

$$X_1 = \left[\frac{\alpha I}{p_1^{\sigma} \left(\alpha p_1^{(1-\sigma)} + (1-\alpha) p_2^{(1-\sigma)} \right)} \right] \tag{A.27}$$

$$X_2 = \left[\frac{(1-\alpha) I}{p_2^{\sigma} \left(\alpha p_1^{(1-\sigma)} + (1-\alpha) p_2^{(1-\sigma)} \right)} \right] \tag{A.28}$$

In the general n goods case the demand equations are as mentioned below

$$X_i = \left[\frac{\alpha_i I}{p_i{}^\sigma\left(\sum_{i=1}^{n}\alpha_i p_i{}^{(1-\sigma)}\right)}\right] \tag{A.29}$$

Let p_U be the price index corresponding to utility U, i.e. $p_U U = I$; then the price index for the above CES function is as follows

$$U = \left(\alpha^{(\frac{1}{\sigma})}\left[\frac{\alpha I}{p_1{}^\sigma B}\right]^{\{\frac{(\sigma-1)}{\sigma}\}} + (1-\alpha)^{(\frac{1}{\sigma})}\left[\frac{(1-\alpha)I}{p_2{}^\sigma B}\right]^{\{\frac{(\sigma-1)}{\sigma}\}}\right)^{\{\frac{\sigma}{(\sigma-1)}\}} \tag{A.30}$$

where

$$B = \left(\alpha p_1{}^{(1-\sigma)} + (1-\alpha)p_2{}^{(1-\sigma)}\right) \tag{A.31}$$

using equations (A.30) and (A.31) the indirect utility function is

$$U = \left(\frac{I}{B}\right)\left(\alpha p_1{}^{(1-\sigma)} + (1-\alpha)p_2{}^{(1-\sigma)}\right)^{\{\frac{\sigma}{(\sigma-1)}\}} \tag{A.32}$$

for the general case the indirect utility function is mentioned below

$$U = I\left(\sum_{i=1}^{n}\alpha_i p_i{}^{(1-\sigma)}\right)^{\{\frac{1}{(\sigma-1)}\}} \tag{A.33}$$

the price index which achieves the above utility level is

$$p_U = \left(\sum_{i=1}^{n}\alpha_i p_i{}^{(1-\sigma)}\right)^{\{\frac{1}{(1-\sigma)}\}} \tag{A.34}$$

Stone Geary

The LES derived from the Stone Geary utility function is similar to the Cobb–Douglas demand system and is as shown below. αs are the coefficients of consumption and C_i is the committed consumption of commodity i. The results for the n goods case are stated as the derivation is similar to the Cobb–Douglas case.

$$U = \prod_{i=1}^{n}(X_i - C_i)^{\alpha_i} \qquad \sum_{i=1}^{n}\alpha_i = 1 \tag{A.35}$$

The consumer solves the following optimisation problem.
Maximise

$$U = (X_1 - C_1)^\alpha (X_2 - C_2)^{(1-\alpha)} \tag{A.36}$$

subject to

$$I = p_1 X_1 + p_2 X_2 \tag{A.37}$$

The demand for the good j is

$$X_j = C_j + \frac{\alpha_j (I - \sum_{i=1}^n p_i C_i)}{p_j} \tag{A.38}$$

let γ be $= \sum_{i=1}^n p_i C_i$, then the indirect utility function is

$$U = (I - \gamma) \prod_{i=1}^n \left(\frac{\alpha_i}{p_i}\right)^{\alpha_i} \tag{A.39}$$

and the price index or expenditure function is

$$p_U = \prod_{i=1}^n \left(\frac{p_i}{\alpha_i}\right)^{\alpha_i} \tag{A.40}$$

Production Functions

The production process of each commodity is modelled as a fixed coefficient of the output. The value added are either *Cobb–Douglas* or *CES* allowing substitutability between the primary factors of *Labour* and *Capital*

The closed form solutions of the producers optimization problems are derived below for the *Cobb–Douglas* and *CES* production functions.

Cobb–Douglas (CD)

The producers Minimise cost

$$p_L L + p_K K \tag{A.41}$$

subject to

$$VA = \phi L^\delta K^{(1-\delta)} \tag{A.42}$$

The lagrangian is

$$\pounds = p_L L + p_K K + \lambda \{ VA - \phi L^\delta K^{(1-\delta)} \} \tag{A.43}$$

differentiating the *lagrangian* w.r.t. the inputs the first order conditions are derived below

$$\frac{\partial \pounds}{\partial L} = 0 \Rightarrow p_L = \lambda \delta \phi L^{(\delta-1)} K^{(1-\delta)} \tag{A.44}$$

$$\frac{\partial \pounds}{\partial K} = 0 \Rightarrow p_K = \lambda (1-\delta) \phi L^\delta K^{-\delta} \tag{A.45}$$

dividing equation (A.44) by equation (A.45)

$$\left(\frac{p_L}{p_K}\right) = \left(\frac{\delta K}{(1-\delta)L}\right) \tag{A.46}$$

using equation (A.46) to express K in terms of other variables $\Rightarrow$

$$K = \left(\frac{(1-\delta)p_L}{\delta p_K}\right)L \tag{A.47}$$

substituting equation (A.47) in the expression for value added

$$VA = \phi L^\delta \left(\frac{(1-\delta)p_L}{\delta p_K}\right)^{(1-\delta)} L^{(1-\delta)} \tag{A.48}$$

simplifying the above expression

$$VA = \phi L \left(\frac{(1-\delta)p_L}{\delta p_K}\right)^{(1-\delta)} \tag{A.49}$$

Using equation (A.49) the reduced form expression for Labour is

$$L = (\frac{VA}{\phi})\left(\frac{\delta p_K}{(1-\delta)p_L}\right)^{(1-\delta)} \tag{A.50}$$

The reduced form equation for Capital is derived using equations (A.47) and (A.50)

$$K = (\frac{VA}{\phi})\left(\frac{(1-\delta)p_L}{\delta p_K}\right)^{\delta} \tag{A.51}$$

Constant Elasticity of Substitution (CES)

The producers Minimise cost

$$p_L L + p_K K \tag{A.52}$$

subject to

$$VA = \phi(\delta L^{\{\frac{(\sigma-1)}{\sigma}\}} + (1-\delta)K^{\{\frac{(\sigma-1)}{\sigma}\}})^{\{\frac{\sigma}{(\sigma-1)}\}} \tag{A.53}$$

The lagrangian is

$$\pounds = p_L L + p_K K + \lambda \left\{ VA - \phi\left(\delta L^{\{\frac{(\sigma-1)}{\sigma}\}} + (1-\delta)K^{\{\frac{(\sigma-1)}{\sigma}\}}\right)^{\{\frac{\sigma}{(\sigma-1)}\}} \right\} \tag{A.54}$$

differentiating the lagrangian w.r.t. the inputs, the first-order conditions are derived below

$$\frac{\partial \pounds}{\partial L} = 0 \Rightarrow p_L = \lambda \phi C^{(\frac{1}{\sigma})} \delta L^{(\frac{-1}{\sigma})} \tag{A.55}$$

$$\frac{\partial \mathcal{L}}{\partial K} = 0 \Rightarrow p_K = \lambda \phi C^{(\frac{1}{\sigma})}(1-\delta)K^{(\frac{-1}{\sigma})} \tag{A.56}$$

where

$$C = \left(\delta L^{\{\frac{(\sigma-1)}{\sigma}\}}(1-\delta)K^{\{\frac{(\sigma-1)}{\sigma}\}} \right) \tag{A.57}$$

dividing equation (A.55) by equation (A.56)

$$\left(\frac{p_L}{p_K}\right) = \left(\frac{\delta}{(1-\delta)}\right)\left(\frac{K}{L}\right)^{(\frac{1}{\sigma})} \tag{A.58}$$

using equation (A.58) to express capital in terms of other variables

$$K = L\left(\frac{(1-\delta)p_L}{\delta p_K}\right)^{\sigma} \tag{A.59}$$

substituting equation (A.59) in the expression for value added

$$VA = \phi\left(\delta L^{\{\frac{(\sigma-1)}{\sigma}\}} + (1-\delta)L^{\{\frac{(\sigma-1)}{\sigma}\}}(\frac{(1-\delta)p_L}{\delta p_K})^{(\sigma-1)} \right)^{\{\frac{\sigma}{(\sigma-1)}\}} \tag{A.60}$$

Using equation (A.60) the reduced form expression for Labour is

$$L = \left(\frac{VA}{\phi}\right)\left(\delta + (1-\delta)[\frac{\delta p_K}{(1-\delta)p_L}]^{(1-\sigma)} \right)^{\{\frac{\sigma}{(1-\sigma)}\}} \tag{A.61}$$

Using equations (A.59) and (A.61) the reduced form expression for Capital is

$$K = \left(\frac{VA}{\phi}\right)\left(\delta[\frac{(1-\delta)p_L}{\delta p_K}]^{(1-\sigma)} + (1-\delta) \right)^{\{\frac{\sigma}{(1-\sigma)}\}} \tag{A.62}$$

Cost Function

The cost functions for the various production functions are derived below. To obtain the cost function, the closed form solutions of factor demands are substituted in the expression for cost.

Cobb–Douglas (CD)

Substituting equation (A.50) and (A.51), which are factor demands for labour and capital respectively in the expression for cost as given in equation (A.41)

$$C = p_L(\frac{VA}{\phi})\left(\frac{\delta p_K}{(1-\delta)p_L}\right)^{(1-\delta)} + p_K(\frac{VA}{\phi})\left(\frac{(1-\delta)p_L}{\delta p_K}\right)^{\delta} \tag{A.63}$$

this $\Rightarrow$

$$C = (\frac{VA}{\phi})\left[p_L{}^\delta p_K{}^{(1-\delta)}\left(\frac{\delta}{(1-\delta)}\right)^{(1-\delta)} + p_L{}^\delta p_K{}^{(1-\delta)}\left(\frac{(1-\delta)}{\delta}\right)^\delta\right] \quad (A.64)$$

$$C = (\frac{VA}{\phi})p_L{}^\delta p_K{}^{(1-\delta)}\left[\left(\frac{\delta}{(1-\delta)}\right)^{(1-\delta)} + \left(\frac{(1-\delta)}{\delta}\right)^\delta\right] \quad (A.65)$$

dividing and multiplying the above expression by δ^δ and $(1-\delta)^{(1-\delta)}$, the expression for cost is

$$C = (\frac{VA}{\phi})(\frac{p_L}{\delta})^\delta(\frac{p_K}{(1-\delta)})^{(1-\delta)}\delta^\delta(1-\delta)^{(1-\delta)}\left[\left(\frac{\delta}{(1-\delta)}\right)^{(1-\delta)} + \left(\frac{(1-\delta)}{\delta}\right)^\delta\right]$$

$$(A.66)$$

simplifying the above expression

$$C = (\frac{VA}{\phi})(\frac{p_L}{\delta})^\delta(\frac{p_K}{(1-\delta)})^{(1-\delta)}\left[\delta + (1-\delta)\right] \quad (A.67)$$

this $\Rightarrow$ the cost function is

$$C = (\frac{VA}{\phi})(\frac{p_L}{\delta})^\delta(\frac{p_K}{(1-\delta)})^{(1-\delta)} \quad (A.68)$$

Constant Elasticity of Substitution (CES)

Substituting equation (A.61) and (A.62), which are factor demands for labour and capital respectively in the expression for cost as given in equation (A.52)

$$C = p_L(\frac{VA}{\phi})\left(\delta + (1-\delta)[\frac{\delta p_K}{(1-\delta)p_L}]^{(1-\sigma)}\right)^{\{\frac{\sigma}{(1-\sigma)}\}}$$
$$+ p_K(\frac{VA}{\phi})\left(\delta[\frac{(1-\delta)p_L}{\delta p_K}]^{(1-\sigma)} + (1-\delta)\right)^{\{\frac{\sigma}{(1-\sigma)}\}} \quad (A.69)$$

this $\Rightarrow$

$$C = p_L(\frac{VA}{\phi})\left[\frac{(\delta[(1-\delta)p_L]^{(1-\sigma)} + (1-\delta)[\delta p_K]^{(1-\sigma)})}{[(1-\delta)p_L]^{(1-\sigma)}}\right]^{\{\frac{\sigma}{(1-\sigma)}\}}$$
$$+ p_K(\frac{VA}{\phi})\left[\frac{(\delta[(1-\delta)p_L]^{(1-\sigma)} + (1-\delta)[\delta p_K]^{(1-\sigma)})}{[\delta p_K]^{(1-\sigma)}}\right]^{\{\frac{\sigma}{(1-\sigma)}\}} \quad (A.70)$$

dividing the numerator and denominator of the above expression by $\delta^{(1-\sigma)}(1-\delta)^{(1-\sigma)}$ $\Rightarrow$

$$C = p_L(\frac{VA}{\phi})\left[\frac{(\delta^\sigma p_L{}^{(1-\sigma)} + (1-\delta)^\sigma p_K{}^{(1-\sigma)})}{[p_L/\delta]^{(1-\sigma)}}\right]^{\{\frac{\sigma}{(1-\sigma)}\}}$$
$$+ p_K(\frac{VA}{\phi})\left[\frac{(\delta^\sigma p_L{}^{(1-\sigma)} + (1-\delta)^\sigma p_K{}^{(1-\sigma)})}{[p_K/(1-\delta)]^{(1-\sigma)}}\right]^{\{\frac{\sigma}{(1-\sigma)}\}} \quad (A.71)$$

factoring the common term results in

$$C = (\frac{VA}{\phi})\left[(\delta^\sigma p_L^{(1-\sigma)} + (1-\delta)^\sigma p_K^{(1-\sigma)})\right]^{\{\frac{\sigma}{(1-\sigma)}\}}\left[p_L(\frac{\delta}{p_L})^\sigma + p_K(\frac{(1-\delta)}{p_K})^\sigma\right]$$

(A.72)

the above expression simplifies to the following cost equation

$$C = (\frac{VA}{\phi})\left[(\delta^\sigma p_L^{(1-\sigma)} + (1-\delta)^\sigma p_K^{(1-\sigma)})\right]^{\{\frac{1}{(1-\sigma)}\}}$$

(A.73)

Welfare Measure

Equivalent Variation (EV)

Let $IU(P,I)$ denote indirect utility in terms of prices P and income I and let $E[P, IU(P,I)]$ denote the expenditure function which stands for the minimum income required to achieve utility IU. The equivalent variation (EV) is defined as[1]

$$EV = E[P^0, IU(P^1, I^1)] - E[P^0, IU(P^0, I^0)]$$

(A.74)

When old prices are a constraint a positive EV means higher expenditure is necessary to reach the consumers utility level, implying welfare gains.

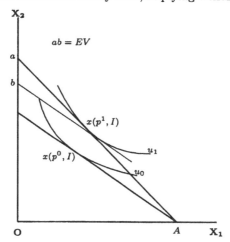

Figure A.1: **Equivalent Variation**

The value of equivalent variation for each of the utility functions is derived.

---

[1] See Figure A.1.

Cobb–Douglas (CD)

The expenditure (I) incurred to achieve indirect utility (IU) at prices p_i (derived in equation (A.15)) is

$$I = IU \prod_{i=1}^{n} \left(\frac{p_i}{\alpha_i}\right)^{\alpha_i} \tag{A.75}$$

Equivalent variation is measured as

$$EV = IU(P^1, I^1) \prod_{i=1}^{n} \left(\frac{p_i^0}{\alpha_i}\right)^{\alpha_i} - IU(P^0, I^0) \prod_{i=1}^{n} \left(\frac{p_i^0}{\alpha_i}\right)^{\alpha_i} \tag{A.76}$$

Using equation (A.14)

$$EV = I^1 \frac{\prod_{i=1}^{n} \left(\frac{\alpha_i}{p_i^1}\right)^{\alpha_i}}{\prod_{i=1}^{n} \left(\frac{\alpha_i}{p_i^0}\right)^{\alpha_i}} - I^0 \tag{A.77}$$

This reduces to

$$EV = I^1 \left[\prod_{i=1}^{n} \frac{p_i^0}{p_i^1}\right]^{\alpha_i} - I^0 \tag{A.78}$$

Constant Elasticity of Substitution (CES)

The expenditure (I) incurred to achieve indirect utility (IU) at prices p_i (derived in equation (A.33)) is

$$I = IU \left(\sum_{i=1}^{n} \alpha_i p_i^{(1-\sigma)}\right)^{\left\{\frac{1}{(1-\sigma)}\right\}} \tag{A.79}$$

For the CES function, equivalent variation is measured as

$$EV = IU(P^1, I^1) \left(\sum_{i=1}^{n} \alpha_i {p^0}_i^{(1-\sigma)}\right)^{\left\{\frac{1}{(1-\sigma)}\right\}} - IU(P^0, I^0) \left(\sum_{i=1}^{n} \alpha_i {p^0}_i^{(1-\sigma)}\right)^{\left\{\frac{1}{(1-\sigma)}\right\}} \tag{A.80}$$

Using equation (A.33)

$$EV = I^1 \frac{\left(\sum_{i=1}^{n} \alpha_i {p^1}_i^{(1-\sigma)}\right)^{\left\{\frac{1}{(1-\sigma)}\right\}}}{\left(\sum_{i=1}^{n} \alpha_i {p^0}_i^{(1-\sigma)}\right)^{\left\{\frac{1}{(1-\sigma)}\right\}}} - I^0 \tag{A.81}$$

This reduces to

$$EV = I^1 \left[\frac{\left(\sum_{i=1}^{n} \alpha_i {p^1}_i^{(1-\sigma)}\right)}{\left(\sum_{i=1}^{n} \alpha_i {p^0}_i^{(1-\sigma)}\right)}\right]^{\left\{\frac{1}{(1-\sigma)}\right\}} - I^0 \tag{A.82}$$

Linear Expenditure System (LES)

The derivation of equivalent variation for the LES is similar to the Cobb–Douglas case. The EV in the LES case is

$$EV = (I^1 - C^1)\left[\prod_{i=1}^{n} \frac{p_i^0}{p_i^1}\right]^{\alpha_i} - (I^0 - C^0) \tag{A.83}$$

Compensating Variation (CV)

Let $IU(P, I)$ denote indirect utility in terms of prices P and income I and let $E[P, IU(P, I)]$ denote the expenditure function which stands for the minimum income required to achieve utility IU. The compensating variation (CV) is defined as[2]

$$CV = E[P^1, IU(P^1, I^1)] - E[P^1, IU(P^0, I^0)] \tag{A.84}$$

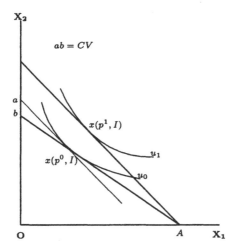

Figure A.2: **Compensating Variation**

Cobb–Douglas (CD)

The expenditure (I) incurred to achieve indirect utility (IU) at prices p_i (derived in equation (A.15)) is

$$I = IU \prod_{i=1}^{n} \left(\frac{p_i}{\alpha_i}\right)^{\alpha_i} \tag{A.85}$$

[2]See Figure A.2.

Compensating variation is measured as

$$EV = IU(P^1, I^1) \prod_{i=1}^{n} \left(\frac{p_i^1}{\alpha_i}\right)^{\alpha_i} - IU(P^0, I^0) \prod_{i=1}^{n} \left(\frac{p_i^1}{\alpha_i}\right)^{\alpha_i} \tag{A.86}$$

Using equation (A.14)

$$EV = I^1 - I^0 \frac{\prod_{i=1}^{n} \left(\frac{\alpha_i}{p_i^0}\right)^{\alpha_i}}{\prod_{i=1}^{n} \left(\frac{\alpha_i}{p_i^1}\right)^{\alpha_i}} \tag{A.87}$$

This reduces to

$$EV = I^1 - I^0 \left[\prod_{i=1}^{n} \frac{p_i^1}{p_i^0}\right]^{\alpha_i} \tag{A.88}$$

Constant Elasticity of Substitution (CES)

Following the derivation for the equivalent variation, the compensating variation for the CES case is given by

$$CV = I^1 - I^0 \left[\frac{\left(\sum_{i=1}^{n} \alpha_i p^0_i{}^{(1-\sigma)}\right)}{\left(\sum_{i=1}^{n} \alpha_i p^1_i{}^{(1-\sigma)}\right)}\right]^{\{\frac{1}{(1-\sigma)}\}} \tag{A.89}$$

Linear Expenditure System (LES)

Following the derivation of equivalent variation, the CV in the LES case is

$$CV = (I^1 - C^1) - (I^0 - C^0) \left[\prod_{i=1}^{n} \frac{p_i^0}{p_i^1}\right]^{\alpha_i} \tag{A.90}$$

Data Set

Introduction

The first requirement of any Computable General Equilibrium (CGE) model is an account of all agents in the economy. The account of all agents should be balanced *i.e.* their incomes should equal their expenditures. Since the data is collected from different data sources, all of which collect data with different objectives in mind, it is highly improbable that they all will be mutually consistent.

What follows is a description of the procedures undertaken to reconcile the different data to produce a single consistent benchmark data set of the Indian economy for the year of analysis *viz.* 1989–90.

The rest of the chapter is organised as follows. First the allocation of income to the factors of production *viz.*, *labour* and *capital* is described. This is followed by a description of the various direct and indirect taxes. The input-output table used in the analysis is mentioned. The national accounts data used to construct a Social Accounting Matrix (SAM) is elucidated with the structure and actual SAM concluding the chapter.

Sectoral Classification

The Input–Output Transactions Table (IOTT) of the economy at the 60 sector level by Planning Commission is used for constructing the SAM. The table shows interindustry transactions at factor cost at 1989–90 prices and is updated based on the IOTT 1983–84 prepared by the Central Statistical Organisation (CSO).

The model analyses the economy at a 19 sector level and the mapping from the 60 sector level to 19 sector level is depicted in Table B.1.

Factor Payments

The Indian economy can be broadly classified as
A: organised and **unorganised**,[1]
This is further sub-classified as
B: primary, secondary and **tertiary**. The *primary* sector consists of three sub-sectors, the *secondary* sector consists of 13 *manufacturing sectors* while the *tertiary* sector comprises of three sub-sectors

The following approach is used. The economy is split first according to classification **A**. The economy thus classified is further split using sub-classification

---

[1]Organised sector is defined as an activity involving 10 or more workers with power or 20 or more workers without power. Unorganised sector is an activity involving less than 10 workers with power or less than 20 workers without power.

Table B.1: **Mapping of 60 Sector Input–Output (IO) Table to 19 Sector Model**

Name	19 Sectors	60 sectors- Name(number)
1 AGRI	Agriculture, Forestry and Fishing.	paddy(1), wheat(2), other cereals(3), pulses(4), sugarcane(5), jute(6), cotton(7), tea(8), coffee(9), rubber(10), other crops(11), animal husbandry(12), forestry and logging(13), fishing(14)
2 CCNG	Coal,Crude and Natural Gas.	coal and lignite(15), crude petroleum and natural gas(16)
3 MINES	Metal and Non-metal Mining.	iron ore(17), other metallic minerals(18), non-metallic and minor minerals(19)
4 FDPR	Food Products	sugar(20), khandsari and boora(21), hydrogenated oil(22), other foods and beaverages(23)
5 TEXT	Textiles and Leather Products	cotton textiles(24), woollen textiles(25), art. silk and synthetic fibre(26) jute, hemp and mesta textiles(27), other textiles(28), leather and leather products(31)
6 PAPER	Wood and Paper Products	wood and wood products(29), paper and paper products(30)
7 CHEM	Rubber, Plastics and Other Chemicals.	rubber products(32), plastic products(33), synthetic fibres and resin(38), other chemicals(39)
8 PETRO	Petroleum and Coal Tar Products.	petroleum products(34), coal tar products(35)
9 FERT	Fertilizer and Pesticides	fertilizer(36), pesticides(37)
10 CEMENT	Cement and Non-Metallic Mineral Products.	cement(40), other non-metallic mineral products(41)
11 METLS	Metals	iron and steel(42), non ferrous metals(43)
12 MECHMC	Non-Electrical Machinery	tractors and other agriculture machinery(44), machine tools(45), other non-electrical machinery(46)
13 ELECMC	Electrical Machinery	electrical machinery(47), communications equipment(48), electronic equipment(49)
14 VEHCL	Transport Equipment	rail equipment(50), motor vehicles(51), other transport equipment(52)
15 OTHMFG	Other Manufacturing	other manufacturing(53)
16 TRNSP	Transport Services	rail transport service(56), other transport service(57)
17 ELEC	Electricity	electricity(55)
18 CONSTR	Construction	construction(54)
19 SRVCE	Other Services	communication(58), trade(59), other services(60)

Source: Author

B. Finally each of the major sectors is split to the level of model disaggregation.

The production side of the economy is modelled as each producer producing only one commodity. The assumption can be relaxed by assuming fixed coefficient joint products. The *Value Added* (VA) is either Cobb–Douglas or CES function of primary factors *labour* and *capital.*

The data on net VA (NVA) is given in the CSO (1994) **National Account Statistics** (NAS), Factor Income (New Series) 1980–81 to 1989–90 (*pp.* 26, 27, 32, 33, 38, 39) by 9 major sectors for both *organised* and *unorganised* sectors. The gross VA (GVA) is obtained from the IO table.

The approach to obtaining consistent factor payments at the 19 sector level is as follows. The economy is classified according to two levels of disaggregation. One at the 7 sector level and the other at the 19 sector level. The mapping from 7 sectors to 19 is outlined in Figure B.1.

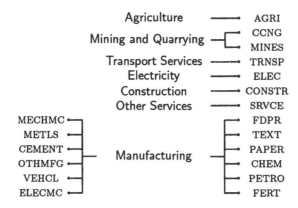

Figure B.1: **Mapping from 7 sectors to 19 sectors**

The economy is first aggregated from 19 to the 7 sector level and consistent accounts at the 7 sector level are obtained. After this the economy is split to the original 19 sector level. The above procedure is adopted in the light of the following. There is no one to one mapping of sectors from NAS to the IO table, both are mapped to a common 7 sector classification.

As shown in Table B.2, to reconcile the difference in NVA between NAS and the IO table, the NAS value added is scaled to match that from the IO table. However in case of *Electricity*, the VA and depreciation figures are taken from the CSO (1993) **Annual Survey of Industries** (ASI) and scaled to the IO level. The value added for Gas and Water Supply is included in *Other Services*. The final figures for VA and depreciation are as per *column e and f* respectively.

The NVA in the IO table is split into *organised* and *unorganised* sectors in the same proportion as the NAS as shown in Table B.3.

Table B.2: **Value Added and Depreciation at 1989–90 prices** *(Rs. Lakhs)*

a b		c	d	e	f
No.	Sector Name	GVA (IO)	NVA (CSO)	New NVA	Depreciation
1	Agriculture	12310107	11928100	11577356	732751
2	Mining and Quarrying	864364	746900	724938	139427
3	Manufacturing	7091581	6504500	6313236	778345
4	Transport Services	2148550	1661500	1612644	535906
5	Electricity	824483	330100	677694	146788
6	Construction	2292503	2260600	2194127	98376
7	Other Services	13991781	12594000	11866374	2125407
8	TOTAL GVA	39523369			
9	depreciation	4557000	4557000	4557000	4557000
10	TOTAL NVA	34966369	36025700	34966369	

Source: National Account Statistics (NAS),
Factor Income (New Series) 1980–81 to 1989–90

Table B.3: **Value Added in Organised and Unorganised Sectors** *(Rs. Crores)*

a b		c	d	$e = c \times \frac{cg}{(c+d)}$	$f = d \times \frac{cg}{(c+d)}$
No.	Sector Name	NVA Org-NAS	NVA Unorg-NAS	New NVA Org-IO	New NVA Unorg-IO
1	Agriculture	5076	114205	4926.74	110846.80
2	Mining and Quarrying	6930	539	6726.24	523.15
3	Manufacturing	39247	25798	38092.95	25039.41
4	Transport Services	6928	9687	6724.28	9402.16
5	Electricity	3150	151	6466.94	310.00
6	Construction	10082	12524	9785.54	12155.73
7	Other Services	58720	67220	55327.42	63336.32
8	TOTAL NVA (NAS)	130133	230124	128050.10	221613.59
9	TOTAL NVA (IO)	349663.69			

Source: Computed from Table B.2 and NAS, Factor Income (New Series) 1980–81 to 1989–90

Organised Sector

In the previous section, Table B.3 shows the NVA in organised and unorganised sectors at the broad 7 sector classification.

This section discusses the methods employed to obtain NVA at the 19 sector level and the corresponding payments to factors for the organised sector.

Primary Sector

This subsection deals with factor payments in the three *primary* sectors.

Agriculture, Forestry and Fishing The model combines agriculture, forestry and fishing into a single *agriculture* sector. The NAS gives the payments to factors in all the three sectors. The payments to factors of *labour* and *capital* are obtained by splitting the NVA from the organised IO table in the same proportion as factor payments in NAS as mentioned in Table B.4.

Table B.4: **Value Added in the Organised Agriculture Sector** *(Rs. Crores)*

a b No. Sector Name	c NAS-Total	d NAS Organised	e IO Organised
1 Agriculture,Forestry and Fishing	119281	5076	4926.74
1a Compensation of Employees	24078	2897	2811.81
1b Operating Surplus	2179	2179	2114.93
1c Mixed Income	93024		

Source: Computed from Table B.3 and NAS, Factor Income (New Series) 1980–81 to 1989–90

Mining and Quarrying An activity like mining and quarrying takes place predominantly in the organised sector. The factor payments in mining and quarrying as per NAS are given in Table B.5.

Table B.5: **Value Added in Mining and Quarrying** *(Rs. Crores)*

a b No. Sector Name	c NVA-CSO	d NVA-IO
1 Mining and Quarrying	7469	7249.38
2 Compensation of Employees	2822	2739.02
3 Operating Surplus	4148	4026.03
4 Mixed Income	499	484.33

Source: Computed from Table B.2 and NAS, Factor Income (New Series) 1980–81 to 1989–90

The mixed income[2] as per the NAS is attributed to capital. The NAS gives *mining and quarrying* as one activity, but in the model there are two sectors in this activity viz. *coal, crude and natural gas* and *metal and non-metal mining.*

---

[2]The notion of mixed income arises in cases where it is difficult to impute payments to the individual factors. The model has only two factors viz. labour and capital and henceforth the mixed income will be distributed over the two.

Table B.6: **Factor Payments in Sectors 2 and 3** *(Rs. Crores)*

a b		c	d	e=c-d	f	g
No.	Sector Name	GVA-IO	NVA	Depreciation	Labour	Capital
1	Coal,Crude,Natural Gas	6959.95	5837.28	1122.68	2205.49	3631.79
2	Metal,Non-metal mining	1683.69	1412.10	271.59	533.53	878.57
3	TOTAL	8643.64	7249.38	1394.27	2739.02	4510.36

Source: Computed from Table B.2 and Table B.5

To obtain factor payments in the two sectors, first the value added in the IO table is split in the same proportion as factor payments as in the NAS for the activity as a whole as in Table B.5. Second, the mining and quarrying activity is split into the two sectors in the ratio of the GVA as per the IO table. The final factor payments in sectors 2 and 3 are outlined in Table B.6.

Secondary Sector

Manufacturing Sector   The primary data source for the manufacturing sector is the ASI, 1989–90. The payments to labour by sectors is given in Table B.7 while those to capital are in Table B.8.

The ASI gives data on factor payments, welfare expenses, contribution to provident fund, depreciation etc. at the 3 digit industrial classification which is mapped to the model sectoral classification.

The purpose of these two tables is as follows. Summation of labour and capital payments gives the net value added in the organised manufacturing sector. The NVA plus depreciation will account for the gross value added. The GVA of the unorganised manufacturing sector is obtained as a residual by subtracting the GVA organised from the GVA in the IO table for each of the manufacturing sectors. A caveat is due here. The IO table is updated from the 1983 − 84 table, and there is a possibility of data mismatch between two sources (*viz.* ASI and IO table), of which ASI is the latest available. In this case the ASI data is made consistent with the IO table. The activities in sectors 8, 9, 11 and 17 take place in the organised sector only. as a result of which the value added in the unorganised sector should be zero. For this the ASI data is scaled to match the IO data.

Given this data the proportion of factor payments in GVA in ASI is used to derive the new factor payments consistent with the IO table. For these sectors and the corresponding factor payments are shown in Table B.9.

Tertiary Sector

This subsection deals with factor payments in the *tertiary* sector comprising of *construction* and *services*.

Construction   To compute factor payments in construction sector, the NVA from the IO table is split in the same proportion as factor payments in NAS. This is

Table B.7: **Payments to Labour in Organised Manufacturing** *(Rs Lakhs)*

a No.	b Sector Name (No.)	c Total Emoluments	d Contribution to PF	e Welfare Expenses	f=c+d+e Labour (gross of tax)
1	FDPR (4)	178010	14473	8248	200731
2	TEXT (5)	289811	38440	11137	339338
3	PAPER (6)	71916	6430	4295	82641
4	CHEM (7)	173811	18771	20330	212912
5	PETRO (8)	20931	1977	3437	26345
6	FERT (9)	38659	3928	6639	49226
7	CEMENT (10)	66270	6614	5792	78676
8	METLS (11)	174946	22672	16785	214403
9	MECHMC (12)	130560	14014	13007	157581
10	ELECMC (13)	120893	12470	14828	148191
11	VEHCL (14)	185229	16697	13171	215097
12	OTHMFG (15)	64695	5835	5047	75577
13	ELEC (17)	304739	29670	8452	342861

Source: Annual Survey of Industries (ASI) Sample Sector 1989–90

Table B.8: **Payments to Capital in Organised Manufacturing** *(Rs Lakhs)*

a No.	b Sector Name (No.)	c Depre- ciation	d Rent Paid	e Interest Paid	f Profits	g=d+e+f Capital (gross of tax)
1	FDPR (4)	71347	7735	90543	202406	300684
2	TEXT (5)	98302	9718	134625	65978	210321
3	PAPER (6)	37821	3677	34698	25785	64160
4	CHEM (7)	119013	14607	134157	169151	317915
5	PETRO (8)	25640	472	12702	152059	165233
6	FERT (9)	61952	2227	73896	−28458	47665
7	CEMENT (10)	58547	4509	80041	−582	83968
8	METLS (11)	110591	4552	112071	102947	219570
9	MECHMC (12)	37357	5154	51888	69650	126692
10	ELECMC (13)	40535	6435	77786	97707	181928
11	VEHCL (14)	48281	3692	55863	36298	95853
12	OTHMFG (15)	19850	2839	35145	39313	77297
13	ELEC (17)	130935	6582	316121	−61062	261641

Source: Annual Survey of Industries (ASI) Sample Sector 1989–90

Table B.9: **New Factor Compositions for Sectors 8, 9, 11 and 17** *(Rs Lakhs)*

a No.	b Sector Name (No.)	c Labour old	d Capital old	e Depr old	f Labour new	g Capital new	h Depr new
1	PETRO (8)	26345	165233	25640	23210.1	145571.0	22588.9
2	FERT (9)	49226	47665	61952	36607.7	35446.9	46071.6
3	METLS (11)	214403	219570	110591	194614.4	199304.5	100383.9
4	ELEC (17)	342861	261641	130935	384374.2	293320.2	146788.4

Source: Computed from Tables B.3, B.7 and B.8

Table B.10: **Value Added in Construction** *(Rs. Crores)*

a b		c	d	e
No.	Sector Name	NAS-Total	NAS Organised	IO Organised
1	Construction	22606	10082	9785.54
1a	Compensation of Employees	17926	8623	8369.44
1b	Operating Surplus	1459	1459	1416.10
1c	Mixed Income	3221		3126.29

Source: Computed from Tables B.2 and B.3

shown in Table B.10.

Transport Services consist of two sectors *viz. railways* and other *transport services*. These two are aggregated to form transport services sector in the model. To obtain the factor payments shown in Table B.11 the same approach is followed as in the case of construction sector.

Table B.11: **Value Added in Transport Services** *(Rs. Crores)*

a b		c	d	e
No.	Sector Name	NAS-Total	NAS Organised	IO Organised
1	Transport Services	16615	6928	6724.28
1a	Compensation of Employees	9265	6301	6115.72
1b	Operating Surplus	627	627	608.56
1c	Mixed Income	6723		

Source: Computed from Tables B.2 and B.3

Other Services comprise of the following sectors *viz. Trade, hotels and restaurants, storage, communication, finance, insurance, real estate* and *miscellaneous other services.* The factor payments are as in Table B.12 computed using the methodology mentioned in the earlier section.

Table B.12: **Value Added in Other Services** *(Rs. Crores)*

a b		c	d	e
No.	Sector Name	NAS-Total	NAS Organised	IO Organised
1	Other Services	125940	58720	55327.42
1a	Compensation of Employees	59388	46823	44117.78
1b	Operating Surplus	11897	11897	11209.64
1c	Mixed Income	54655		

Source: Computed from Tables B.2, B.3 and NAS, Factor Income (New Series)

Unorganised Sector

Primary Sector

In this case unlike the organised sector, there is only one sector. The reason being the other sectors wholly belong to the organised sector.

Agriculture, Forestry and Fishing As can be seen from the table B.13, the major activity takes place in the unorganised sector.

Table B.13: **Value Added in the Unorganised Agriculture Sector** *(Rs. Crores)*

a b No. Sector Name	c NAS Total	d NAS UnOrganised	e IO UnOrganised
1 Agriculture,Forestry and Fishing	119281	114205	110846.8
1a Compensation of Employees	24078	21181	20558.2
1b Operating Surplus	2179		
1c Mixed Income	93024	93024	90288.6

Source: Computed from Tables B.2 and B.3 and NAS, Factor Income (New Series)

The concept of *mixed income* is typical of unorganised sectors. For the model this mixed income will have to be split into payments to factors of labour and capital. To impute the share of labour in mixed income, the wage rate of agricultural labourers is calculated using population of agricultural labourers from the census data by Census Commissioner (1992) and compensation of employees from Table B.13. The same wage rate is assumed to hold for cultivators whose population is also obtained from the census. The payments to capital is imputed as a residual from mixed income once the labour income is calculated. Due to the lack of data for forestry and fishing, the same ratio of labour to mixed income in the case of agriculture is used to derive payments to labour and capital in these sectors. The factor payments are shown in Table B.14.

Table B.14: **Factor Payments: Unorganised Agriculture, Forestry and Fishing** *(Rs. Crores)*

a b No. Heading	c Agriculture	d Forestry	e Fishing	f Total
1 Compensation of employees	19904.0		654.2	20558.2
2 Operating Surplus				
3 Mixed Income	81725.1	6078.8	2484.7	90288.6
4 Population of Labourers *(lakhs)*	745.9			
5 Wage of Labourers *(Rs)*	2668.2			
6 Population of Cultivators *(lakhs)*	1107			
7 Wage income of Cultivators	29537.3	2197.0	898.0	32632.4
8 Capital income of Cultivators	52187.7	3881.8	1586.7	57656.2
9 Labour Income	49441.3	2197.0	1552.2	53190.6
10 Capital Income	52187.7	3881.8	1586.7	57656.2

Source: Computed from Table B.13 and Census

Secondary Sector

Manufacturing Sectors   The unorganised manufacturing sector is further classified on the basis of number of workers employed. Based on this classification the following distribution results.

1. Own Account Enterprises (OAE): Only one worker.

2. Non-Directory Establishments (NDE): up to 5 workers.

3. Directory Establishments (DE): with workers ranging from 6 to 10.

The data source for the NDE which deal with manufacturing (NDME) is the NSSO (1995) **National Sample Survey Organisation**, 45th round, July 1989 to June 1990, No. 396/1, Part I.

The data for the remaining falls under the jurisdiction of the CSO and has not yet been released.

To calculate the payments to capital it is necessary to compute the depreciation in the unorganised sector. To calculate this the following is done. Of the total depreciation in the Manufacturing sector, the depreciation in the organised sector is subtracted to residually give the depreciation in the unorganised sector. This total figure is split into depreciation of various sectors using shares of depreciation of various sectors in the organised sector. The depreciation in the unorganised sector is as shown in Table B.15.

Table B.15: **Depreciation in Unorganised Manufacturing** *(Rs Lakhs)*

a No.	b Sector Name (No.)	c Depreciation Organised	d=c/c10 Share	e=d*e10 Depreciation Unorganised	f=c+e Depr. Total
1	FDPR (4)	71347	0.134	10512.6	81859.6
2	TEXT (5)	98302	0.185	14484.2	112786.2
3	PAPER (6)	37821	0.071	5572.7	43393.7
4	CHEM (7)	119013	0.224	17535.9	136548.9
5	CEMENT (10)	58547	0.110	8626.6	67173.6
6	MECHMC (12)	37357	0.070	5504.3	42861.3
7	ELECMC (13)	40535	0.076	5972.6	46507.6
8	VEHCL (14)	48281	0.091	7113.9	55394.9
9	OTHMFG (15)	19850	0.037	2924.8	22774.8
10	TOTAL	531053	1.000	78247.5	609300.5

Source: Computed from Tables B.8 and B.9

The NDME survey of the NSSO gives the number of units, full time employment, part time employment, VA per unit, wage rate for both rural and urban units at the 2 digit level. The total employment is calculated as the sum of the number of units (accounting for the entrepreneur assuming the same wage rate as workers), full time employment and half of part time employment (assuming part time employment gets half the wage rate as full time employment). The wage rate times the total employment gives the payments to labour in the various industries. This 2 digit level is mapped to the IO sectoral classification and the rural and urban units are aggregated to arrive at the labour payments in the unorganised manufacturing sector. The total VA is calculated using the data on number of units and VA per unit. The ratio of labour payments to total VA is used to calculate the share of labour in VA in the unorganised manufacturing sector. This ratio is applied to the NVA in the unorganised manufacturing sector to compute payments to factors.

The following is done to obtain the factor payments in the unorganised manufacturing sector. First NVA is obtained by subtracting depreciation as mentioned in Table B.15 from the GVA. Then the ratio of labour to VA from Table B.16 is applied to the NVA calculated above to give payments to labour. The payment to capital is obtained as a residual difference between NVA and labour payments.

Table B.16: **Labour Share in Unorganised Manufacturing** *(Rs Lakhs)*

a b No. Sector Name (No.)	c Value Added	d Labour Payments	e=d/e Ratio of Labour to Value Added
1 FDPR (4)	94231.5	32767.0	0.354
2 TEXT (5)	154696.0	65808.7	0.425
3 PAPER (6)	67652.1	29525.5	0.436
4 CHEM (7)	18695.1	6398.0	0.342
5 CEMENT (10)	11133.9	4216.6	0.379
6 METLS (11)	3710.5	1397.9	0.377
7 MECHMC (12)	28009.2	9683.0	0.346
8 ELECMC (13)	8757.8	3211.5	0.367
9 VEHCL (14)	4225.9	2032.0	0.481
10 OTHMFG (15)	68132.1	28842.1	0.423

Source: Computed

The final factor payments are shown in Table B.17.

Table B.17: **Factor Payments in Unorganised Manufacturing** *(Rs. Crores)*

a b No. Sector Name (No.)	c GVA	d Deprec- iation	e=c-d NVA	f Ratio of L to VA	g=e*f Labour	h=e-g Capital
1 FDPR (4)	525.49	105.13	420.36	0.354	149.02	271.34
2 TEXT (5)	13121.22	144.84	12976.38	0.425	5520.24	7456.14
3 PAPER (6)	1089.62	55.73	1033.89	0.436	451.22	582.67
4 CHEM (7)	477.97	175.36	302.61	0.342	103.56	199.05
5 CEMENT (10)	1492.53	86.26	1406.27	0.379	532.58	873.69
6 MECHMC (12)	540.64	55.04	485.60	0.346	167.87	317.72
7 ELECMC (13)	3137.56	59.73	3077.83	0.367	1128.64	1949.19
8 VEHCL (14)	2363.89	71.14	2292.75	0.481	1102.46	1190.29
9 OTHMFG (15)	5122.21	29.25	5092.96	0.423	2155.98	2936.98

Source: Computed from Tables B.9 and B.16.

Tertiary Sector

As in the case of organised sector, the tertiary sector comprises of construction and services. First the factor payments to construction are computed followed by services.

Construction   There is no data available on the factor payments in the unorganised construction sector. In this case the mixed income arising here is split in the same proportion of labour to capital as in the organised sector. The final payments to labour and capital in the unorganised construction sector are shown in Table B.18.

Table B.18: **Factor Payments in the Unorganised Construction Sector** *(Rs. Crores)*

a	b	c	d	e=c*d	f=c-e
No.	Sector Name (No.)	Mixed income	Ratio of labour to Value added	Labour	Capital
1	Construction **(18)**	3126.29	0.8553	2673.87	452.42

Source: Computed from Table B.10

Of the total VA in the unorganised construction sector of Rs 12155.73 crores, mixed income is Rs 3126.29 crores, implying labour payments to be a residual of Rs 9029.44 crores. The total labour payment works out to Rs 11703.31 (9029.44+ 2673.87) crores.

Transport Services   In the model there are two service sectors viz. Transport Services (no. 16) and Other Services (no. 19). To obtain payments to primary factors the same methodology is adopted as before for other unorganised sectors. The latest available data for unorganised service sector is from the various issues of the Enterprise Survey by the Central Statistical Organisation (CSO) 1983-84. For the model purposes the same ratio of labour to value added in the above mentioned data is used to compute the shares of primary factors. Table B.19 shows the data on the unorganised transport service sector.

Table B.19: **Unorganised Transport Services** *(Rs 000's)*

a	b	c	d	e	f=c+d+e
No.	Sector	DE	NDE	OAE	Total
1	Transport Services				
1a	labour	947742	663730	1146	1612618
1b	VA	2753085	662435	3176432	8591952
1c	ratio of Labour to VA	0.34	0.25	0.00036	0.19

Source: Enterprise Survey, 1983-84

Other Services   Table B.20 shows the data on unorganised other services sector. Using tables B.19 and B.20 the payment to labour in the two service sectors is calculated using the ratio of labour to value added in the unorganised sector and is shown in Table B.21.

Table B.20: **Unorganised Other Services** *(Rs 000's)*

a	b	c	d	e	f=c+d+e
No.	Sector	DE	NDE	OAE	Total
1	Total Other Service Sector				
1a	labour	5995513	2948903	108750	9053166
1b	VA	13606569	8619867	9824891	32051327
1c	ratio of Labour to VA	0.44	0.34	0.01	0.28

Source: Enterprise Survey, 1983–84

Table B.21: **Factor Payments in Unorganised Other Services** *(Rs lakhs)*

a	b	c	d	e=c*d	f=c-e
No	Sector Name	NVA unorganised	Ratio of L to VA	Labour	Capital
1	Transport	940215.5	0.19	176468.1	763747.4
2	Other Services	6333632.0	0.28	1773417.0	4560215.0

Source: Tables B.3, B.19 and B.20

Tax Payments

Direct and Factor Taxes

Labour Payments and Labour Tax

The organised sector has to contribute to the provident fund (PF) of the employees. This data for the manufacturing sector is given in the ASI and mentioned in Table B.22.

For the sectors where this data is not available a rate of 8.33% is assumed to be the contribution of the employer to the provident fund. The reason is that the employer has to contribute at least a months salary of an employee to PF which works out to 8.33%. The contribution of PF is modelled as an "ad-valorem" tax on the use of labour inputs in the organised sector. This is because for every additional unit of labour requirement the producer has to contribute to PF.

The **Indian Economic Statistics-Public Finance** IES-PF (1991), 1991 shows that the government received Rs. 6999.60 crores as special deposits of non-government PF. (Table 1.1, p. 4, IES-PF). The contribution to PF as calculated by procedures in the above paragraph do not match the total mentioned in IES-PF.

There is no contribution to PF in the unorganised sector hence the tax rate for the unorganised sector is zero. In the model there is no distinction between organised and unorganised sector. Hence the tax rate computed for model purposes underestimates the actual tax rate in that the base for calculating the

Table B.22: **Contribution to Provident Fund (PF)** *(Rs Lakhs)*

a	b	c
	Sector name	Provident Fund
1	AGRI	21629.26
2	CCNG	16965.23
3	MINES	4104.07
4	FDPR	14473.00
5	TEXT	38440.00
6	PAPER	6430.00
7	CHEM	18771.00
8	PETRO	1741.75
9	FERT	2921.12
10	CEMENT	6614.00
11	METLS	20579.46
12	MECHMC	14014.00
13	ELECMC	12470.00
14	VEHCL	16697.00
15	OTHMFG	5835.00
16	TRNSP	47043.83
17	ELEC	33262.41
18	CONSTR	64380.09
19	SRVCE	339366.30
20	TOTAL	685737.50
21	Total IES-PF	699960.00

Source: ASI 1989–90 and IES-PF

rate is the sum of organised and unorganised labour. In addition to the above contribution of non government provident fund there is a contribution of state government to the provident fund. This is an additional Rs 2972.94 crores (Table 1.1 B, p. 4, IES-PF 1991) as state provident fund net. Thus the total contribution to provident fund from both non-government and government sources is Rs 9972.54 crores. Apart from the employer's contribution to PF, the employees also contribute a month's salary to the provident fund. The total amount collected is then invested as per the guidelines set by the government. Not all the collection is invested in government securities, but may be invested in other instruments specified by the government. Thus the PF collection with the government is potentially less than the total PF collected from employees and employers. Since the total PF collection was Rs. 9972.54 crores, the amount of Rs. 3115.16 crores is assumed to be that part of the employees own contribution that was invested with the government. For modelling purposes this is modelled as a transfer from households to the government.

Capital Payment and Capital Tax

As far as capital goes both the organised as well as the unorganised sectors have to pay taxes on the profits earned. The taxes on profits are modelled as an ad-valorem tax on the use of capital. The calculation of the tax rates on capital is explained below.

Taxes Table B.23 from IES-PF 1991 gives data on direct taxes.

Table B.23: **Direct Taxes** *(Rs. Crores)*

a b	c
Direct Taxes	Revenue
1 Corporation Tax	4728.92
2 Taxes on Income	5079.10
3 Estate Duty	4.27
4 Interest Tax	3.94
5 Wealth Tax	178.51
6 Gift Tax	8.06
7 Land Revenue	690.85
8 Agricultural Tax	92.59
9 Hotel Receipts Tax	0.00
10 Others (profession tax, non urban immovable property etc)	378.36
11 TOTAL	11164.60

Source: IES-PF Table 1.2, p5

The source of data for the direct taxes is the **All India Income Tax Statistics** AIITS (1995) Assessment Year 1990-91. The AIITS gives in Table 5 (pp. 12-24) Number of Returns, Gross Income and Gross Tax - By Source, Range of Returned Income and Status. Table B.24 shows the total gross income and gross tax by status as compiled from Table 5 of the AIITS.

Table B.24: **Gross Income and Gross Tax by Status**

a b	c	d	e=d/c	f=d/d7	g
Status	Gross Income	Gross Tax	Average Tax Rate	Share in Gross Tax of Non-Company	Tax Payable
1 Individual	19903.9	3550.3	0.1783	0.7725	3923.9
2 Hindu Undivided Family	1513.8	297.0	0.1962	0.0646	328.3
3 Registered Firm	5948.2	687.2	0.1155	0.1495	759.5
4 Others	204.4	60.9	0.2978	0.0134	67.3
5 Company	11831.6	5792.2	0.4895	na	na
6 TOTAL	39401.9	10387.5	0.2636	na	na
7 Non Company Total	27570.3	4595.3	0.1667	1	5079.1

Source: AIITS (Table 5) and Computed.

As mentioned in Table B.23 the IES-PF does not give a break up of taxes on income accruing from different status as mentioned in Table B.24. In the model income tax is modelled as a direct tax on the income of agents while tax on capital is modelled as an ad- valorem tax on use of capital. Hence it is necessary to split the "Non-Company" into two groups viz. "Individual and Hindu Undivided Family" and "Registered Firms and Others". The former will be mapped to agents in the model while the latter to producers who will be paying a tax on use of capital.

The total "Taxes on Income" as per IES-PF is Rs 5079.1 crores while that given by AIITS is Rs 4595.3038 crores. Hence the figures given by AIITS are scaled to match those given in IES-PF and are shown in column g, Table B.24. Hence the total tax on capital is Rs 5555.74 crores (Rs 4728.92: CIT and Rs 826.82: registered firms and others). The tax on capital unlike tax on labour is paid by both organised as well as unorganised sector.

The AIITS gives in Table 9, pp. 32-42 Number of returns, Gross Income and Gross Tax from Business and Profession - By nature of Business. This is mapped to the input–output sectoral classification and is used as a proxy for calculating tax paid by each sector as shown in Table B.25. The data given by AIITS is scaled to match the data given by IES-PF and the result is as shown in columns f, g and h of Table B.25.

Table B.25: **Gross Tax Paid by Sectors** *(Rs Lakhs)*

a	b	c	d	e=c+d	f	g	h=f+g
No	Sector Name	AIITS Non-Company	AIITS Company	AIITS Total	Actual Non Company	Actual Company	Actual Total
1	AGRI	38.54	2015.67	2054.21	14.9	1469.3	1484.2
2	CCNG	10.84	45909.70	45920.54	4.2	33465.3	33469.5
3	MINES	129.09	4042.56	4171.65	50.0	2946.8	2996.7
4	FDPR	8572.06	46367.61	54939.67	3318.3	33799.1	37117.4
5	TEXT	2970.86	23470.78	26441.64	1150.0	17108.8	18258.8
6	PAPER	2169.05	11259.91	13428.96	839.7	8207.8	9047.4
7	CHEM	6541.78	70504.30	77046.08	2532.4	51393.3	53925.6
8	PETRO	13.97	16020.15	16034.12	5.4	11677.7	11683.1
9	FERT	5.32	2136.42	2141.74	2.1	1557.3	1559.4
10	CEMENT	822.53	7060.08	7882.61	318.4	5146.4	5464.8
11	METLS	1551.61	49836.61	51388.22	600.6	36327.8	36928.4
12	MECHMC	1699.27	24474.38	26173.65	657.8	17840.3	18498.1
13	ELECMC	657.35	30111.34	30768.69	254.5	21949.3	22203.8
14	VEHCL	351.79	68454.63	68806.42	136.2	49899.2	50035.4
15	OTHMFG	3911.14	8515.90	12427.04	1514.0	6207.6	7721.6
16	TRNSP	3299.90	2927.11	6227.01	1277.4	2133.7	3411.1
17	ELEC	5.21	2532.18	2537.39	2.0	1845.8	1847.8
18	CONSTR	6385.68	12888.33	19274.01	2471.9	9394.8	11866.7
19	SRVCE	174456.05	220213.24	394669.29	67532.8	160521.8	228054.6
20	TOTAL	213592.04	648740.90	862332.94	82682.5	472892.0	555574.5

Source: AIITS (pp. 32-42) and Computed.

Subsidies Apart from taxes the government also gives subsidies to public sector units which are modelled as ad-valorem subsidies on the use of capital.

The IES-PF gives data on subsidies in Table 8.5, p.73. A part of it is reproduced in Table B.26.

Table B.26: **Subsidies in Central Budget** *(Rs. Crores)*

a	b	c	d
No	Subsidies	Value	Mapped to Sector
1	Subsidy on Controlled Cloth	10	5
2	Subsidy to Railways	233	16
3	Subsidy to Industrial Units in backward areas	101	4to15
4	Subsidy for River Dredging	21	16
5	Subsidy to GIC for central crop insurance fund	90	19
6	Subsidy to SCI for running shipping service	10	16
7	Subsidy for vegetable oil (to NAFED and others)	4	4
8	Subsidy to Jute corporation of India	12	5
9	Interest subsidy	524	all
10	TOTAL	1005	

Source: IES-PF, Table 8.5, p. 73.

The remaining subsidies are modelled as either subsidy on final consumption (food subsidy) or as input subsidy in intermediate use (fertiliser subsidy). The Table B.26 shows the various subsidies and their mapping to various sectors.

In the case of subsidy to industrial units in backward areas, the subsidy is distributed to each sector in the proportion of its value added in the total manufacturing. In case of interest subsidy, the subsidy is distributed to each sector in the proportion of the share of value added in the public sector as shown in Table B.27.

Table B.27: **Total Subsidies to Sectors** *(Rs Lakhs)*

a	b	c	d	e	f
No	Sector Name	Ind. Units	Interest	Total	
1	AGRI			1849.1	1849.1
2	CCNG			4466.4	4466.4
3	MINES			1080.5	1080.5
4	FDPR	400	1343.9	507.8	2251.7
5	TEXT	2200	1520.5	1591.8	5312.3
6	PAPER		433.2	238.4	671.6
7	CHEM		1524.8	566.5	2091.3
8	PETRO		449.0	155.4	604.4
9	FERT		277.2	95.9	373.1
10	CEMENT		519.0	300.8	819.8
11	METLS		1159.8	401.5	1561.3
12	MECHMC		754.7	305.1	1059.8
13	ELECMC		869.7	555.8	1425.5
14	VEHCL		842.9	483.7	1326.6
15	OTHMFG		405.3	556.2	961.5
16	TRNSP	26400		3811.5	30211.5
17	ELEC			2943.8	2943.8
18	CONSTR			2189.3	2189.3
19	SRVCE	9000		30300.4	39300.4
20	TOTAL	38000	10100.0	52400.0	100500.0

Source: Computed

Net tax paid by each sector shown in Table B.28 is the sum of tax paid by each sector minus the subsidy received by it.

Table B.28: **Tax on Capital** *(Rs Lakhs)*

a b		c	d	e
No	Sector Name	Tax	Subsidy	Net Tax
1	AGRI	1484.2	1849.1	−364.9
2	CCNG	33469.5	4466.4	29003.1
3	MINES	2996.7	1080.5	1916.3
4	FDPR	37117.4	2251.7	34865.7
5	TEXT	18258.8	5312.3	12946.5
6	PAPER	9047.4	671.6	8375.8
7	CHEM	53925.6	2091.3	51834.3
8	PETRO	11683.1	604.4	11078.7
9	FERT	1559.4	373.1	1186.3
10	CEMENT	5464.8	819.9	4644.9
11	METLS	36928.4	1561.3	35367.1
12	MECHMC	18498.1	1059.8	17438.3
13	ELECMC	22203.8	1425.5	20778.3
14	VEHCL	50035.4	1326.6	48708.8
15	OTHMFG	7721.6	961.5	6760.1
16	TRNSP	3411.1	30211.5	−26800.4
17	ELEC	1847.8	2943.8	−1096.0
18	CONSTR	11866.7	2189.3	9677.4
19	SRVCE	228054.6	39300.4	188754.2
20	TOTAL	555574.5	100500.0	455074.5

Source: Computed

Indirect Taxes

The model incorporates all the major indirect taxes as outlined in Table B.29.

Table B.29: **Indirect Taxes and their Model Treatment** *(Rs Crore)*

a b		c d	
No	Tax Head	Collection	Treatment
1	Excise	22406.30	Ad-valorem tax on Output of Goods
2	Tariff	18036.13	Ad-valorem tax on use of imports
3	Sales Tax	15648.72	Ad-valorem tax on sales of Goods
4	State Excise	4059.18	Ad-valorem tax on liquor
5	Motor Vehicles Tax	1454.21	Ad-valorem tax on use of vehicles
6	Tax on Goods/Pass.	941.10	Ad-valorem tax on transport service
7	Electricity Duty	1086.74	Ad-valorem tax on use of electricity
8	Stamp Duty	2363.37	Ad-valorem tax on financial services
9	Sugarcane Tax	90.86	Ad-valorem tax on use of sugarcane
10	Entertainment Tax	427.49	Ad-valorem tax on final consumption of Other services.

Source: Author and IES-PF

To calculate the tax rates the actual collections of various taxes was divided by the tax base as mentioned in the table above. To arrive at the sales tax rates however a different approach was adopted. The levying of the sales tax falls under the jurisdiction of each state and there are different sales tax rates for the same item in different states. The impact of different sales tax rates on the flow of commodities between states is beyond the scope of this study even though it very much takes place. For the modelling purposes only one rate is assumed to exist. The rates are selected from NIPFP (1991) data which gives sales tax rates for different commodities by various states. Tax rates were selected such that they matched the tax collection matched the actual collection with a difference of about 20 crores.

Consistent Set of Factor Payments

The above discussion explained the various procedures adopted to achieve a consistent set of accounts on the production side of the economy. The final consistent data set on payments to labour and capital and the respective taxes is outlined in this section. This is merely a compilation of the final values obtained at the various stages of procedures adopted in the earlier analysis.

The taxes on labour are depicted in Table B.30 while capital taxes on each sector are outlined in Table B.31.

Table B.30: **Labour Payment and Tax on Labour** *(Rs. Crores)*

a b	c	d	e=c+d	f	g=e-f	h=f/g
	organised labour	unorganised labour	Total Labour	Labour Tax	Labour Net	tax rate
1 AGRI	2811.81	53190.60	56002.41	216.29	55786.12	0.0038
2 CCNG	2205.49	0.00	2205.49	169.65	2035.84	0.0833
3 MINES	533.53	0.00	533.53	41.04	492.49	0.0833
4 FDPR	2007.31	149.02	2156.33	144.73	2011.60	0.0719
5 TEXT	3393.88	5520.24	8914.12	384.40	8529.72	0.0451
6 PAPER	826.41	451.22	1277.63	64.30	1213.33	0.0529
7 CHEM	2129.12	103.56	2232.68	187.71	2044.97	0.0918
8 PETRO	232.10	0.00	232.10	17.42	214.68	0.0811
9 FERT	366.08	0.00	366.08	29.21	336.87	0.0867
10 CEMENT	786.76	532.58	1319.34	66.14	1253.26	0.0528
11 METLS	1946.14	0.00	1946.14	205.79	1740.35	0.1182
12 MECHMC	1575.81	167.88	1743.69	140.14	1603.55	0.0874
13 ELECMC	1481.91	1128.64	2610.55	124.70	2485.85	0.0501
14 VEHCL	2150.97	1102.46	3253.43	166.97	3086.46	0.0541
15 OTHMFG	755.77	2155.97	2911.74	58.35	2853.39	0.0204
16 TRNSP	6115.72	1764.68	7880.40	470.43	7409.97	0.0635
17 ELEC	3843.74	0.00	3843.74	332.62	3511.12	0.0947
18 CONSTR	8369.44	11703.31	20072.75	643.85	19428.95	0.0331
19 SRVCE	44117.78	17734.17	61851.95	3393.66	58458.29	0.0581
20 TOTAL	85649.78	95704.33	181354.14	6857.35	174496.80	

Source: Computed

Table B.31: **Capital Payment and Tax on Capital** *(Rs. Crores)*

a	b	c	d	e	f=c+d+e	g	h=f-g	i=g/h
	Sector name	org capital	unorg capital	deprec-iation	Total capital	Capital Tax	Capital Net	tax rate
1	AGRI	2114.9	57656.2	7327.5	67098.6	−3.6	67102.3	−0.00005
2	CCNG	3631.8	0.0	1122.7	4754.5	290.0	4464.4	0.06496
3	MINES	878.6	0.0	271.6	1150.2	19.2	1131.0	0.01697
4	FDPR	3006.8	271.3	818.6	4096.7	348.7	3748.0	0.09303
5	TEXT	2103.2	7456.1	1127.9	10687.2	129.5	10557.7	0.01226
6	PAPER	641.6	582.7	433.9	1658.2	83.8	1574.4	0.05323
7	CHEM	3179.2	199.0	1365.5	4743.7	518.3	4225.4	0.12263
8	PETRO	1455.7	0.0	225.9	1681.6	110.8	1570.8	0.07053
9	FERT	354.5	0.0	460.7	815.2	11.9	803.3	0.01481
10	CEMENT	839.7	873.7	671.7	2385.1	46.4	2338.7	0.01984
11	METLS	1993.0	0.0	1003.8	2996.9	353.7	2643.1	0.13382
12	MECHMC	1266.9	317.7	428.6	2013.2	174.4	1838.8	0.09484
13	ELECMC	1819.3	1949.2	465.1	4233.6	207.8	4025.8	0.05162
14	VEHCL	958.5	1190.3	553.9	2702.7	487.1	2215.6	0.21985
15	OTHMFG	773.0	2937.0	227.7	3937.7	67.6	3870.1	0.01746
16	TRNSP	608.6	7637.5	5359.1	13605.1	−268.0	13873.2	−0.01932
17	ELEC	2933.2	0.0	1467.9	4401.1	−11.0	4412.1	−0.00249
18	CONSTR	1416.1	452.4	983.8	2852.3	96.8	2755.5	0.03513
19	SRVCE	11209.6	45602.2	21254.1	78065.9	1887.5	76178.4	0.02477
20	TOTAL	41184.2	127125.3	45570.0	213879.5	4550.7	209328.6	

Source: Computed

Input–Output Table

The input–output table forms the basis of large scale economic analysis. A brief outline of the procedures followed by the Central Statistical Organisation (CSO) in constructing an input–output table and subsequent manipulations on it to arrive at the data required for the model is necessary.

The CSO prepares the IO table at 115 sectors comprising of Agriculture (1-17), Animal Husbandry (18-20), Forestry and Logging (21), Fishing (22), Mining and Quarrying (23-32), Manufacturing (33-98) and Tertiary Sectors (99-115). Final Demand comprises of Private Final Consumption Expenditure (PFCE), Government Final Consumption Expenditure (GFCE), Gross Fixed Capital Formation (gfcf), Change in Stocks (CIS), Exports (EXP) and Imports (IMP).

Matrices in the IO table

The Input–Output Transactions Table (IOTT) has 2 matrices. The *commodity × industry* matrix or absorption matrix and the *industry × commodity* matrix or make matrix. The absorption matrix shows the input of commodity i in industry j. Thus steel used by a heavy engineering company would be a part of this matrix. Consumable like diesel for running a captive power plant or ATF for a private commercial aircraft would also be a part of this matrix. The make matrix shows the primary and other secondary products produced by an industry. Thus reactors, pressure vessels and other fabrication goods will be the main commodity produced by the heavy engineering company, but surplus power sold to the grid from captive power operations, or lending the aircraft when not in use, would be secondary output of electricity and transport services by the heavy engineering firm. Based on these 2 matrices rest of the relationships are determined.

The structure of the input–output table is shown in Table B.32.

Table B.32: **Input–Output (IO) Accounting Framework**

	commodity	industry	final demand	total
commodity		X	f	q
industry	M			g
primary i/p		y'		
total	q'	g'		

Source: CSO (1990) p. 48.

where,

- q_j : output of the jth commodity

- g_i : output (main + byproducts) of the ith industry

- f_j : final demand of the jth commodity

- x_{jk} : output of the jth commodity used in k^{th} sector

- m_{ij} : output of the jth commodity produced by i^{th} industry

- y_j : value of primary inputs (factor incomes) j^{th} industry

- $'$: denotes transpose

Table B.33 derives other matrices from the basic input–output table.

Table B.33: **Input–Output (IO) Derived Matrices**

	commodity	industry	final demand
commodity	A	$B=X(\bar{g})^{-1}$	
	$W=A\bar{q}$		
industry	$C=M'(\bar{g})^{-1}$	E	
	$D=M(\bar{q})^{-1}$	$Z=E\bar{g}$	e

Source: CSO (1990) p. 49.

To derive the *commodity* × *commodity* and *industry* × *industry* table, using various assumptions, the flow matrices and outputs are computed as follows.[3] Industries produce many commodities that include a main product and possibly many by-products. The production process of producing commodities will vary between industries. This leads to two assumptions on technology.

---

[3]Table B.34 shows the derivations.

1. Commodity Technology Assumption – the input structure of the industry producing the byproduct is the same as that of an industry producing the same commodity as a main product. To cite an example, power generate using a captive power plant (using diesel generator sets) in a cement industry and sold to the grid would be assumed to be produced using the same inputs as that used by power generation industry (using gas/steam turbines).

2. Industry Technology Assumption – the input structure of the industry producing the byproduct is the same as that of the main product. To give the same example, power generated in a captive power plant used in cement industry will generate power using turbines rather than diesel generator sets.

Table B.34: **Derivation of Flow and Output**

commodity × commodity table		
commodity technology	$q = (BC^{-1})q + f$	$W = (BC^{-1})\bar{q}$
industry technology	$q = (BD)q + f$	$W = (BD)\bar{q}$
commodity technology	net indirect taxes : $T_2 = T_1(\bar{g})^{-1}C^{-1}q$	
industry technology	net indirect taxes : $T_2 = T_1(\bar{g})^{-1}Dq$	
commodity technology	value added : $l = (D)^{-1}y$	
industry technology	value added : $l = Cy$	
industry × industry table		
commodity technology	$g = (C^{-1}B)g + e$	$Z = (C^{-1}B)\bar{g}$
industry technology	$g = (DB)g + e$	$Z = (DB)\bar{g}$
commodity technology	final demand : $e = C^{-1}f$	
industry technology	final demand : $e = Df$	

where,

- $\bar{g}$, diagonal matrix with elements of g on the diagonal

- $\bar{q}$, diagonal matrix with elements of q on the diagonal

- e, final demand for output of industry

- A : *commodity × commodity* coefficient matrix

- B : *commodity × industry* coefficient matrix, values in absorption matrix used as coefficients $= X(\bar{g})^{-1}$

- C : product mix matrix, columns of which show proportion of various commodities produced by a particular industry, $= M'(\bar{g})^{-1}$

- D : market share matrix, columns of which show proportion of various industries producing a particular commodity, $= M'(\bar{q})^{-1}$

- E : *industry × industry* coefficient matrix

- W : *commodity × commodity* flow matrix recording the value of purchases of commodities by commodities

- Z: *industry × industry* flow matrix recording the value of purchases of industry output by industries

The 60 sector input–output table for the year 1989–90 is aggregated to 19 sectors as mentioned in Table B.1. The table supplied by the Planning Commission gives the transactions in millions of rupees of *commodity i* used by *industry j* along with the *make matrix* which gives the different commodities produced by each industry. The model assumes that each industry produces only one commodity. So the *commodity × industry* table is converted to a *commodity × commodity* table using the procedures outlined in CSO (1990). The final input–output transactions table at 19 sectors under one industry one product assumption is as shown.

$$FD_j = PFCE_j + GFCE_j + INV_j + EXPORTS_j - IMPORTS_j \quad (B.1)$$

where $PFCE_j$ is private final consumption expenditure on good j, $GFCE_j$ is government final consumption expenditure on good j, INV_j is investment plus change in stocks of good j, $EXPORTS_j$ is export of good j and $IMPORTS_j$ is import of good j.

$$IUse_j = \sum_{i=1}^{n} A_{ij} \quad (B.2)$$

$$GO_j = IUse_j + FD_j \quad (B.3)$$

$$NIT_i = GO_i - GVA_i - \sum_{j=1}^{n} A_{ij} \quad (B.4)$$

where, FD_j is final demand for good j, $I\,Use_j$ is intermediate use of good j, GO_j is gross output of good j and NIT_i is net indirect tax paid by industry i.

Table B.35: **Nineteen Sector Input–Output (IO) Table** *(Million Rs.)*

	AGRI	CCNG	MINES	FDPR	TEXT
AGRI	359917.437	0.000	2.121	14096.9403	75313.538
CCNG	750.550	699.200	18.698	1695.641	3755.675
MINES	0.243	453.400	21.003	1006.039	27.955
FDPR	12185.704	0.000	0.057	42456.181	689.649
TEXT	4611.313	1.100	6.535	3781.574	156766.685
PAPER	319.909	622.000	70.273	3127.468	5003.667
CHEM	1380.968	1966.501	379.629	6299.610	29981.346
PETRO	17257.748	2576.193	971.508	3820.016	7639.454
FERT	73129.799	0.000	0.000	52.749	3.926
CEMENT	6.684	510.696	14.635	796.742	35.139
METLS	25.922	0.200	6.422	387.328	1155.202

continued on next page

continued from previous page

MECHMC	7246.414	7574.794	410.510	1100.409	2813.780
ELECMC	70.086	0.000	1.115	0.571	4.303
VEHCL	2279.712	600.300	6.700	1.793	5.019
OTHMFG	1171.882	1913.301	312.008	6234.597	5489.661
TRNSP	21329.406	2955.500	390.214	10625.851	21482.139
ELEC	13309.208	6252.702	1244.835	3655.424	28764.778
CONSTR	34106.105	2265.284	61.751	2101.126	2330.840
SRVCE	68431.720	7397.979	779.239	45477.690	81973.031

	PAPER	CHEM	PETRO	FERT	CEMENT
AGRI	16532.877	13060.989	120.349	65.339	800.813
CCNG	1767.255	1986.897	91448.138	2344.320	6037.270
MINES	670.631	2703.569	56.319	4097.846	10884.157
FDPR	135.185	4964.800	17.014	30.955	22.830
TEXT	1079.409	6691.897	188.846	2042.169	2636.322
PAPER	30990.219	8192.769	243.097	236.762	673.034
CHEM	3736.532	66539.660	3882.775	10170.369	1700.070
PETRO	1007.244	9847.735	19357.502	8531.162	5709.488
FERT	0.074	106.068	0.001	7740.143	1.847
CEMENT	52.629	1297.754	5.781	56.098	5596.116
METLS	1575.249	3157.133	12.477	78.393	2434.041
MECHMC	507.244	861.895	89.126	239.285	488.808
ELECMC	9.713	13.425	0.090	0.380	45.352
VEHCL	12.417	71.559	0.082	0.346	1.195
OTHMFG	1388.312	7720.394	1913.273	1810.695	1619.564
TRNSP	3336.062	9272.301	6323.542	3169.160	7007.020
ELEC	3798.813	9837.323	1862.114	5768.461	4197.293
CONSTR	392.143	1222.075	391.454	306.203	940.859
SRVCE	12746.665	34409.616	14894.898	10707.801	13004.577

	METLS	MECHMC	ELECMC	VEHCL	OTHMFG
AGRI	299.122	494.621	46.823	344.877	628.276
CCNG	6366.805	213.901	92.054	571.160	1133.625
MINES	9453.258	7.711	8.778	3.744	454.012
FDPR	1.157	0.455	0.494	9.121	35.125
TEXT	198.440	141.364	147.484	213.425	766.493
PAPER	123.425	512.083	1758.861	821.980	1706.440
CHEM	2128.410	1959.546	3649.566	5917.936	3210.209
PETRO	11525.543	1437.139	1213.621	2686.211	1987.176
FERT	0.453	0.170	0.157	0.229	19.328
CEMENT	457.839	38.372	358.198	222.429	635.292
METLS	52829.556	28052.811	24321.072	22574.179	32137.666
MECHMC	701.732	18816.723	509.731	2029.241	870.657
ELECMC	404.860	2787.849	26776.602	2392.542	2563.361
VEHCL	142.932	704.450	177.806	22435.062	2299.438
OTHMFG	15118.506	4792.108	6284.432	4850.050	11895.488
TRNSP	8902.338	3299.539	2895.700	3053.287	3985.755
ELEC	12511.617	2095.362	1752.453	2818.158	3718.796
CONSTR	2012.472	924.756	797.366	2639.466	765.208
SRVCE	21520.735	18868.552	14484.366	14141.265	16021.196

	TRNSP	ELEC	CONSTR	SRVCE	GVA

continued on next page

continued from previous page

AGRI	674.911	308.435	18212.900	46882.373	1231010.7135
CCNG	2146.464	27660.457	0.000	3752.799	69599.5240
MINES	0.000	50.954	30034.800	465.555	16836.8800
FDPR	500.900	7.101	0.000	8044.456	62531.1409
TEXT	523.845	77.545	1146.800	18244.034	196013.3149
PAPER	2717.867	577.161	16247.700	22589.768	29358.4307
CHEM	6467.179	327.929	8712.600	30380.110	69763.7429
PETRO	39572.611	3547.928	11271.900	2953.320	19137.0069
FERT	1.281	1.082	812.000	415.743	11812.6291
CEMENT	210.413	239.829	36517.500	511.927	37044.4615
METLS	1009.362	802.072	66589.600	5614.323	49430.2736
MECHMC	822.720	2342.985	845.600	1729.877	37569.4571
ELECMC	3287.326	5278.833	20011.400	3349.858	68441.0105
VEHCL	34594.683	63.792	515.300	2875.484	59562.0863
OTHMFG	4308.236	2954.626	1076.500	21165.243	68494.5507
TRNSP	27967.991	9693.781	23080.900	66317.225	214854.9546
ELEC	5656.155	53338.515	9735.700	14682.476	82448.2753
CONSTR	9802.391	4151.120	71.600	36325.466	229250.3448
SRVCE	31486.334	9988.638	60736.200	119729.751	1399178.1281

	PFCE	GFCE	INV	EXPORTS	IMPORTS
AGRI	1076219.8	1392.8	44803.4	28992.0	16277.0
CCNG	2073.5	72.4	536.0	89.0	46516.0
MINES	0.0	0.0	5359.0	4899.0	48582.0
FDPR	272101.6	195.9	678.0	10914.0	5061.0
TEXT	339763.0	742.4	36597.8	73189.0	4530.0
PAPER	14237.7	8276.3	2738.6	389.0	8504.0
CHEM	76920.3	2067.6	35751.4	23403.0	43711.0
PETRO	42136.5	9966.3	953.0	5310.0	15878.0
FERT	0.0	618.7	2702.0	661.0	13204.0
CEMENT	12864.6	0.8	912.2	48373.0	1712.0
METLS	0.0	0.0	13242.4	3164.0	44678.0
MECHMC	1093.7	3930.3	158240.0	13033.0	90594.0
ELECMC	18050.4	952.3	106118.2	10060.0	33494.0
VEHCL	11995.3	2589.0	94636.0	7213.0	21404.0
OTHMFG	33673.0	21828.8	32744.2	8419.0	28655.0
TRNSP	172484.6	13178.0	5608.8	30960.0	39484.0
ELEC	17140.6	12962.8	0.0	67.0	0.0
CONSTR	0.0	46616.9	413738.8	0.0	0.0
SRVCE	740816.8	386500.4	35547.5	98926.0	26746.0

Source: Planning Commission and Computed.

National Accounts

This section deals with the accounts of the government (both central and state). The various expenditure and receipts of the government are consolidated at one place to facilitate the construction of the social accounting matrix (SAM). The activities of the government can be classified under receipts (revenue and capital) and expenditures (domestic and external). The revenue and capital receipts of the government are depicted in Table B.36.

Table B.36: **Capital and Revenue Receipts of the Government**

Revenue Receipts		Capital Receipts	
Tax Head	Rs. Crore	Head	Rs. Crore
1A Indirect Tax		A	
i Excise	22406.30	i Market Loans	9707.64
ii Tariff	18036.13	ii Small Savings	7958.20
iii Sales Tax	15648.72	iii ppf	616.70
iv State Excise	4059.18	iv Repayments loans/adv	3130.45
v MVT	1454.21	v Transfers from ROW	3567.05
vi Tax goods/pass	941.1	Total A	**24980.04**
vii Electricity Duty	1086.74		
viii Stamp Duty	2363.37		
ix Sugarcane Tax	90.86		
x Entertainment Tax	427.49		
Total Indirect Tax	**66514.10**		
1B Direct Tax		B	
i CIT + Oth. Tax	5555.74	i PF (non govt.)	6999.60
ii Income Tax + Oth	5608.86	ii PF (state govt.)	2972.94
Total Direct Tax	**11164.60**	Total PF	**9972.54**
1 *Tax Revenue*	**77678.70**		
2A Rev from govt Service		C	
i public sector	−1121.17	i loans LIC/RBI	554.96
ii fiscal services	835.74	ii borrowing from RBI	−105.60
iii general services	1579.89	iii treasury bills	173.60
iv social services	744.09	iv Total C	**622.96**
v economic services	4864.98		
Total Govt. Services	**6903.53**		
2B Other revenue			
i Interest Receipts	6626.02		
2 *Non Tax Revenue*	**13529.55**		
Revenue Receipts	**91208.25**	**Capital Receipts**	**35575.54**
Total Domestic Receipts			126783.79
Borrowings from Abroad			2958.00
Miscellaneous Cap Receipts			2924.95
Total Government Revenue			**132666.74**

Source: Author and IES-PF

The government has borrowed from the central bank and floated treasury bills, which are not accounted in a real model. So in the construction of the SAM, this amount is deducted from the government income.

Apart from planned and non planned expenditure on commodities which forms a part of government final consumption expenditure (GFCE) as mentioned in the input–output table, the government also gives subsidies and transfers to individuals and institutions. This expenditure is classified in Table B.37 is deducted from the income in addition to GFCE.

Table B.37: **Government Subsidies and Transfers to Households**

Subsidies		Transfers	
Head	Rs. Crore	Head	Rs. Crore
1A Provision in Central Budget		A	
i on controlled cloth	10	i pension	2958.45
ii to railways	233	ii relief(non-planned)	517.52
iii industrial units in		iii relief(planned)	−21.77
backward areas	101		
iv for river dredging	21	iv comp. to landholders	2.79
v to GIC	90	v social security(NP)	1801.04
vi to SCI	10	vi social security(P)	1478.31
vii for vegetable oil	4	vii interest payments	18942.93
viii to jute corp of India	12	viii rural development	5302.23
ix interest	524	Total Transfers	**36389.68**
Total	**1005**		
1B Other Subsidies			
i fertiliser domestic	3771		
ii fertiliser imported	830		
iii agriculture	7868.34		
iv exports	2483.65		
v food subsidy	2512.32		
Total	**17465.31**		
Total Subsidies	**18470.31**		

Source: Author and IES-PF

On the external front the economy imports and exports goods leading to a current account deficit or surplus as the case may be. This deficit or surplus is financed from transfers or borrowing from the rest of the world, net of interest obligations. This external account is shown in Table B.38.

Table B.38: **External Account**

Expenditure		Receipts	
Head	Rs. Crore	Head	Rs. Crore
i Imports	48903.0	i Transfers to households	4000.20
ii NRI interest	1558.2	ii Transfer to Government	3567.05
Total	**50461.2**	iii Borrowings	2958.00
		iv Misc. Capital Receipts	2924.95
		v Exports	37011.00
		Total	**50461.20**

Source: Author, RBI Bulletin and IES-PF

Social Accounting Matrix for India

All the accounts of various agents are put together at one place in a *Social Accounting Matrix* (SAM). Dervis, deMelo, and Robinson (1982) give the basic format of a SAM. The SAM provides a consistent picture of the flow-of-funds accounts of separate actors/institutions in the economy. A SAM is always a square matrix as opposed to an input–output table, with the row sum equal to the column sum in a SAM. An entry in a column in the SAM depicts the expenditures made by an actor/institution, while the row entry shows the receipts accruing to the actor/institution. A SAM does not mean a consistent model, but a consistent model always implies a SAM. It is as shown in the Table B.39 with some modifications.

Table B.39: **Format of a Social Accounting Matrix**

	A	B	C	D	E	F	G	H	I
A		Domestic Commodity Supplies				Export Subsidy		Exports	
B	Intermediate Inputs				Private Consumption	Government Consumption	Investment		
C	Wages								
D	Rentals								
E			Labour Income	Capital Income		Transfers	Capital Inflow		
F	Indirect Taxes			Capital Taxes	Direct Taxes	Sales Taxes	Sales Taxes	Sales Taxes	
G					Private Saving	Government Saving			
H		Imports				Reserve Accumulation			
I	Total Costs	Total Absorption	Factor Income	Factor Income	Household Income	Government Expenditure	Investment	Foreign Exchange Inflow	

Source: Author and Dervis, deMelo, and Robinson (1982)
Key
A: Activities   B: Commodities   C: Labour
D: Capital   E: Households   F: Government
G: Investment   H: Rest of the World   I: Total

The SAM is prepared using the input–output table, factor payments and factor taxes and national accounts. The actual SAM is shown in Table B.40.

Table B.40: **Social Accounting Matrix for India**

	A	B	C	D	E	F	G	H	I
A		721637.59						36806.10	758443.69
B	337103.55				283157.14	51189.17	99090.73		770540.59
C	174518.48								174518.48
D	209306.99								209306.99
E			174518.48	202403.46		36389.68		4000.20	417311.82
F	37514.67			6903.53	48094.15	2100.74	9305.58	9654.90	113573.57
G					86060.53	22335.78			108396.31
H		48903.00				1558.20			50461.20
I	758443.69	770540.59	174518.48	209306.99	417311.82	113573.57	108396.31	50461.20	

Source: Author

Appendix C
Calibration and Parameters

Introduction

In the last chapter the description of the procedures to construct a benchmark data set were outlined. Apart from a consistent data set various other parameters are required for implementing a general equilibrium model. These parameters are either selected from literature search or are estimated. Once the crucial parameters are selected or estimated the residual parameters are calculated to replicate the benchmark observation, year 1989–90 in this case. This procedure known as calibration is used by most modellers.

The chapter is outlined as follows. First the estimates of production functions used in the model are explained. This is followed by the details of various exogenous parameters used. Finally in the last section calibration procedures are outlined.

Estimation of Production Functions

There have been a plethora of studies estimating the production functions of the Indian manufacturing sector at various levels of disaggregation and at various points of time. The host of issues addressed in those studies ranged from estimating elasticities of substitution, returns to scale, technical progress and cost functions which have been summarised by Barua (1985). Similar survey of estimates of production functions in different countries was undertaken by Caddy (1976). In all studies of production functions on the Indian manufacturing sector the functional forms were specified *a priori*.

Model Used

The model structure used below is similar to Bairam (1991)

$$VA = f(L, K) \tag{C.1}$$

where VA is the value added, L is the labour in person days and K is the capital, a sum of fixed and working capital. The function is homogeneous of degree n, the returns to scale.

The methodology used to estimate the model is a time series cross section pooled analysis of the following specification as mentioned in Kmenta (1986)

$$Y_{it} = X_{it}{}^{\mathrm{T}}\beta + \epsilon_{it}; \quad \text{for } i = 1, ..., N, \quad t = 1, ..., T \tag{C.2}$$

where β is the $k \times 1$ vector of unknown parameters and ϵ_{it} is a random vector. The model makes the following assumptions on the disturbance covariance matrix that gives a cross sectionally heteroscedastic and time wise autoregressive model. The assumptions of the Kmenta model are

1. $E(\epsilon_{i,t}{}^2) = \sigma_i{}^2$; heteroscedasticity.

2. $E(\epsilon_{i,t}\epsilon_{j,t}) = 0$ for $i \neq j$; cross section independence.

3. $\epsilon_{i,t} = \rho_i\epsilon_{j,t-1} + v_{it}$, autoregression.

4. $E(v_{i,t}) = 0$ $E(v_{i,t}{}^2) = \phi_{ii}$.

5. $E(v_{i,t}v_{j,t}) = 0$ for $i \neq j$.

6. $E(v_{i,t}v_{i,s}) = 0$ for $t \neq s$ and $E(\epsilon_{i,t-1}v_{jt})$.

The following equation was used and iterated over values of λ from 0 to 1. The value of λ was close to 0 implying a log-linear functional form.

$$\frac{(VA^\lambda - 1)}{\lambda} = a + b\frac{L^\lambda}{\lambda} + c\frac{K^\lambda}{\lambda} \tag{C.3}$$

where $n = b + c$ stands for the *returns to scale* with $b, c > 0$ and $-\infty < \lambda < \infty$. The elasticity of substitution σ between labour and capital is given by $\frac{1}{1-\lambda}$. To satisfy properties of production function $\lambda \leq 1$.

Data and Procedure

The exercise of estimation was undertaken to decide the functional form for the production functions in the organised manufacturing sector. This functional form is then used for calibration. It is important to note that the parameter estimates obtained will not be used for the model as the classification is different, but will be calibrated from the base case given the estimated functional form.

A Box-Cox procedure, was used to arrive at the functional form. The data for estimation purposes is taken from various issues of the Annual Survey of Industries CSO (8 89) at the 3 digit level. This is then mapped to the appropriate 2 digit level and the pooled data from 1980 − 81 to 1988 − 89 is used. The sum of fixed and working capital is used as capital and person days is used as a proxy for labour. The data set was not adjusted for capacity utilisation rates. The value of λ is very close to 0, implying the elasticity of substitution is 1. The production functions are Cobb–Douglas. The log linear form suitable to estimate the production function is

$$\ln(VA) = a + b\ln L + c\ln K \tag{C.4}$$

Table C.1 shows the estimates of production functions.

Table C.1: **Production Function Estimation – Organised Manufacturing Sector**

ASI	Industry Name	Constant	Labour	Capital	n	D.W.	R^2	DF	ρ
20-21	Food Products	−0.86 (−3.07)[a]	0.35 (7.60)	0.67 (18.16)	1.02	1.82	0.995	168	−0.046
22	Beverages and Tobacco	−1.09 (−3.89)	0.38 (8.82)	0.71 (17.4)	1.09	1.95	0.989	87	−0.061
23	Cotton Textiles	−1.85 (−8.10)	0.45 (5.34)	0.66 (8.31)	1.11	1.86	0.998	53	−0.039
24	Man-made Textiles	−1.46 (−7.32)	0.60 (7.48)	0.50 (7.17)	1.10	1.99	0.996	87	−0.078
25	Jute and Other Vegetable Textiles	−0.25 (−1.04)[b]	0.82 (13.2)	0.09 (1.13)[b]	0.91	1.99	0.975	21	−0.108
26	Textile Products	−0.02 (−0.05)[b]	0.61 (3.79)	0.29 (2.07)	0.90	1.98	0.971	67	−0.041
27	Wood and Wood Products	−0.05 (−1.89)[c]	0.39 (6.52)	0.58 (9.78)	0.97	1.80	0.983	69	−0.014
28	Paper and Paper Products	−0.53 (−2.11)	0.58 (8.22)	0.43 (6.99)	1.01	1.95	0.993	78	−0.061
29	Leather and Leather Products	−1.11 (−2.56)	0.48 (2.79)	0.61 (4.11)	1.09	1.77	0.989	33	−0.048
30	Basic Chemicals	−1.21 (−1.91)[c]	0.14 (1.812)[c]	0.68 (13.91)	0.82	1.95	0.996	61	−0.094
31	Rubber, Plastic, Petro/Coal Products	−2.47 (−2.47)	0.55 (4.28)	0.67 (17.4)	1.22	1.94	0.998	87	−0.099
32	Non-Metallic Mineral Products	−0.55 (−1.91)[c]	0.37 (4.58)	0.62 (9.99)	0.99	1.79	0.990	67	−0.027
33	Basic Metal and Alloy Industries	−0.24 (−0.57)[b]	0.58 (6.14)	0.41 (4.56)	0.99	1.60	0.998	61	−0.033
34	Metal Products and Parts	−0.12 (−0.25)[b]	0.27 (2.98)	0.70 (8.57)	0.97	1.87	0.997	60	−0.106
35	Non-Electrical Machinery	1.12 (−2.94)	0.18 (5.77)	0.67 (16.7)	0.85	1.73	0.999	77	−0.016
36	Electrical Machinery	−1.16 (4.69)	0.32 (3.63)	0.76 (17.1)	1.08	1.73	0.999	45	−0.058
37	Transport Equipment and Parts	−1.26 (−5.09)	0.79 (13.7)	0.31 (6.15)	1.10	1.56	0.994	67	−0.056
38	Other Manufacturing Industries	0.23 (−0.443)[b]	0.73 (5.831)	0.24 (2.944)	0.97	1.35	0.988	42	−0.086
40-74	Electricity,Gas and Water Supply	−1.03 (−1.965)[c]	0.54 (2.195)[d]	0.47 (2.719)	1.01	1.85	0.997	29	−0.054
97	Repair Services	0.10 (0.649)[b]	0.62 (9.190)	0.34 (5.720)	0.96	1.51	0.994	37	−0.093

a numbers in brackets denote t statistics @ 1% significance level
b significant @ 2.5 %
c significant @ 5%
d insignificant @ 10%

Exogenous Parameters

Ogaki, Ostry, and Reinhart (1996) study the relationship between real interest rates, savings and growth. They estimate a model in which the inter-temporal elasticity of substitution varies with the level of wealth using macroeconomic data for a cross-section of countries. The estimated parameters are used to calculate the responsiveness of savings to real interest rate changes for countries at different stages of development.

The model requires the elasticity of savings with respect to the real rate of return η. Ballard, Fullerton, Shoven, and Whalley (1985) use the value of 0.4

Table C.2: **Intertemporal Elasticity of Substitution**

Country	Level (a)	GNP per equivalent adult in 1985$ 1980–87 average As a share of US level (b)	Intertemporal Elasticity of Substitution Lower bound (c)	Point estimate (d)	Upper bound (e)
India	829.1	0.046	0.233	0.336	0.440
USA	18194.5	1.000	0.440	0.636	0.831

Source: Table 5, Ogaki, Ostry, and Reinhart (1996)

for all households. For sensitivity analyses the value of η is varied from 0.20 to 0.45 using the results of Ogaki, Ostry, and Reinhart (1996) as mentioned in the Table C.2

Calibration

This section deals with procedures undertaken to replicate the benchmark data set and is structured as follows. First the calibration procedure for the production functions is outlined. Following this the tax model is calibrated for labour leisure choice, savings choice and demand system at various nests. In the concluding part the trade model is calibrated beginning with the demand system and later followed with economies of scale and market imperfections.

Production Function Calibration

As outlined in Section C.2, the production functions are Cobb–Douglas. In this case the functional form for the value added is as depicted in equation (A.39). Manipulating the first order conditions as per Section A.2.1 results in

$$\frac{\delta}{(1-\delta)} = \frac{p_L L}{p_K K} \tag{C.5}$$

this $\Rightarrow$

$$\delta = \frac{p_L L}{p_L L + p_K K} \tag{C.6}$$

It follows from equations (A.38) and (A.39) that

$$\phi = \frac{(1+t_l)L + (1+t_k)K}{L^\delta K^{(1-\delta)}} \tag{C.7}$$

since $p_L = (1+t_l)w$ and $p_K = (1+t_K)r$. The values of ϕ and δ are given in Table C.3.

Table C.3: **Calibration of Production Functions**

Sector Number	Sector Name	ϕ	δ
1	AGRI	1.995331	0.454930
2	CCNG	1.999409	0.316883
3	MINES	1.936800	0.316883
4	FDPR	2.067776	0.344841
5	TEXT	2.045713	0.454771
6	PAPER	2.088599	0.435185
7	CHEM	2.082805	0.320035
8	PETRO	1.550833	0.121284
9	FERT	1.924937	0.309903
10	CEMENT	1.978142	0.356151
11	METLS	2.201511	0.393715
12	MECHMC	2.177164	0.464124
13	ELECMC	2.043293	0.381430
14	VEHCL	2.243013	0.546226
15	OTHMFG	2.014691	0.425107
16	TRNSP	1.950324	0.367789
17	ELEC	2.078668	0.466201
18	CONSTR	1.504527	0.875584
19	SRVCE	2.064854	0.442059

Source: Computed

Tax Model Calibration

The utility function of the *representative* consumer has to be calibrated. The utility function has four nests. The savings–consumption choice at nest 1, followed by labour–leisure choice at nest 2. Nest 3 is the demand system for the 19 composite goods while nest 4 determines the domestic–imported choice for each good. The calibration of each of the nests follows.

Labour–Leisure Choice

Let e be the elasticity of labour supply with respect to the net wage rate P_l. Let ê be the elasticity of leisure consumption with respect to its price P_l. The ratio of labour endowment to labour supply is $\xi \Rightarrow \xi = E/L$, where $L = E - l$.

Labour supply elasticity is

$$e = \frac{\partial(E-l)}{\partial P_l} \frac{P_l}{(E-l)} = \left(\frac{\partial E}{\partial P_l} - \frac{\partial l}{\partial P_l}\right) \frac{P_l}{(E-l)} \tag{C.8}$$

This $\Rightarrow$

$$e = -\frac{\partial l}{\partial P_l} \frac{P_l}{l} \frac{l}{(E-l)} \Rightarrow \frac{(E-l)}{l} = -\frac{\partial l}{\partial P_l} \frac{P_l}{l} \tag{C.9}$$

since $\partial E/\partial P_l = 0$ The elasticity of leisure demand is

$$\hat{e} = \frac{\partial l}{\partial P_l} \frac{P_l}{l} \tag{C.10}$$

from the above two equations it $\Rightarrow$

$$\hat{e} = -e\frac{(E-l)}{l} = -e\frac{L}{(E-L)} = -e\frac{1}{(\xi-1)} \tag{C.11}$$

With $e = 0.15$ and $\xi = 1.75$, the elasticity of leisure demand $\hat{e} = -0.20$

The labour–leisure choice nest has two parameters *viz.* β and σ_2. For benchmark calibration one of these parameters has to be estimated/calculated before the other can be obtained using consistency procedures.

First the elasticity of substitution between present consumption and present leisure σ_2 will be evaluated in terms of other known parameters. Reproducing equation (3.73), which gives demand for leisure

$$l = \frac{\beta(I_{Max} - P_S S)}{P_l^{\sigma_2}\Delta_2} \tag{C.12}$$

In the above equation the share parameter β and price of savings P_S are independent of P_l. Differentiating the above equation with respect to P_l,

$$\frac{\partial l}{\partial P_l} = -\frac{\beta(I_{Max} - P_S S)\sigma_2}{\Delta_2 P_l^{(\sigma_2+1)}} + \frac{\beta}{P_l^{\sigma_2}\Delta_2}\left[\frac{\partial I_{Max}}{\partial P_l} - P_S\frac{\partial S}{\partial P_l}\right] - \frac{\beta(I_{Max} - P_S S)}{P_l^{\sigma_2}\Delta_2^2}\frac{\partial\Delta_2}{\partial P_l} \tag{C.13}$$

There is a simultaneity problem between the order of present-future consumption and labour–leisure choice. At nest 1, since the amount of leisure is not known, the income is undetermined and hence savings is undetermined. If one were to allocate the labour–leisure choice at nest one, then income would be determined but for a given level of prices if the requisite savings were not available, the labour–leisure choice would have to be revised. More formally, value of savings from equation (3.69) is reproduced below.

$$S = \frac{(1-\alpha)I_{Max}}{P_S(\frac{P_G}{r\gamma})^{(\sigma_3-1)}\Delta_1} \tag{C.14}$$

The net wage P_l affects savings in two ways. The direct price effect due to labour endowment term E in I_{Max}. Hence $\partial I_{Max}/\partial P_l = E$. There is a cross price effect due to the presence of P_H in Δ_1. P_H also contains a P_l term. To resolve this problem the cross price effect is neglected as it is likely to be small. So the following approximation is used

$$\frac{\partial S}{\partial P_l} = \frac{(1-\alpha)E}{P_S(\frac{P_G}{r\gamma})^{(\sigma_3-1)}\Delta_1} = \frac{SE}{I_{Max}} \tag{C.15}$$

substituting equation (C.12) in equation (C.10)

$$\frac{\partial l}{\partial P_l} = -\frac{\beta(I_{Max} - P_S S)\sigma_2}{\Delta_2 P_l^{(\sigma_2+1)}} + \frac{\beta}{P_l^{\sigma_2}\Delta_2}\left[E - \frac{P_S SE}{I}\right] - \frac{\beta(I_{Max} - P_S S)}{P_l^{\sigma_2}\Delta_2^2}\frac{\partial\Delta_2}{\partial P_l} \tag{C.16}$$

using equation (C.9), it follows

$$\frac{\partial l}{\partial P_l} = -\frac{l\sigma_2}{P_l} + \frac{\beta}{P_l^{\sigma_2}\Delta_2}\left[E - \frac{P_S SE}{I_{Max}}\right] - \frac{l}{\Delta_2}\left(\frac{\partial \Delta_2}{\partial P_l}\right) \tag{C.17}$$

The term to be evaluated is $\partial \Delta_2/\partial P_l$. The expression for Δ_2 reproduced from equation (1.39) is

$$\Delta_2 = \beta P_l^{(1-\sigma_2)} + (1-\beta)P_G^{(1-\sigma_2)} \tag{C.18}$$

differentiating with respect to P_l

$$\frac{\partial \Delta_2}{\partial P_l} = \frac{\beta(1-\sigma_2)}{P_l^{\sigma_2}} \tag{C.19}$$

equation (C.14) and equation (C.16) $\Rightarrow$

$$\frac{\partial l}{\partial P_l} = -\frac{l\sigma_2}{P_l} + \frac{\beta}{P_l^{\sigma_2}\Delta_2}\left[E - \frac{P_S SE}{I_{Max}}\right] - \frac{l\beta(1-\sigma_2)}{P_l^{\sigma_2}\Delta_2} \tag{C.20}$$

from equation (C.7) elasticity of leisure demand is

$$\hat{e} = \frac{\partial l}{\partial P_l}\frac{P_l}{l} = -\sigma_2 + \frac{\beta P_l^{(1-\sigma_2)}}{l\Delta_2}\frac{E}{I_{Max}}(I_{Max} - P_S S) - \frac{\beta(1-\sigma_2)P_l^{(1-\sigma_2)}}{\Delta_2} \tag{C.21}$$

rewriting equation (C.9) as

$$\frac{P_l l}{(I_{Max} - P_S S)} = \frac{\beta P_l^{(1-\sigma_2)}}{\Delta_2} \tag{C.22}$$

using the above expression, elasticity of leisure demand $\hat{e}$ is

$$\hat{e} = -\sigma_2 + \frac{P_l E}{I_{Max}} - \frac{P_l l(1-\sigma_2)}{I_{Max} - P_S S} \tag{C.23}$$

simplifying the above expression to solve for σ_2

$$\sigma_2 = \left[-\hat{e} + \frac{P_l E}{I_{Max}} - \frac{P_l l}{(I_{Max} - P_S S)}\right] \Big/ \left[1 - \frac{P_l l}{(I_{Max} - P_S S)}\right] \tag{C.24}$$

The value of σ_2 can be easily computed as all the variables either appear in the benchmark data set or are computed as $\hat{e}$ and P_l.

After obtaining σ_2 from above, the scale factor in the labour–leisure choice β is obtained by calibration. Reproducing equation (3.74) which is the demand for composite good X_G.

$$X_G = \frac{(1-\beta)(I_{Max} - P_S S)}{P_G^{\sigma_2}\Delta_2} \tag{C.25}$$

dividing equation (C.9) by (C.22) yields

$$\frac{l}{X_G} = \frac{\beta}{(1-\beta)} \frac{P_G^{\sigma_2}}{P_l^{\sigma_2}} \tag{C.26}$$

solving the above for $\beta \Rightarrow$

$$\beta = \frac{l P_l^{\sigma_2}}{l P_l^{\sigma_2} + X_G P_G^{\sigma_2}} \tag{C.27}$$

X_G is obtained from equation (3.74) while P_G is obtained from equation (3.79), thus obtaining β from the above equation.

Consumption–Saving Choice

Having calibrated the parameters for the labour–leisure choice at nest 2, the parameters for nest 1 addressing the consumption–savings choice have to be calibrated. Similar to the earlier section, the elasticity of savings η with respect to the real rate of return ror is specified exogenously. Hence $\eta = (\partial S/\partial ror)(ror/S)$, where $ror = r\gamma/P_S$. The elasticity of substitution at nest 1, σ_3 is a function of η. To evaluate σ_3 in terms of η analytically as for nest 2 is very difficult. The expression for savings is reproduced below.

$$S = \frac{(1-\alpha)I_{Max}}{P_S(\frac{P_G}{r\gamma})^{(\sigma_3-1)}\Delta_1} \tag{C.28}$$

Savings is a function of I_{Max}, P_S and P_G. These are in turn functions of r, which is a function of capital-labour ratios. In order to obtain $\partial S/\partial ror$ a numerical approach is selected. First the values of S and ror are calculated with all prices equal to 1. Then r is arbitrarily increased by 1% and the values of S and ror are calculated. This 1% increase in r results in changes in S and ror. These changes are used to compute $\eta = \Delta S/\Delta(ror).(ror)/S$. If η thus obtained is greater than required σ_3 is scaled down and vice-versa. For simulation purposes different values of η were chosen and the model calibrated to each. This was done to analyse the sensitivity of the results to the value of η. The values of σ_3 for various values of η are shown in Table C.4.

To complete the calibration of utility functions at nest 1, the share parameter α needs to be evaluated. The expressions for present consumption H and future consumption C_F reproduced below are necessary.

$$H = \frac{\alpha I_{Max}}{P_H^{\sigma_3}\Delta_1} \tag{C.29}$$

Let price of future consumption $P_{CF} = P_S P_G/r\gamma$

$$C_F = \frac{(1-\alpha)I_{Max}}{(\frac{P_S P_G}{r\gamma})^{\sigma_3}\Delta_1} = \frac{(1-\alpha)I_{Max}}{P_{CF}^{\sigma_3}\Delta_1} \tag{C.30}$$

Table C.4: **Elasticity of Substitution at Nest 1**

Number	η	σ_3
1	0.20	1.3350
2	0.25	1.4150
3	0.30	1.4975
4	0.35	1.5800
5	0.40	1.6650
6	0.45	1.7475

Source: Computed

Dividing equation (C.26) by (C.27)

$$\frac{H}{C_F} = \frac{\alpha}{(1-\alpha)} \frac{P_{CF}^{\sigma_3}}{P_H^{\sigma_3}} \tag{C.31}$$

solving for α

$$\alpha = \frac{H P_H^{\sigma_3}}{H P_H^{\sigma_3} + C_F P_{CF}^{\sigma_3}} \tag{C.32}$$

Demand System

The calibration of parameters of the demand system at nest 3 is explained below. The demand system at nest 3 being Cobb–Douglas the parameter λ_i of the ith good is equal to the share of expenditure of that good in total expenditure. Therefore

$$\lambda_i = \frac{PC_i C_i}{\sum_{i=1}^{n} PC_i C_i} \tag{C.33}$$

The shares for private consumption, investment and government consumption are mentioned in Table C.5

The calibration of demand parameters at nest 4 is similar to those at nest 3, the demand system being Cobb–Douglas. The parameters are

$$\epsilon_i = \frac{PFD_i FD_i}{PC_i C_i} \tag{C.34}$$

The shares for domestic and imported consumption for private, investment and government purposes is mentioned in Table C.6.

Trade Model Calibration

This subsection will deal with the calibration of the extended version of the trade model incorporating increasing returns to scale since the production function calibration is same for both the tax as well as the trade model.

Table C.5: **Share of Consumption of Goods at Nest 3**

Sector	PVT	INV	GOV
AGRI	0.344	0.040	0.003
CCNG	0.001	0.001	0.000
MINES	0.000	0.005	0.000
FDPR	0.117	0.001	0.000
TEXT	0.120	0.035	0.001
PAPER	0.005	0.003	0.017
CHEM	0.035	0.041	0.005
PETRO	0.022	0.001	0.028
FERT	0.000	0.001	0.001
CEMENT	0.005	0.001	0.000
METLS	0.000	0.014	0.000
MECHMC	0.000	0.176	0.009
ELECMC	0.009	0.118	0.002
VEHCL	0.005	0.104	0.006
OTHMFG	0.015	0.039	0.055
TRNSP	0.060	0.005	0.025
ELEC	0.006	0.000	0.026
CONSTR	0.000	0.382	0.087
SRVCE	0.256	0.033	0.735

Source: Computed

Table C.6: **Share of Consumption of Goods at Nest 4**

Sector	PVT(d)	PVT(m)	INV(d)	INV(m)	GOV(d)	GOV(m)
AGRI	0.990	0.010	1.000	0.000	0.998	0.002
CCNG	1.000	0.000	1.000	0.000	1.000	0.000
MINES	0.000	0.000	1.000	0.000	0.000	0.000
FDPR	0.979	0.021	1.000	0.000	0.977	0.023
TEXT	0.990	0.010	1.000	0.000	0.984	0.016
PAPER	0.776	0.224	1.000	0.000	0.750	0.250
CHEM	0.782	0.218	0.993	0.007	0.808	0.192
PETRO	0.726	0.274	1.000	0.000	0.726	0.274
FERT	0.000	0.000	1.000	0.000	1.000	0.000
CEMENT	0.918	0.082	0.978	0.022	1.000	0.000
METLS	0.000	0.000	1.000	0.000	0.000	0.000
MECHMC	0.426	0.574	0.489	0.511	0.445	0.555
ELECMC	0.314	0.686	0.782	0.218	0.776	0.224
VEHCL	0.979	0.021	0.826	0.174	0.924	0.076
OTHMFG	0.577	0.423	0.608	0.392	0.577	0.423
TRNSP	0.815	0.185	1.000	0.000	0.884	0.116
ELEC	1.000	0.000	0.000	0.000	1.000	0.000
CONSTR	0.000	0.000	1.000	0.000	1.000	0.000
SRVCE	0.969	0.031	1.000	0.000	0.999	0.001

Source: Computed

Table C.7: **Share of Domestic and Imported Goods in Consumption**

Sector	TOTAL	Domestic	Imported
AGRI	0.232	0.990	0.010
CCNG	0.001	1.000	0.000
MINES	0.001	1.000	0.000
FDPR	0.076	0.979	0.021
TEXT	0.086	0.991	0.009
PAPER	0.006	0.791	0.209
CHEM	0.033	0.845	0.155
PETRO	0.017	0.731	0.269
FERT	0.000	1.000	0.000
CEMENT	0.004	0.922	0.078
METLS	0.003	1.000	0.000
MECHMC	0.043	0.487	0.513
ELECMC	0.034	0.704	0.296
VEHCL	0.029	0.845	0.155
OTHMFG	0.026	0.589	0.411
TRNSP	0.043	0.826	0.174
ELEC	0.007	1.000	0.000
CONSTR	0.101	1.000	0.000
SRVCE	0.259	0.980	0.020

Source: Computed

Demand System

The calibration of demand parameters is similar to the tax model, the reason being the demand system is Cobb–Douglas.

$$\delta_i = \frac{PFD_i FD_i}{PC_i C_i} \tag{C.35}$$

The share in expenditure on domestic, imported and total consumption is mentioned in Table C.7.

Increasing Returns to Scale

In the basic trade model constant marginal costs $\Rightarrow$ price equals marginal cost. Under increasing returns total costs equal variable costs plus fixed costs.

$$TC_i = FC_i + CV_i \tag{C.36}$$

and,

$$CV_i = INTC_i + P\tilde{V}C_i \tag{C.37}$$

where PVC_i is primary variable costs under increasing returns and is calibrated using

$$P\tilde{V}C_i = PVC_i - CDR_i \times TC_i \tag{C.38}$$

where CDR is the cost disadvantage ratio defined as $(CDR = FC/TC)$ and PVC is primary variable costs as shown in equations (1.2) and (1.3). Labour share in fixed costs is assumed to be the same as labour share in value added. Thus

$$LSFC = \frac{wL_i}{VA_i} \tag{C.39}$$

Hence fixed labour and capital costs are

$$\overline{LF}_i = LSFC_i \frac{FC_i}{w}, \qquad \overline{KF}_i = (1 - LSFC_i)\frac{FC_i}{r} \tag{C.40}$$

To replicate the base case value added is reduced by the amount of fixed costs by subtracting the fixed cost component of labour and capital from labour and capital in each sector with increasing returns. The value added thus obtained is used in calibration of the production function parameters, the procedure being outlined in equation (C.4.1).

For modelling the various market structures it is necessary to calculate the value of conjectures in the benchmark. The conjecture is given by

$$\Omega_i = N_i \epsilon_i{}^d \left[1 - \frac{C_i'}{P}\right] \tag{C.41}$$

for Cobb–Douglas demand system $\epsilon_i{}^d$ equals 1 and each industry is assumed to have one representative firm. Thus conjecture is calibrated from the above equation. This concludes the changes brought about to the calibration of the basic trade model.

Programming Appendix

Introduction

This chapter aims to explain in brief the basics of fixed point algorithms.[1] It then outlines the use of Merrill's algorithm to compute a vector of prices for a general equilibrium model.

Homotopy and Fixed Point Nomenclature

Computable general equilibrium models seek to obtain a price vector that clears the market, wherein supply equals demand. The equations for price and excess demand are non-linear.

Let R^n denote the Euclidean n space. A function F: $R^n \rightarrow R^n$ implies $F(x)$ has n components, i.e., $F(\mathbf{x}) = F_1(\mathbf{x}), F_2(\mathbf{x}), \ldots, F_n(\mathbf{x})$ and $\mathbf{x}$ is a vector of n components $\mathbf{x} = (x_1, x_2, \ldots, x_n)$. such that $F_i(\mathbf{x}) = F_i(x_1, x_2, \ldots x_n), i = 1, 2, \ldots, n$ One needs to solve the $n \times n$ system of nonlinear equations $F(\mathbf{x})=0$. In this case $\mathbf{x}$ will be a vector of excess demands of the various commodities. The system of equations can be depicted as

$$F_1(x_1, x_2, \ldots, x_n) = 0$$
$$F_2(x_1, x_2, \ldots, x_n) = 0$$
..
..
..
$$F_n(x_1, x_2, \ldots, x_n) = 0$$

to obtain a vector $\mathbf{x}^*$

To cite a concrete example, $F(x)$ is the excess demand function (demand - supply) at each price, for different commodities. If one works in the realm of factor prices (wage rate $\mathbf{w}$ and price of capital $\mathbf{r}$), the $\mathbf{x} = \{\mathbf{w}, \mathbf{r}\}$. Thus $F(\mathbf{x}) = \{F_l(w, r), F_r(w, r)\}$, where F_l and F_r are excess demands for labour (l) and capital (r).

Homotopy

Consider the system $H(\mathbf{x}, t)$, $0 \leq t \leq 1$, where H: $R^{(n+1)} \rightarrow R^n$ implies $H(x)$ has n components of $\mathbf{x}$ and 1 t.

$$H(\mathbf{x}, t) = (1 - t)E(\mathbf{x}) + tF(\mathbf{x}) = 0 \qquad (D.1)$$

For $t = 0$, the problem reduces to finding solution to $E(\mathbf{x})=0$ and at $t = 1$, the original problem $F(\mathbf{x})=0$. One needs to find a path for t from $t = 0$ to $t = 1$, to obtain a solution to the original problem.

---

[1]Part of this chapter follows Zangwill and Garcia (1981).

Newton Homotopy

$$\begin{aligned} H(\mathbf{x}, t) &= F(\mathbf{x}) - (1-t)F(\mathbf{x}^0) \\ E(\mathbf{x}) &= F(\mathbf{x}) - F(\mathbf{x}^0) \end{aligned} \tag{D.2}$$

For $x = x^0$, E has a solution, therefore one can begin at an arbitrary point x^0.

Fixed-Point Homotopy

$$\begin{aligned} H(\mathbf{x}, t) &= (1-t)(\mathbf{x} - \mathbf{x}^0) + tF(\mathbf{x}) \\ E(\mathbf{x}) &= \mathbf{x} - \mathbf{x}^0 = 0 \end{aligned} \tag{D.3}$$

For $x(0) = x^0$, E has a solution, therefore one can begin at an arbitrary point x^0.

Linear Homotopy

$$\begin{aligned} H(\mathbf{x}, t) &= (1-t)E(\mathbf{x}) + tF(\mathbf{x}) \\ H(\mathbf{x}, t) &= E(\mathbf{x}) + t\{F(\mathbf{x}) - E(\mathbf{x})\} \end{aligned} \tag{D.4}$$

When $E(\mathbf{x})=\mathbf{x}-\mathbf{x}^0$, the linear homotopy reduces to the fixed point and when $E(\mathbf{x})=F(\mathbf{x})-F(\mathbf{x}^0)$, the linear homotopy reduces to newton homotopy.

Path Existence

To move to the solution of $F(\mathbf{x})=0$ from the initial $E(\mathbf{x})=0$, a path must exist from $t = 0$ to $t = 1$. Define

$$H^{-1} = \{(\mathbf{x}, t) | H(\mathbf{x}, t) = 0\}$$

as the set of all solutions $(\mathbf{x},t) \in R^{(n+1)}$ to the system $H(\mathbf{x},t)=0$. H^{-1} consists of both $\mathbf{x}$ and t. Let

$$H^{-1}(t) = \{(\mathbf{x}) | H(\mathbf{x}, t) = 0\}$$

$H^{-1}(t)$ has points $\mathbf{x} \in R^n$. For a function $H(\mathbf{x},t)$: $R^{(n+1)} \rightarrow R^n$, denote its Jacobian $(n \times (n+1))$ matrix by

$$H'(\mathbf{x}, t) = \begin{bmatrix} \frac{\partial H_1}{\partial x_1} & \frac{\partial H_1}{\partial x_2} & \cdots & \frac{\partial H_1}{\partial x_n} & \frac{\partial H_1}{\partial t} \\ \frac{\partial H_2}{\partial x_1} & \frac{\partial H_2}{\partial x_2} & \cdots & \frac{\partial H_2}{\partial x_n} & \frac{\partial H_2}{\partial t} \\ \cdots & \cdots & \cdots & \cdots & \cdots \\ \cdots & \cdots & \cdots & \cdots & \cdots \\ \cdots & \cdots & \cdots & \cdots & \cdots \\ \frac{\partial H_n}{\partial x_1} & \frac{\partial H_n}{\partial x_2} & \cdots & \frac{\partial H_n}{\partial x_n} & \frac{\partial H_n}{\partial t} \end{bmatrix} \tag{D.5}$$

Split $H'(\mathbf{x},t)$ into matrix $H'_x(\mathbf{x},t)$ $(n \times n)$ and vector $\frac{\partial H}{\partial t}$.

$$H'_x(\mathbf{x},t) = \begin{bmatrix} \frac{\partial H_1}{\partial x_1} & \frac{\partial H_1}{\partial x_2} & \cdots & \frac{\partial H_1}{\partial x_n} \\ \frac{\partial H_2}{\partial x_1} & \frac{\partial H_2}{\partial x_2} & \cdots & \frac{\partial H_2}{\partial x_n} \\ \cdots & \cdots & \cdots & \cdots \\ \cdots & \cdots & \cdots & \cdots \\ \frac{\partial H_n}{\partial x_1} & \frac{\partial H_n}{\partial x_2} & \cdots & \frac{\partial H_n}{\partial x_n} \end{bmatrix} \quad \frac{\partial H}{\partial t} = \begin{bmatrix} \frac{\partial H_1}{\partial t} \\ \frac{\partial H_2}{\partial t} \\ \cdots \\ \cdots \\ \frac{\partial H_n}{\partial t} \end{bmatrix} \tag{D.6}$$

Using the Jacobian linearise H^{-1} around any arbitrary point $(\overline{\mathbf{x}}, \overline{t})$ such that $H(\overline{\mathbf{x}}, \overline{t}) = 0$. Therefore

$$H(\mathbf{x},t) \approx H(\overline{\mathbf{x}}, \overline{t}) + \sum_{i=1}^{n} \frac{\partial H(\overline{\mathbf{x}}, \overline{t})}{\partial x_j}(x_j - \overline{x}_j) + \frac{\partial H(\overline{\mathbf{x}}, \overline{t})}{\partial t}(t - \overline{t}) \tag{D.7}$$

Assuming that the Jacobian is non-singular (invertible)

$$(x - \overline{x}) = -[H'_x]^{-1}\frac{\partial H}{\partial t}(t - \overline{t}) \tag{D.8}$$

There are n equations corresponding to each $x_i, i = 1, 2, ..., n$ and $n+1$ unknowns (n x's plus t). Thus the solution is not a unique point $\mathbf{x}^*$, but a line segment or a **path** through $(\overline{\mathbf{x}}, \overline{t})$

In economic terms one is interested in finding an equilibrium vector of prices p^* and quantities q^* such that the vector of excess demands of commodities is always zero. Brouwer's fixed point theorem states the conditions under which $x^* \in R^n$ and a function $F(x) \in R^n$, such that

$$F(x^*) = x^* \tag{D.9}$$

Intuitively p^* is a vector of prices such that in equilibrium the vector of excess demands is always zero. The function $F(\mathbf{p})$ computes the prices to obtain equilibrium.

The objective then is to practically implement algorithms that enable one to compute the economic equilibria, having chosen an appropriate homotopy function and the fact that jacobian of excess demands is non-singular.

Simplices

Simplices are a collection of points or vertices such that any vertex cannot be expressed as a convex combination of the other vertices. A n simplex has $n + 1$ vertices and can be denoted by $s = \{v^0, v^1, v^2, ..., v^n\}$. Any point in the n dimension simplex can be expressed as a convex combination of the vertices. Thus a point w can be expressed as $w = \sum_{i=1}^{n} \lambda_i v^i$ with $\sum_{i=1}^{n} \lambda_i = 1$ and $\lambda_i \geq 0$. Few simplices are illustrated in Figure D.1.

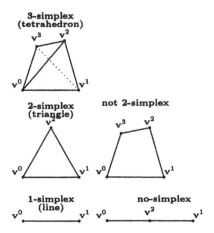

Figure D.1: **Simplices**

Another common simplex is the **unit** simplex, consisting of vertices x_i such that $\{\sum_{i=1}^{n} x_i \leq 1, x_i \geq 0\}$. Triangulation of a unit simplex is shown in Figure D.2.

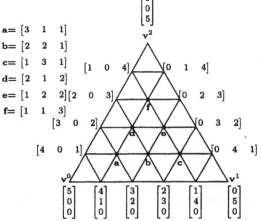

Figure D.2: **Triangulation on Unit Simplex**

The objective of the exercise is to approximate the solution path (non-linear) by approximating it by a line, such that the line does not deviate too far from the path. The simplices are responsible for dividing the entire region into smaller subsets where the union of the simplices spans the entire region and the path is approximated over each simplex.

Function Approximation

Given a homotopy function $H\colon R^{n+1} \to R^n$, $s = \{v^i\}_0^{n+1}$ be an $(n+1)$ simplex in R^{n+1}. In order to specify a function $G\colon s \to R^n$ that approximates H on the simplex s one needs to choose a point w interior to the simplex such that w is a convex combination of the vertices v^i, $w = \sum_{i=0}^{n+1} \lambda_i v^i$, with $\sum_{i=0}^{n+1} \lambda_i = 1$ and $\lambda_i \geq 0$. Defining $G(w) = \sum_{i=0}^{n+1} \lambda_i H(v^i)$, we can obtain G. Since the function H is user defined, $H(v^i)$ is available at $i = 0, 1, ..., n+1$.

Obtaining a Path

$G(w) = 0$ approximates $H(y) = 0$ and is easier to solve as it is a linear combination of the weights λ_i. Given $H(v^i)$ and with $\sum_{i=0}^{n+1} \lambda_i = 1$ and $\lambda_i \geq 0$ obtain λ_i. From these λ_i obtain $w = \sum_{i=0}^{n+1} \lambda_i v^i$. One cannot get a unique point, but a line as there are $(n+2)$ $\lambda_i s$, n equations for H and 1 equation normalising sum of all λs to 1. Thus the solution to $G(w) = 0$ is a line, which approximates the path over the simplex.

Simplicial Algorithms

A j simplex has $j+1$ vertices. In a j simplex a union of some vertices $k < j+1$ is termed as a **face**. A **face** with j vertices in a j simplex is termed as a **facet**. Simplicial algorithms move from one facet of a simplex to another another facet of an adjacent simplex till the solution is obtained. Consider a facet $B^j = \{v^0, v^1, .., v^n\}$ of simplex $s^j = B^j \cup \{v^{n+1}\}$. The algorithm will begin (see Figure D.3) with a point w^0 on say facet $B^0 = \{v^0, v^1\}$ of simplex $s^0 = \{v^0, v^1, v^2\}$ and a path will be generated to facet $B^1 = \{v^1, v^2\}$ on simplex s^0. Another simplex $s^1 = \{v^1, v^2, v^3\}$ will be constructed which contains facet B^1 with another new vertex v^3. This is illustrated in Figure D.3.

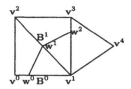

Figure D.3: **Path Generation Across Simplices**

The problem is to find out which vertex leaves the simplex and which comes in to form a new simplex. If the new vertex is chosen arbitrarily the algorithms are termed as flex simplicial algorithms. If the new vertex is chosen in a fixed manner with a pre-specified formula, the algorithm is termed as fixed or triangulation algorithms.

Data Set used in Simulation

Table D.1 shows the illustrative data set with 4 industries, each producing a homogenous commodity. The economy has 3 consumers, who pay income taxes and receive transfers. There is no government or the role is just restricted to collecting taxes and refunding the whole as transfers. The gross income, taxes and transfers are shown in Table D.2. There are indirect taxes on use of commodity i in industry j, in addition to taxes on use of labour (L) and capital (K) by industry. The consumers also pay sales taxes on the use of any commodity. The demand for commodity i by consumer k is shown in Table D.3.

Table D.1: Benchmark Data

A_{ij}	1	2	3	4	IUse	FD	O/P
1	50	10	10	40	110	90	200
2	10	60	40	20	130	210	340
3	10	50	80	20	160	150	310
4	30	40	40	80	190	190	380
NIT	6	20	24	14	64		
L	60	80	60	100	300		
K	20	60	40	80	200		
t_L	6	8	6	10	30		
t_K	8	12	10	16	46		
VA	100	180	140	220	640		
O/P	200	340	310	380			
t_{excise}	0.00	0.10	0.20	0.10			
t_{sales}	0.05	0.10	0.10	0.05			

Source: Author

Table D.2: Factor Income

Agent	a L	b K	c=a+b Gross	d Tax	e=c-d Net Transfer	f	g=e+f Total
C_1	50	120	170	17	153	63	216
C_2	100	60	160	16	144	83	227
C_3	150	20	170	17	153	94	247
Total	300	200	500	50	450	240	690

Source: Author

Table D.3: **Demand System**

Agent	1	2	3	4	T$_s$	Total
C$_1$	40	70	50	40	16	216
C$_2$	30	70	60	50	17	227
C$_3$	20	70	40	100	17	247
	90	210	150	190	640	
T$_s$	4.5	21	15	9.5	50	
Total	94.5	231	165	199.5		690

Source: Author

Merrill's Algorithm

Labelling Rule

1. If the vertex is on the **original** layer (initial co-ordinate 0), then Evaluate **excess demand**(=demand-supply) for the given vertex.[2]

$$\begin{bmatrix} variable & & ed \\ & 0 & \\ 1 & 8 & -0.1887840 \\ 2 & 8 & -0.2824583 \\ 3 & 14 & +0.1256635 \end{bmatrix}$$

2. label=order of first variable with +ve excess demand. Variable 3 is the first variable with positive **excess demand** (+0.1256635). Therefore label = **3**.

3. If the vertex is on the **artificial** layer (initial co-ordinate 1, then compare the values of the variables of this vertex with the vertex on original layer. The vertex will carry a label equal to that variable which has its value **less than** the corresponding vertex on the original layer. To cite an example, the initial vertex is $[0, 8, 8, 14]^T$. The label for vertex 1 is **3**, since variable 3 is the first variable with positive excess demand (+0.1256635). The remaining vertices are $2 = [1, 7, 8, 14]^T$, $3 = [1, 8, 7, 14]^T$, $5 = [0, 8, 7, 15]^T$ and $6 = [1, 7, 7, 15]^T$. The labels for these vertices are vertex 2 ⇒ label 1 (variable 1 = 7 < variable 1 on base layer = 8), vertex 3 ⇒ label 2 (variable 2 = 7 < variable 1 on base layer = 8) and vertex 6 ⇒ label 1 (variable 1 = 7 < variable 1 on base layer = 8) and vertex 5 ⇒ label 3 (positive excess

---

[2]Part of this section follows Shoven and Whalley (1992).

demand for variable 3 = +0.0664154).

$$
\begin{bmatrix}
 & & & & & ed \\
1 & 2 & 3 & 4 & & vertex \\
3 & 1 & 2 & 3 & & label \\
0 & 1 & 1 & 1 & & layer \\
8 & 7 & 8 & 8 & -0.1887840 \\
8 & 8 & 7 & 8 & -0.2824523 \\
14 & 14 & 14 & 13 & +0.1256635
\end{bmatrix}
\begin{bmatrix}
 & & & & & ed \\
6 & 2 & 3 & 5 & & vertex \\
1 & 1 & 2 & 3 & & label \\
1 & 1 & 1 & 0 & & layer \\
7 & 7 & 8 & 8 & -0.2711940 \\
7 & 8 & 7 & 7 & -0.0252990 \\
15 & 14 & 14 & 15 & +0.0664154
\end{bmatrix}
$$

Replacement Rule

1. Simplex at any iteration consists of $(n + 1)$ vertices $[v^0, v^1, ..., v^n]$, with each vertex having $(n + 1)$ elements. After the vertex to be dropped has been decided a new vertex is to be introduced in the simplex. This is done by the replacement rule.

$$
\begin{bmatrix}
v_0^0 & v_0^1 & v_0^2 & v_0^3 & .. & v_0^n \\
v_1^0 & v_1^1 & v_1^2 & v_1^3 & .. & v_1^n \\
v_2^0 & v_2^1 & v_2^2 & v_2^3 & .. & v_2^n \\
v_3^0 & v_3^1 & v_3^2 & v_3^3 & .. & v_3^n \\
.. & .. & .. & .. & .. & .. \\
v_n^0 & v_n^1 & v_n^2 & v_n^3 & .. & v_n^n
\end{bmatrix}
$$

2. If the vertex to be replaced belongs to columns 2 to n-1, the old vertex is substituted by the **new** vertex using the following rule $v_{new}^j = v^{j-1} + v^{j+1} - v_{old}^j, \forall j \in \{2, ..n - 1\}$

$$
\begin{bmatrix}
\textbf{new} \\
v_0^j \\
v_1^j \\
v_2^j \\
v_3^j \\
.. \\
v_n^j
\end{bmatrix}
=
\begin{bmatrix}
v_0^{j+1} \\
v_1^{j+1} \\
v_2^{j+1} \\
v_3^{j+1} \\
.. \\
v_n^{j+1}
\end{bmatrix}
+
\begin{bmatrix}
v_0^{j-1} \\
v_1^{j-1} \\
v_2^{j-1} \\
v_3^{j-1} \\
.. \\
v_n^{j-1}
\end{bmatrix}
-
\begin{bmatrix}
\textbf{old} \\
v_0^j \\
v_1^j \\
v_2^j \\
v_3^j \\
.. \\
v_n^j
\end{bmatrix}
$$

3. If the vertex to be replaced belongs to **first** column, the old vertex is substituted by the **new** vertex using the following rule $v_{new}^0 = v^1 + v^n - v_{old}^0$

$$
\begin{bmatrix}
\textbf{new} \\
v_0^0 \\
v_1^0 \\
v_2^0 \\
v_3^0 \\
.. \\
v_n^0
\end{bmatrix}
=
\begin{bmatrix}
v_0^1 \\
v_1^1 \\
v_2^1 \\
v_3^1 \\
.. \\
v_n^1
\end{bmatrix}
+
\begin{bmatrix}
v_0^n \\
v_1^n \\
v_2^n \\
v_3^n \\
.. \\
v_n^n
\end{bmatrix}
-
\begin{bmatrix}
\textbf{old} \\
v_0^0 \\
v_1^0 \\
v_2^0 \\
v_3^0 \\
.. \\
v_n^0
\end{bmatrix}
$$

4. If the vertex to be replaced belongs to **last** column, the old vertex is substituted by the **new** vertex using the following rule $v_{new}^n = v^0 + v^{n-1} - v_{old}^n$

$$\begin{bmatrix} \text{new} \\ v_0^n \\ v_1^n \\ v_2^n \\ v_3^n \\ .. \\ v_n^n \end{bmatrix} = \begin{bmatrix} v_0^0 \\ v_1^0 \\ v_2^0 \\ v_3^0 \\ .. \\ v_n^0 \end{bmatrix} + \begin{bmatrix} v_0^{n-1} \\ v_1^{n-1} \\ v_2^{n-1} \\ v_3^{n-1} \\ .. \\ v_n^{n-1} \end{bmatrix} - \begin{bmatrix} \text{old} \\ v_0^n \\ v_1^n \\ v_2^n \\ v_3^n \\ .. \\ v_n^n \end{bmatrix}$$

Algorithm

1. Select a grid size D, a factor β and tolerance limit ϵ. Begin with an initial vertex $v^0 = [0, v_1^0, v_2^0, v_i^0, .., v_n^0]$, such that $\sum_{i=0}^n v_i = D$. To give an example, select D=30, $\beta = 4$, $\epsilon = 0.000001$ and initial vertex $[v^0]^T = [0, 8, 8, 14]$, corresponding to 3 variables with initial values $\frac{8}{30}$, $\frac{8}{30}$ and $\frac{14}{30}$.

2. Create the initial simplex

$$\begin{bmatrix} 0 & 1 & 1 & 1 \\ v_1^0 & v_1^0 - 1 & v_1^0 & v_1^0 \\ v_2^0 & v_2^0 & v_2^0 - 1 & v_2^0 \\ v_3^0 & v_3^0 & v_3^0 & v_3^0 - 1 \end{bmatrix} = \begin{bmatrix} 0 & 1 & 1 & 1 \\ 8 & 7 & 8 & 8 \\ 8 & 8 & 7 & 8 \\ 14 & 14 & 14 & 13 \end{bmatrix}$$

3. Label each vertex of the simplex as per the labelling rule described earlier. One obtains the following

$$\begin{bmatrix} & & & & & \text{ed} \\ \text{counter} & 1 & 2 & 3 & 4 & \\ \text{label} & 3 & 1 & 2 & 3 & \\ \text{layer} & 0 & 1 & 1 & 1 & \\ \text{variable1(r)} & 8 & 7 & 8 & 8 & -0.1887840 \\ \text{variable2(w)} & 8 & 8 & 7 & 8 & -0.2824523 \\ \text{variable3(T)} & 14 & 14 & 14 & 13 & +0.1256635 \end{bmatrix}$$

4. Replace the vertex on the artificial layer using the replacement rule described previously. In the above case vertex 4 with label 3 has to be replaced as it is the same as vertex 1. Since vertex 4 is the last column j=n, the new vertex using the replacement rule is

$$\begin{bmatrix} \text{new} \\ v_0^n = 0 \\ v_1^n = 8 \\ v_2^n = 7 \\ v_3^n = 15 \end{bmatrix} = \begin{bmatrix} v_0^0 = 0 \\ v_1^0 = 8 \\ v_2^0 = 8 \\ v_3^0 = 14 \end{bmatrix} + \begin{bmatrix} v_0^{n-1} = 1 \\ v_1^{n-1} = 8 \\ v_2^{n-1} = 7 \\ v_3^{n-1} = 14 \end{bmatrix} - \begin{bmatrix} \text{old} \\ v_0^n = 1 \\ v_1^n = 8 \\ v_2^n = 8 \\ v_3^n = 13 \end{bmatrix}$$

5. Evaluate the label for this vertex. If all vertices except 1 are on the **original** layer and are **completely labelled** i.e. labels are distinct and vary from 1 to n, go to step 7. Else go to step 6.

6. Replace the **old** vertex that has the same label as the newly added vertex and calculate the label of the newly added vertex. Go to step 5.

7. If all vertices are on the original layer and completely labelled, check if excess demands < tolerance (ϵ). If **yes** stop, else increase the grid size D by a factor β. Thus $D := D\beta$. Go to step 2.

Demonstration of Merrill's Algorithm

[original $\Rightarrow$ 0 and artificial $\Rightarrow$ 1]

$$\begin{bmatrix} 0 & 1 & 1 & 1 \\ 8 & 7 & 8 & 8 \\ 8 & 8 & 7 & 8 \\ 14 & 14 & 14 & 13 \end{bmatrix}$$

dtot= 30
r1= 0.2666667 w1= 0.2666667 t= 0.4666667 walras= 4.563756E-007

					ed						ed
counter	1	2	3	4		1	2	3	5	
label	3	1	2	3		3	1	2	3	
layer $\rightarrow$	0	1	1	1	$\rightarrow$	0	1	1	0	
variable1(r)	8	7	8	8	−0.1887840	8	7	8	8	−0.2711940
variable2(w)	8	8	7	8	−0.2824523	8	8	7	7	+0.0252990
variable3(T)	14	14	14	13	+0.1256635	14	14	14	15	+0.0664154

			ed					ed
6	2	3	5		6	7	3	5
1	1	2	3		1	2	2	3
1	1	1	0	$\rightarrow$	1	1	1	0
7	7	8	8		7	8	8	8
7	8	7	7		7	6	7	7
15	14	14	15		15	15	14	15

			ed					ed
6	7	8	5		6	9	8	5
1	2	2	3		1	3	2	3
1	1	0	0	$\rightarrow$	1	0	0	0
7	8	8	8	0.3552805	7	7	8	8	−0.0331921
7	6	6	7	0.4379563	7	7	6	7	−0.0496614
15	15	16	15	0.0071505	15	16	16	15	+0.0193327

simplex on original level not completely labelled

			ed					ed
6	9	8	10		11	9	8	10
1	3	2	1		2	3	2	1
1	0	0	1	$\rightarrow$	0	0	0	1
7	7	8	7		7	7	8	7	−0.1295769
7	7	6	6		6	7	6	6	+0.3509564
15	16	16	16		17	16	16	16	−0.0399565

simplex on original level not completely labelled

$$
\begin{bmatrix}
11 & 9 & 12 & \mathbf{10} \\
2 & 3 & 1 & \mathbf{1} \\
0 & 0 & 1 & \mathbf{1} \\
7 & 7 & 6 & \mathbf{7} \\
6 & 7 & 7 & \mathbf{6} \\
17 & 16 & 16 & \mathbf{16}
\end{bmatrix}^{\mathbf{ed}}
\rightarrow
\begin{bmatrix}
11 & 9 & 12 & 13 & \\
2 & 3 & 1 & 1 & \\
0 & 0 & 1 & 0 & \\
7 & 7 & 6 & 6 & +0.2871025 \\
6 & 7 & 7 & 7 & -0.1274576 \\
17 & 16 & 16 & 17 & -0.2768010
\end{bmatrix}^{\mathbf{ed}}
$$

simplex on original level completely labelled
    writing new b r1= 0.2000000 w1= 0.2333333 t= 0.5666667

$$
\begin{bmatrix}
0 \\
18 \\
21 \\
51
\end{bmatrix}
\rightarrow
\begin{bmatrix}
1 & \mathbf{2} & 3 & 4 & \\
1 & \mathbf{1} & 2 & 3 & \\
0 & \mathbf{1} & 1 & 1 & \\
18 & \mathbf{17} & 18 & 18 & +0.2871025 \\
21 & \mathbf{21} & 20 & 21 & -0.1274576 \\
51 & \mathbf{51} & 51 & 50 & -0.2768010
\end{bmatrix}^{\mathbf{ed}}
\rightarrow
\begin{bmatrix}
1 & 5 & 3 & 4 & \\
1 & 1 & 2 & 3 & \\
0 & 0 & 1 & 1 & \\
18 & 19 & 18 & 18 & +0.1334124 \\
21 & 20 & 20 & 21 & +0.0162930 \\
51 & 51 & 51 & 50 & -0.0317851
\end{bmatrix}^{\mathbf{ed}}
$$

$$
\begin{bmatrix}
6 & 5 & \mathbf{3} & 4 \\
2 & 1 & \mathbf{2} & 3 \\
1 & 0 & \mathbf{1} & 1 \\
19 & 19 & \mathbf{18} & 18 \\
20 & 20 & \mathbf{20} & 21 \\
50 & 51 & \mathbf{51} & 50
\end{bmatrix}^{\mathbf{ed}}
\rightarrow
\begin{bmatrix}
6 & \mathbf{5} & 7 & 4 & \\
2 & \mathbf{1} & 1 & 3 & \\
1 & \mathbf{0} & 0 & 1 & \\
19 & \mathbf{19} & 19 & 18 & +0.1687360 \\
20 & \mathbf{20} & 21 & 21 & -0.1011572 \\
50 & \mathbf{51} & 50 & 50 & -0.1201832
\end{bmatrix}^{\mathbf{ed}}
$$

$$
\begin{bmatrix}
6 & 8 & 7 & \mathbf{4} \\
2 & 3 & 1 & \mathbf{3} \\
1 & 1 & 0 & \mathbf{1} \\
19 & 19 & 19 & \mathbf{18} \\
20 & 21 & 21 & \mathbf{21} \\
50 & 49 & 50 & \mathbf{50}
\end{bmatrix}^{\mathbf{ed}}
\rightarrow
\begin{bmatrix}
\mathbf{6} & 8 & 7 & 9 & \\
\mathbf{2} & 3 & 1 & 2 & \\
\mathbf{1} & 1 & 0 & 0 & \\
\mathbf{19} & 19 & 19 & 20 & +0.02904463 \\
\mathbf{20} & 21 & 21 & 20 & +0.04345512 \\
\mathbf{50} & 49 & 50 & 50 & -0.01611078
\end{bmatrix}^{\mathbf{ed}}
$$

$$
\begin{bmatrix}
10 & 8 & \mathbf{7} & 9 & \\
1 & 3 & \mathbf{1} & 2 & \\
0 & 1 & \mathbf{0} & 0 & \\
20 & 19 & \mathbf{19} & 20 & +0.6256247 \\
21 & 21 & \mathbf{21} & 20 & -0.7523727 \\
49 & 49 & \mathbf{50} & 50 & +0.3652990
\end{bmatrix}^{\mathbf{ed}}
$$

simplex on original level not completely labelled

$$
\begin{bmatrix}
10 & 8 & 11 & \mathbf{9} \\
1 & 3 & 2 & \mathbf{2} \\
0 & 1 & 1 & \mathbf{0} \\
20 & 19 & 20 & \mathbf{20} \\
21 & 21 & 20 & \mathbf{20} \\
49 & 49 & 49 & \mathbf{50}
\end{bmatrix}^{\mathbf{ed}}
\rightarrow
\begin{bmatrix}
10 & \mathbf{8} & 11 & 12 \\
1 & \mathbf{3} & 2 & 3 \\
0 & \mathbf{1} & 1 & 1 \\
20 & \mathbf{19} & 20 & 20 \\
21 & \mathbf{21} & 20 & 21 \\
49 & \mathbf{49} & 49 & 48
\end{bmatrix}^{\mathbf{ed}}
$$

$$
\begin{bmatrix}
& & & & \text{ed} \\
10 & 13 & 11 & 12 & \\
1 & 2 & 2 & 3 & \\
0 & 0 & 1 & 1 & \\
20 & 21 & 20 & 20 & -0.06507778 \\
21 & 20 & 20 & 21 & +0.07025909 \\
49 & 49 & 49 & 48 & -0.00042796
\end{bmatrix}
\rightarrow
\begin{bmatrix}
& & & & \text{ed} \\
10 & 13 & 14 & 12 & \\
1 & 2 & 3 & 3 & \\
0 & 0 & 0 & 1 & \\
20 & 21 & 21 & 20 & -0.03319216 \\
21 & 20 & 21 & 21 & -0.04966140 \\
49 & 49 & 48 & 48 & +0.01933277
\end{bmatrix}
$$

simplex on original level completely labelled

Table D.4: **Iterations in Merrill's Algorithm – Initial Vector**

iter	w	r	T	D
3	63	63	144	270
4	183	186	441	810
5	555	552	1323	2430
6	1656	1659	3975	7290
7	4971	4968	11931	21870
8	14910	14913	35787	65610
9	44736	44733	107361	196830
10	134202	134205	322083	590490
11	402609	402606	966255	1771470
12	1207821	1207824	2898765	5314410
13	3623466	3623460	8696304	15943230
14	10870390	10870390	26088910	47829690

Source: Author

The algorithm converges in 14 iterations. Table D.4 shows the initial vector at each iteration. The final values for factor prices are as follows. $r = 0.2272728$, $w = 0.2272729$ and $T = 0.5454543$. The value of excess demand as per Walras' law $= 3.630464 \times 10^{-7}$. After normalising the wage rate $w = 1$, the other factor prices are $r = 0.9999998$ and $T = 2.3999970$. The data set is scaled so that all variables are close to unity.

Counterfactual simulations are performed by eliminating excise taxes and applying a uniform sales tax (τ) on all commodities of 25%. The results of the base case and the counterfactual are tabulated in Tables D.5, D.6 and D.7

Table D.5: **Final Consumption, Output and Prices**

	a1	a2	a3	FD	O/P	P_p	P_m
c1	0.4000	0.3000	0.2000	0.9000	1.9999	1.0000	1.0500
c1	0.7000	0.7000	0.7000	2.0999	3.3999	1.0000	1.1100
c1	0.5000	0.6000	0.4000	1.4999	3.0999	1.0000	1.1100
c1	0.4000	0.5000	1.0000	1.9000	3.8000	1.0000	1.0500
			$\tau = 0.25$				
c1	0.3751	0.2837	0.1894	0.8482	1.9252	0.9297	1.1620
c2	0.7170	0.7230	0.7240	2.1639	3.4878	0.8917	1.1147
c3	0.5299	0.6412	0.4281	1.5992	3.3284	0.8618	1.0773
c4	0.3757	0.4735	0.9484	1.7976	3.6918	0.9283	1.1604

Source: computed

Table D.6: **Income of Agents**

Agent	l	k	wages	capital	Taxes	Transfer	Disp Inc
			$w=1.000$; $r=1.000$				
a1	0.5	1.2	0.5	1.2	0.1700	0.6300	2.1600
a2	1.0	0.6	1.0	0.6	0.1600	0.8300	2.2700
a3	1.5	0.2	1.5	0.2	0.1700	0.9400	2.4700
			$\tau=0.25$; $w=1.000$; $r=1.002$				
a1	0.5	1.2	0.5	1.2	0.1702	0.7093	2.2419
a2	1.0	0.6	1.0	0.6	0.1601	0.9345	2.3758
a3	1.5	0.2	1.5	0.2	0.1700	1.0583	2.5888

Source: computed

Table D.7: **Taxes and Transfers**

Taxes		Transfers	
Head		Head	
Labour Tax	0.30	Agent 1	0.6300
Capital Tax	0.46	Agent 2	0.8300
Factor Tax	0.76	Agent 3	0.9400
Consumption Tax	0.50		
Income Tax	0.50		
Excise Tax	0.64		
Total Tax	2.40	**Total Transfers**	2.40
		$\tau=0.25$	
Labour Tax	0.30	Agent 1	0.7093
Capital Tax	0.46	Agent 2	0.9345
Factor Tax	0.76	Agent 3	1.0583
Consumption Tax	1.44		
Income Tax	0.50		
Excise Tax	0.00		
Total Tax	2.70	**Total Transfers**	2.70

Source: computed

Computing Equilibria

1. Begin with a set of factor prices [w, r and T]. Compute the labour and capital requirements per unit output for the specified functional form (Cobb–Douglas, CES).

   - Cobb–Douglas: The reduced form expression for *Labour* is

$$l = (\frac{VA}{\phi})\left(\frac{\delta p_k}{(1-\delta)p_l}\right)^{(1-\delta)} \tag{D.10}$$

   The reduced form equation for *Capital* is

$$k = (\frac{VA}{\phi})\left(\frac{(1-\delta)p_l}{\delta p_k}\right)^{\delta} \tag{D.11}$$

- CES: The reduced form expression for *Labour* is

$$l = (\frac{VA}{\phi})\left(\delta + (1-\delta)[\frac{\delta p_k}{(1-\delta)p_l}]^{(1-\sigma)}\right)^{\{\frac{\sigma}{(1-\sigma)}\}} \tag{D.12}$$

The reduced form expression for *Capital* is

$$k = (\frac{VA}{\phi})\left(\delta[\frac{(1-\delta)p_l}{\delta p_k}]^{(1-\sigma)} + (1-\delta)\right)^{\{\frac{\sigma}{(1-\sigma)}\}} \tag{D.13}$$

2. Calculate the value added in each industry.

$$va = l \times p_l + k \times p_k \quad p_l = w \times (1+t_l) \quad p_k = r \times (1+t_k) \tag{D.14}$$

3. Compute product prices from factor prices

$$\mathbf{p} = [I - A^{\mathrm{T}} \times (1+t_I)]^{-1}VA \tag{D.15}$$

where A^{T} is the transpose of the A_{ij} input–output coefficient matrix, t_I is the diagonal matrix of taxes on intermediate inputs and VA is the vector of value added in each industry.

4. Compute income of each agent.

$$Y_i = (1-t_{inc})(w \times L_i + r \times K_i) + tr \times T \tag{D.16}$$

where t_{inc} is the income tax on each individual, L_i and K_i are labour and capital endowments, T is the tax revenue and tr is the fraction of the revenues transferred to each consumer.

5. From the producer prices (p_i) determine market prices (p_i^m) using sales tax rates t_i^s. Income (Y_i) and market prices determine the demand for each commodity i by consumer j.

$$p_i^m = p_i \times (1+t_i^s)$$

- Cobb–Douglas:

$$X_i = \frac{\alpha_i Y_i}{p_i^m}$$

- CES:

$$X_i = \left[\frac{\alpha_i Y_i}{p_i^{m\sigma}(\sum_{i=1}^n \alpha_i p_i^{m(1-\sigma)})}\right]$$

- LES:

$$X_j = C_j + \frac{\alpha_j(Y_i - \sum_{i=1}^n p_i^m C_i)}{p_j^m} \tag{D.17}$$

6. Compute the final demand (**FD**) for each commodity

$$\mathbf{FD} = \sum_{j=1}^{m} X_j \tag{D.18}$$

7. Compute the output of each industry.

$$\mathbf{O} = [I - A]^{-1}\mathbf{FD} \tag{D.19}$$

8. Compute the factor demand in each industry. Evaluate the aggregate factor demand

$$l_i^d = l \times \mathbf{O} \quad k_i^d = k \times \mathbf{O}$$

$$L_d = \sum_{i=1}^{n} l_i^d \quad K_d = \sum_{i=1}^{n} k_i^d \tag{D.20}$$

9. Calculate excess demands for factors

$$\rho_l = L_d - L_s$$

$$\rho_k = K_d - K_s$$

$$revenue = \sum_{i=1}^{n}(w \times t_l \times l_i^d + r \times t_k \times k_i^d)$$

$$+ \sum_{j=1}^{n}\sum_{i=1}^{n} p_i \times t_i \times A_{ij} \times O_j$$

$$+ \sum_{i=1}^{n} pm_i \times t_i^s \times FD_i$$

$$+ \sum_{i=1}^{m} t_{inc} \times Y_i$$

$$\rho_t = revenue - T \tag{D.21}$$

Walras' law is given by $w \times \rho_l + r \times \rho_k + \rho_t$.

Appendix E

India – A Brief Background

Introduction

This chapter is written for the reader not familiar with India.[1] It covers the basic political system prevalent today and some economic facts.

Politics

India was constituted into a *Sovereign, Socialist, Secular*,[2] *Democratic, Republic* on November 26, 1949. Undivided India was a British colony and gained independence from the British on the midnight of August 15, 1947.

India comprises of 29 states and 6 union territories and has a federal form of government. The details of the states are mentioned in Table E.1. It is the world's largest functioning democracy with a central and state governments. The central government is also called as the Parliament and the state government is termed as the legislative assembly. Voting is based on the principle of adult suffrage with every individual above the age of 18 eligible to vote.

Central Government

Parliament consists of the President and the two Houses – the Council of States (*Rajya Sabha*) and the House of the People (*Lok Sabha*).

Lok Sabha (House of the People) is composed of representative of the people chosen by direct election on the basis of adult suffrage. The maximum strength of the House envisaged by the Constitution is 552 - upto 530 members to represent the States, up to 20 members to represent the Union Territories and not more than two members of the Anglo-Indian Community to be nominated by the President, if, in his opinion, that community is not adequately represented in the House. The total elective membership is distributed among the States in such a way that the ratio between the number of seats allotted to each State and the population of the State is, so far as practicable, the same for all States. The qualifying age for membership of Lok Sabha is 25 years.

The Lok Sabha at present consists of 545 members including the Speaker and two nominated members. Lok Sabha, unless sooner dissolved, continues for five years from the date appointed for its first meeting and the expiration of the period of five years operates as dissolution of the House. However, while a Proclamation of Emergency is in operation, this period may be extended by Parliament by law for a period not exceeding one year at a time and not extending, in any case,

---

[1]Figure E.1 shows India's political map.
[2]Through the Constitution Act (42nd Amendment) 1976.

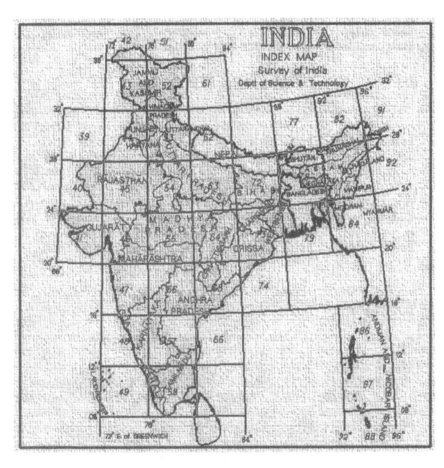

Figure E.1: **India's Political Map**

Table E.1: **Indian States and Union Territories**

No. State	Area sq. km.	No. of Districts	Lok Sabha seats	Rajya Sabha seats	Legislative Assembly seats	Population Census 2001 nos.
			States			
1 Andhra Pradesh	275069	23	42	18	294	75727541
2 Arunachal Pradesh	83743	13	2	1	60	1091117
3 Assam	78438	23	14	7	126	26638407
4 Bihar	94163	37	54	16	243	82878796
5 Chhatisgarh	135191	16		5	90	20795956
6 Delhi	1483	9	7	3	70	13782976
7 Goa	3702	2	2	1	40	1343998
8 Gujarat	196024	25	26	11	182	50596992
9 Haryana	44212	19	10	5	90	21082989
10 Himachal Pradesh	55673	12	4	3	68	6077248
11 Jammu and Kashmir	222236	14	6	4	87	10069917
12 Jharkhand	79714	18		6	81	26909428
13 Karnataka	191791	27	28	12	224	52733958
14 Kerala	38863	14	20	9	140	31838619
15 Madhya Pradesh	308245	45	40	11	230	60385118
16 Maharashtra	307577	35	48	19	288	96752247
17 Manipur	22327	9	2	1	60	2388634
18 Meghalaya	22429	7	2	1	60	2306069
19 Mizoram	21087	8	1	1	40	891058
20 Nagaland	16579	8	1	1	60	1988636
21 Orissa	155707	30	21	10	147	36706920
22 Punjab	50362	17	13	7	117	24289296
23 Rajasthan	342239	32	25	10	200	56473122
24 Sikkim	7096	4	1	1	32	540493
25 Tamil Nadu	130058	30	39	18	234	62110839
26 Tripura	10486	4	2	1	60	3191168
27 Uttar Pradesh	240928	70	85	31	403	166052859
28 Uttaranchal	53483	13		3	70	8479562
29 West Bengal	88752	18	42	16	294	80221171
TOTAL STATES	156808	582	537	232	4090	1024345134
			Union Territories			
1 Andaman and Nicobar Islands	8248	2	1			356265
2 Chandigarh	114	1	1			900914
3 Dadra and Nagar Haveli	491	1	1			220451
4 Daman and Diu	112	2	1			158059
5 Lakshadweep	32	1	1			60595
6 Pondicherry	480	4	1	1	30	973829
TOTAL UTs	9477	11	6	1	30	2670113
TOTAL INDIA	3175762	593	543	233	4120	1027015247

Source: Government of India

beyond a period of six months after the proclamation has ceased to operate. The first general elections under the new Constitution (adopted January 26, 1950) were held during the year 1951-52 and the first elected Parliament came into being in April, 1952. In all India has witnessed twelve general elections with the Lok Sabha being elected in April 1952, April 1957, April 1962, March 1967, March 1971, March 1977, January 1980, December 1984, December 1989, June 1991, May 1996 and March 1998.

Rajya Sabha (Council of States) is elected by the elected representatives of the legislative councils of states.

The maximum strength of the Rajya Sabha is 250 out of which 12 members are nominated by the President and 238 are representatives of the States and of the Union territories. The members nominated by the President are persons having special knowledge or practical experience in respect of such matters as literature, science, art and social service. The allocation of seats to be filled by representatives of States and the Union territories is laid down in the Fourth Schedule to the Constitution. The representatives of States are elected by the elected members of the Legislative Assemblies of the respective States in accordance with the system of proportional representation by means of the single transferable vote.

Basic Economic Indicators

This section outlines the basic economic indicators to highlight the structure of the economy.

Table E.2 shows the population that is employed in rural and urban India by sex. Total workers comprise of main and marginal workers.[3]

Table E.2: Labour – 2001 Census

	Total population	Total workers	Main workers	Marginal workers	Non-workers
			India		
Persons	1025251059	402512190	313173394	89338796	622738869
Males	530422415	275463736	240520672	34943064	254958679
Females	494828644	127048454	72652722	54395732	367780190
			India-Rural		
Persons	740255371	310655339	229672348	80982991	429600032
Males	380438194	199199602	169333233	29866369	181238592
Females	359817177	111455737	60339115	51116622	248361440
			India-Urban		
Persons	284995688	91856851	83501046	8355805	193138837
Males	149984221	76264134	71187439	5076695	73720087
Females	135011467	15592717	12313607	3279110	119418750

Source: Government of India

---

[3]Data on total population mentioned in Table E.2 differs from that mentioned in Table E.1 on account of the earthquake where a population enumeration census was not conducted in the state of Gujarat (entire Kutchh district and some parts of Rajkot and Jamnagar districts).

Table E.3 shows the occupation of main and marginal workers in rural and urban India by sex.

Table E.3: Labour Specialisation – 2001 Census

	Total workers	Cultivators	Agricultural Labourers	Household Industry workers	Other workers
			India		
Persons	402512190	127628287	107447725	16395870	151040308
Males	275463736	86328447	57354281	8312191	123468817
Females	127048454	41299840	50093444	8083679	27571491
			India-Rural		
Persons	310655339	124682055	103122189	11709533	71141562
Males	199199602	84046644	54749291	5642112	54761555
Females	111455737	40635411	48372898	6067421	16380007
			India-Urban		
Persons	91856851	2946232	4325536	4686337	79898746
Males	76264134	2281803	2604990	2670079	68707262
Females	15592717	664429	1720546	2016258	11191484

Source: Government of India

Table E.4 shows the various deficits of the central government.

Table E.4: Deficit of the Central Government (*Rs. Crores*)

		2000–01 Actuals	2001–02 BE	2001–02 RE	2002–03 BE
1	Revenue Receipts	192624	231745	212572	245105
2	Tax Revenue (net to centre)	136916	163031	142348	172965
3	Non-Tax Revenue	55708	68714	70224	72140
4	Capital Receipts(5+6+7)	132987	143478	151864	165204
5	Recoveries of Loans	12046	15164	15143	17680
6	Other Receipts	2125	12000	5000	12000
7	Borrowings and other liabilities	118816	116314	131721	135524
8	Total Receipts (1+4)	325611	375223	364436	410309
9	Non-Plan Expenditure	242942	275123	265282	296809
10	On Revenue Account of which	226782	250341	242471	270169
11	Interest Payments	99314	112300	107257	117390
12	On Capital Account	16160	24782	22811	26640
13	Plan Expenditure	82669	95100	99154	113500
14	On Revenue Account	51076	60225	61834	70313
15	On Capital Account	31593	34875	37320	43187
16	Lump sum provision for Additional Plan expenditure linked to disinvestment receipts	5000			
17	Total Expenditure (9+13+16)	325611	375223	364436	410309
18	Revenue Expenditure(10+14)	277858	310566	304305	340482
19	Capital Expenditure(12+15+16)	47753	64657	60131	69827
20	Revenue Deficit (18-1)	85234	78821	91733	95377
21	Fiscal Deficit (17-1-5-6)	118816	116314	131721	135524
22	Primary Deficit (21-11)	19502	4014	24464	18134

Source: Government of India

Table E.5 shows the various deficits of the state governments.

Table E.5: **Deficit of States** (*Rs. Crores*)

States	1999–2000 (Accounts)			2000–2001 (RE)			2001–2002 (BE)		
	Receipts	Expen-diture	Deficit	Receipts	Expen-diture	Deficit	Receipts	Expen-diture	Deficit
Andhra Pradesh	16804.6	21781.0	4976.4	19717.4	26926.8	7209.5	22406.0	31303.1	8897.0
Arunachal Pradesh	1020.0	1079.3	59.3	1136.1	1360.8	224.7	1143.1	1295.5	152.4
Assam	4840.9	6446.7	1605.8	6870.9	8794.3	1923.5	6648.8	9183.5	2534.7
Bihar	12578.6	18686.3	6107.7	11384.7	16269.1	4884.3	11569.0	14966.3	3397.3
Chhattisgarh	-	-	-	2247.6	2578.5	330.9	4727.4	5681.9	954.5
Goa	1227.9	1568.9	341.0	1558.6	2054.3	495.7	1929.0	2369.8	440.8
Gujarat	13900.3	20692.3	6792.0	16371.4	24793.5	8422.0	20485.4	30504.7	10019.3
Haryana	5766.8	7899.3	2132.5	7035.9	9441.8	2405.9	8114.3	10484.3	2370.0
Himachal Pradesh	3715.3	3904.9	189.6	3350.8	4924.8	1574.0	3216.0	5309.7	2093.7
Jammu and Kashmir	5513.6	6852.1	1338.6	6350.2	6975.3	625.1	6336.2	7092.7	756.5
Jharkhand	-	-	-	-	-	-	5695.8	6933.0	1237.2
Karnataka	12906.5	17182.9	4276.5	14911.9	19060.0	4148.2	17328.1	22455.6	5127.5
Kerala	7941.8	12478.4	4536.6	9332.1	13695.7	4363.7	10626.2	13863.5	3237.3
Madhya Pradesh	13203.7	17115.1	3911.4	13792.0	17454.4	3662.5	12459.7	16205.7	3746.0
Maharashtra	25269.5	36975.6	11706.2	30271.0	40263.8	9992.9	34152.3	40768.0	6615.7
Manipur	1069.9	1725.7	655.8	1281.9	1513.3	231.4	1220.2	1492.3	272.2
Meghalaya	943.7	1152.7	209.1	1237.2	1517.3	280.1	1331.1	1691.3	360.2
Mizoram	953.7	1132.8	179.1	1081.8	1279.4	197.6	933.9	1113.1	179.3
Nagaland	1144.0	1393.1	249.0	1419.8	1778.6	358.8	1506.9	1804.5	297.7
Orissa	5884.6	9630.7	3746.1	7510.8	10516.3	3005.5	8533.8	11791.6	3257.8
Punjab	7467.9	10662.6	3194.7	10288.8	14749.2	4460.4	11299.3	15701.2	4401.9
Rajasthan	9789.6	15150.8	5361.2	12507.1	17304.3	4797.3	13261.1	18543.6	5282.5
Sikkim	1511.8	1604.4	92.6	1112.6	1165.7	53.1	978.3	1008.4	30.1
Tamil Nadu	16327.5	21709.9	5382.3	18396.0	24176.5	5780.6	20909.5	27260.6	6351.2
Tripura	1438.5	1728.8	290.3	1777.3	2204.6	427.3	1963.2	2671.1	707.9
Uttaranchal	-	-	-	-	-	-	2532.9	4235.8	1703.0
Uttar Pradesh	21495.1	32593.9	11098.7	27623.9	39903.1	12279.2	30454.4	39847.5	9393.0
West Bengal	10211.1	21877.5	11666.4	15580.5	26801.5	11220.9	16912.6	27857.2	10944.6
NCT Delhi	4274.3	5655.9	1381.6	5466.7	7388.9	1922.2	6457.5	7318.6	861.1
All States	207201.2	298681.6	91480.5	249615.0	344891.8	95277.3	285132.0	380754.1	95622.4

Source: Government of India
RE: Revised Estimates; BE: Budget Estimates

Table E.6 shows the quarterly GDP at constant 1993-94 prices by major sectors.

Table E.6: **Quarterly GDP @ 1993–94 Prices** (*Rs. Crores*)

	agri forestry fishing	mining quarrying	mfg	elect gas water supply	const	trade, hotels transport communication	finance insurance real estate	community social services	GDP@ factor cost
1996-97	276091	23370	177013	23383	46452	202936	109995	110843	970083
Q1	64156	5486	42923	5714	11075	47469	26682	24176	227679
Q2	46470	5334	42834	5674	11223	46035	26990	23833	208392
Q3	91763	5953	44040	5929	11490	53615	27395	24928	265113
Q4	73702	6597	47216	6066	12665	55817	28929	37906	268898
1997-98	269383	25667	179689	25224	51208	218627	122784	123817	1016399
Q1	63727	6010	43141	6109	12137	50956	29806	25155	237042
Q2	47091	5891	43543	6238	12062	49633	29683	26357	220498
Q3	88825	6597	45334	6248	13073	57952	30531	27874	276433
Q4	69740	7168	47670	6628	13936	60087	32764	44431	282425
1998-99	286094	26391	184578	26988	54389	235482	131892	136658	1082472
Q1	66038	6303	44501	6732	13202	54535	31372	29290	251972
Q2	48964	6156	44884	6581	12868	54606	31774	32848	238683
Q3	94101	6735	46057	6634	13609	61926	33230	30537	292829
Q4	76990	7197	49137	7040	14710	64415	35516	43983	298988
1999-00	289842	26908	192404	28637	58815	253506	145865	152523	1148500
Q1	69546	6271	45979	6984	14084	58788	34705	33331	269688
Q2	49876	6352	46683	7190	13833	58444	35112	34811	252301
Q3	94253	6809	48119	7062	14634	66757	36872	35643	310150
Q4	76167	7476	51622	7402	16264	69516	39176	48738	316361
2000-01	289194	27796	205220	30406	62801	266817	150051	161637	1193922
Q1	70779	6572	49706	7481	15837	63535	35977	34405	284292
Q2	51821	6582	49989	7510	15216	62142	36467	38227	267954
Q3	93454	7099	51542	7718	15681	69971	37639	37442	320545
Q4	73140	7544	53983	7697	16067	71169	39968	51562	321131
2001-02	305181	28315	210697	31724	65717	283784	163960	171297	1260676
Q1	72428	6569	50857	7731	16238	66867	39527	36550	296769
Q2	53562	6621	51154	7874	15833	66006	40467	40545	282063
Q3	100522	7318	53018	8008	16372	74587	40677	39763	340265
Q4	78669	7807	55668	8111	17273	76324	43289	54439	341580
2002-03									
Q1	74731	6900	52961	8182	16814	71368	42211	38700	311867

Source: Government of India
Q1: Apr-Jun, Q2: Jul-Sep, Q3: Oct-Dec, Q4: Jan-Mar
100,000=1 lakh; 1 million=10 lakh; 100 lakhs=1 crore; 100 crores=1 billion

Table E.7 shows the quarterly GDP at current prices by major sectors.

Table E.7: **Quarterly GDP @ Current Prices** (*Rs. Crores*)

	agri forestry fishing	mining quarrying	mfg	elect gas water supply	const	trade, hotels transport communication	finance insurance real estate	community social services	GDP@ factor cost
1996-97	362605	27702	220675	29962	62807	255285	137583	146927	1243546
Q1	80765	6174	53191	7322	14642	58415	32591	31019	284118
Q2	60994	6442	53263	7271	15219	58044	33834	31567	266633
Q3	122275	7156	54939	7597	15638	67926	34492	33343	343365
Q4	98571	7930	59282	7773	17309	70900	36666	50998	349429
1997-98	387008	33427	231981	35288	77824	292051	156801	175768	1390148
Q1	89698	8289	55346	8547	18195	67269	37538	34782	319665
Q2	67297	7326	56138	8727	18239	66066	37704	36861	298358
Q3	127644	8471	58614	8741	19951	77759	39159	39569	379908
Q4	102369	9341	61882	9273	21439	80957	42400	64556	392217
1998-99	442494	35675	252240	43622	92009	333330	181143	217564	1598077
Q1	97425	7456	60009	10932	21955	76105	42384	45006	361271
Q2	76241	8209	61250	10437	21783	77477	43684	52325	351406
Q3	152413	9728	63077	10521	23276	88634	46134	49856	443638
Q4	116416	10282	67904	11733	24995	91114	48942	70376	441762
1999-00	460547	40520	266890	43886	105440	365735	220561	252059	1755638
Q1	108363	10088	63215	10531	24802	83603	51591	53927	406120
Q2	79895	10213	64586	10842	24648	84041	52808	57189	384223
Q3	151148	9605	67056	10649	26461	97143	56230	59586	477879
Q4	121141	10614	72033	11865	29529	100947	59932	81356	487417
2000-01	471981	44648	299753	49526	116431	399623	236645	277236	1895843
Q1	116796	9869	71221	11654	28674	93287	55516	57922	444938
Q2	84630	10731	72536	11969	27851	92169	56843	65035	421763
Q3	152338	11574	75922	12704	29535	106477	60268	65009	513827
Q4	118217	12474	80074	13199	30371	107690	64019	89271	515315
2001-02	516510	47362	313365	57994	126262	437931	268496	305341	2073259
Q1	121634	10451	75520	13378	30999	102978	64661	64194	483815
Q2	90672	11055	76265	14056	30482	102353	66637	72350	463871
Q3	171751	12507	78894	15181	31620	115904	66783	71452	564091
Q4	132453	13349	82685	15379	33161	116696	70415	97345	561483
2002-03	516510	47362	313365	57994	126262	437931	268496	305341	2073259
Q1	128144	11524	79570	15346	32687	111499	69888	69947	518605

Source: Government of India
Q1: Apr-Jun, Q2: Jul-Sep, Q3: Oct-Dec, Q4: Jan-Mar
100,000=1 lakh; 1 million=10 lakh; 100 lakhs=1 crore; 100 crores=1 billion

Bibliography

Adelman, I. and S. Robinson (1978). *Income Distribution Policy in Developing Countries: A Case Study of Korea.* Oxford University Press.

AIITS (1995, May). *All India Income Tax Statistics, Assessment Year 1990-91.* Directorate of Income Tax, Research, Statistics, Publications and Public Relations, Government of India.

Aksoy, A. (1990, November). India: A Strategy for Trade Reform. Sector Report 8998-IN, Industry and Finance Division, Asia Country Department, The World Bank.

Atkinson, A. B. (1991). *The International Library of Critical Writings in Economics 15: Modern Public Finance (Volumes. I & II).* Edward Elgar.

Atkinson, A. B. and J. E. Stiglitz (1976, July-August). The Design of Tax Structure: Direct Versus Indirect Taxation. *Journal of Public Economics 6*(1,2), 55–75.

Atkinson, A. B. and J. E. Stiglitz (1987). *Lectures on Public Economics.* McGraw Hill, International Students Edition.

Auerbach, A. J. and L. J. Kotlikoff (1987). *Dynamic Fiscal Policy.* Cambridge University Press.

Bairam, E. (1991). Elasticity of Substitution, Technical Progress and Returns to Scale in Branches of Soviet Industry: A New CES Function Approach. *Journal of Applied Econometrics 6*, 91–96.

Ballard, C. L., D. Fullerton, J. B. Shoven, and J. Whalley (1985). *A General Equilibrium Model for Tax Policy Evaluation.* Chicago: The University of Chicago Press for NBER.

Bandara, J. S. (1991). Computable General Equilibrium Models for Development Policy Analysis in LDCs. *Journal of Economic Surveys 5*(1), 3–69.

Barro, R. J. (1974). Are Government Bonds Net Wealth? *Journal of Political Economy 82*(6), 1095–1117.

Barua, A. (1985). Production Functions: A Survey of the Estimates for Indian Manufacturing. Discussion Paper 66, University of Warwick.

Bettendorf, L. (1994). *A Dynamic Applied General Equilibrium Model for a Small Open Economy.* Ph.D. dissertation, Katholieke Universeteit Leuven.

Bhagwati, J. (1965). On the equivalence of tariffs and quotas. In *Trade, Growth and the Balance of Payments: Essays in Honour of Gottfried Haberler*, pp. 53–67. Rand McNally & Co. and North Holland.

Bhagwati, J. N. and T. N. Srinivasan (1980, December). Revenue Seeking: A Generalisation of the Theory of Tariffs. *Journal of Political Economy 88*(6), 1069–1087.

Bhattacharya, S. C. (1996). Applied general equilibrium models for energy studies: a survey. *Energy Economics 18*, 145–164.

Borges, A. M. and L. H. Goulder (1984). Decomposing the impacts of higher energy prices on long-term growth. In H. E. Scarf and J. B. Shoven (Eds.), *Applied General Equilibrium Analysis*, Chapter 8, pp. 319–362. Cambridge University Press.

Brander, J. A. and B. J. Spencer (1985, February). Export Subsidies and International Market Share Rivalry. *Journal of International Economics 18*(1/2), 83–100.

Bruno, M. (1972, Jan-Feb). Domestic Resource Costs and Effective Protection: Clarification and Synthesis. *Journal of Political Economy 80*(1), 16–33.

Burgess, R. and N. Stern (1993, July). A VAT in India: Problems and Options. EF No. 4, STICERD, London School of Economics.

Caddy, V. (1976). Empirical Estimation of Elasticity of Substitution: A Review. Working Paper No. OP-09, Industries Assistance Commission, Melbourne.

Census Commissioner (1992). *Census of India - 1991, Final Population Totals: Brief Analysis of Primary Census Abstract*. Registrar General and Census Commissioner, Government of India.

Corlett, W. and D. C. Hague (1953). Complementarity and the Excess Burden of Taxation. *Review of Economic Studies XXI*(1), 21–30.

CSO (1980-81 to 1988-89). *Annual Survey of Industries, Summary Results for Factory Sector*. Central Statistical Organisation, Ministry of Planning, Government of India.

CSO (1990). *Input Output Transactions Table 1983-84*. Central Statistical Organisation, Department of Statistics, Ministry of Planning, Government of India.

CSO (1993, April). *Annual Survey of Industries 1989-90, Summary Results for Factory Sector*. Central Statistical Organisation, Ministry of Planning, Government of India.

CSO (1994). *National Account Statistics 1980-81 to 1989-90, Factor Income (New Series)*. Central Statistical Organisation, Ministry of Planning and Programme Implementation, Government of India.

Deardorff, A. V. (1986). Comments. In T. N. Srinivasan and J. Whalley (Eds.), *General Equilibrium Trade Policy Modelling*, Chapter IV, pp. 311–317. The MIT Press.

Deardorff, A. V. and R. M. Stern (1986). *The Michigan Model of World Production and Trade*. The MIT Press.

Decaluwé, B. and A. Martens (1988). CGE Modeling and Developing Economies: A Concise Empirical Survey of 73 Applications to 26 Countries. *Journal of Policy Modelling 10*(4), 529–568.

DeJanvry, A. and K. Subbarao (1986). *Agriculture Price Policy and Income Distribution in India*. Oxford University Press: Delhi.

deMelo, J. and D. Tarr (1992). *A General Equilibrium Analysis of US Foreign Trade Policy*. The MIT Press.

Dervis, K., J. deMelo, and S. Robinson (1982). *General Equilibrium Models for Development Policy*. The World Bank.

Devarajan, S. and D. Rodrik (1989, May). Trade Liberalisation in Developing Countries: Do Imperfect Competition and Scale Economies Matter? *American Economic Review 79*(2), 283–287.

Diamond, P. A. (1965). National Debt in a Neoclassical Growth Model. *American Economic Review LV*, 1126–1150.

Diamond, P. A. and J. A. Mirlees (1971). Optimal Taxation and Public Production I: Production Efficiency and II: Tax Rules. *American Economic Review LXI*, 8–27 and 261–278.

Dixit, A. (1983). The Multi Country Transfer Problem. *Economics Letters 13*, 49–53.

Dixit, A. and V. Norman (1972, August). Gains from Trade Without Lump-Sum Compensation. *Journal of International Economics 21*(1/2), 111–122.

Dixon, P. B. (1991, April). The Mathematical Programming Approach to Applied General Equilibrium Modelling: Notes and Problems. Working Paper I-50, Centre of Policy Studies, Monash University.

Dixon, P. B., B. R. Parmenter, A. A. Powell, and P. J. Wilcoxen (1992). *Notes and Problems in Applied General Equilibrium Economics*. North Holland.

Eaton, J. and G. M. Grossman (1986, May). Optimal Trade and Industrial Policy Under Oligopoly. *Quarterly Journal of Economics CI*(2), 383–406.

Fehr, H., C. Rosenberg, and W. Wiegard (1995). *Welfare Effects of Value Added Tax Harmonisation in Europe: A Computable General Equilibrium Approach*. Springer Verlag.

Fehr, H. and W. Wiegard (1996). A cge examination of worldwide agricultural liberalisation policies: Model structure and preliminary results. In A. Fossati (Ed.), *Economic Modelling Under Applied General Equilibrium Approach*, Chapter 7, pp. 143–211. Aldershot: Avebury.

Feldstein, M. (1976, July-August). On the Theory of Tax Reform. *Journal of Public Economics 6*(1,2), 77–104.

Findlay, R. and S. Wellisz (1982). Endogenous tariffs, the political economy of trade restrictions, and welfare. In J. N. Bhagwati (Ed.), *Import Competition and Response*, Chapter 8, pp. 223–234. Chicago: University of Chicago Press.

Frenkel, J. A., A. Razin, and S. Symansky (1991, December). International VAT Harmonisation. *IMF Staff Papers 38*(4), 789–827.

Fullerton, D., Y. K. Henderson, and J. B. Shoven (1984). A comparison of methodologies in empirical general equilibrium models of taxation. In H. E. Scarf and J. B. Shoven (Eds.), *Applied General Equilibrium Analysis*, Chapter 9, pp. 367–410. Cambridge University Press.

Ginsburgh, V. and M. A. Keyzer (1997). *The Structure of Applied General Equilibrium Models*. The MIT Press.

Goosens, M., F. Mittelbach, and A. Samarin (1994). *The LATEX Companion*. Addison-Wesley Publishing Company.

Goulder, L. H. and L. H. Summers (1989). Tax Policy, Asset Prices and Growth A General Equilibrium Analysis. *Journal of Public Economics 38*, 265–296.

Guesnerie, R. and K. Roberts (1984, January). Effective Policy Tools and Quantity Controls. *Econometrica 52*(1), 59–86.

Gunning, J. W. and M. A. Keyzer (1993, May). Applied General Equilibrium Models for Policy Analysis. Research Memorandum RM - 93 - 05, Stichting Onderzoek Wereldvoedselvoorziening van de Vrije Universiteit.

Guzel, H. A. and S. N. Kulshreshtha (1995). Effects of Real Exchange Rate Changes on Canadian Agriculture: A General Equilibrium Evaluation. *Journal of Policy Modelling 17*(6), 639–657.

Harberger, A. C. (1962, June). The Incidence of the Corporation Income Tax. *Journal of Political Economy 70*(3), 215–240.

Harris, R. (1984). Applied General Equilibrium Analysis of Small Open Economies with Scale Economies and Imperfect Competition. *American Economic Review 74*, 1016–1032.

Harris, R. (1985, November). Why Voluntary Export Restraints are Voluntary. *Canadian Journal of Economics XVIII*(4), 799–809.

Harrison, G. W., T. F. Rutherford, and D. G. Tarr (1997, September). Quantifying the Uruguay Round. *The Economic Journal 107*, 1405–1430.

Hayashi, F. (1982, January). Tobin's Marginal *q* and Average *q*: A Neoclassical Interpretation. *Econometrica 50*(1), 213–224.

Horstmann, I. J. and J. R. Markusen (1986, May). Up the Average Cost Curve: Inefficient Entry and the New Protectionism. *Journal of International Economics 20*(3/4), 225–247.

Hudson, E. and D. W. Jorgenson (1974). US Energy Policy and Economic Growth, 1975-2000. *The Bell Journal of Economics and Management Science 5*, 461–514.

IES-PF (1991). *Indian Economic Statistics, Public Finance*. Ministry of Finance, Department of Economic Affairs, Economic Division, Government of India.

IES-PF (1995). *Indian Economic Statistics, Public Finance*. Ministry of Finance, Department of Economic Affairs, Economic Division, Government of India.

Johansen, L. (1974). *A Multi-Sectoral Study of Economic Growth* (Second Enlarged ed.). North Holland Publishing Company.

Jorgenson, D. W. and P. J. Wilcoxen (1990). Intertemporal General Equilibrium Modeling of US Environmental Regulation. *Journal of Policy Modelling 12*, 715–744.

Keyzer, M. A. (1990, January). Technical Specification of Indonesia Model. Research Memorandum RM - 90 - 01, Stichting Onderzoek Wereldvoedselvoorziening van de Vrije Universiteit.

King, M. (1983, July). Welfare Analysis of Tax Reforms Using Household Data. *Journal of Public Economics 21*(2), 183–214.

Kmenta, J. (1986). *Elements of Econometrics* (2 ed.). Macmillan.

Kreuger, A. O. (1974, June). The Political Economy of the Rent Seeking Society. *American Economic Review 64*(3), 291–303.

Manne, A. (Ed.) (1985). *Economic Equilibrium: Model Formulation and Solution*. The Netherlands: Elsevier Science.

Mercenier, J. and N. Schmitt (1996, August). On Sunk Costs and Trade Liberalisation in Applied General Equilibrium. *International Economic Review 37*(3), 553–571.

Mirlees, J. A. (1971, April). An Exploration in the Theory of Optimal Income Taxation. *Review of Economic Studies XXXVIII*(2), 175–208.

Mitra, P. K. and S. D. Tendulkar (1986). Coping with internal and external exogenous shocks: India, 1974-84. Discussion Paper 1986-21, World Bank CPD.

Modigliani, F. (1961, December). Long Run Implications of Alternative Fiscal Policies and the Burden of the National Debt. *Economic Journal 71*, 730–755.

Mundell, R. A. (1968). The classical system; transfers, productivity and taxes. In *International Economics*, Chapter 1-2, pp. 3–42. Macmillian.

Narayana, A. V. C., A. Bagchi, and R. C. Gupta (1991). *The Operation of MODVAT*. Vikas Publishing House for National Institute of Public Finance and Policy.

Narayana, N. S. S., K. S. Parikh, and T. N. Srinivasan (1991). *Agriculture, Growth and Redistribution of Income. Policy Analysis with an Applied General Equilibrium Model*. North Holland.

Neary, J. P. (1995). *The International Library of Critical Writings in Economics 59: International Trade (Volume I)*. Edward Elgar.

Neary, J. P. and K. W. S. Roberts (1980). The Theory of Household Behaviour Under Rationing. *European Economic Review 13*(1), 25–42.

Neary, P. (1988, February-November). Tariffs, Quotas and Voluntary Export Restraints With and Without Internationally Mobile Capital. *Canadian Journal of Economics XXI*, 714–735.

Negishi, T. (1960). Welfare economics and existence of an equilibrium for a competitive economy. *Metroeconomica 12*, 92–97.

NIPFP (1991). *Sales Tax Systems in India: A Profile*. National Institute of Public Finance and Policy.

Norman, V. D. (1990). Assessing Trade and Welfare Effects of Trade Liberalization. *European Economic Review 10*(34), 725–751.

NSSO (1995). *Tables with Notes on Unorganised Manufacture: Non-Directory Establishments and Own Account Enterprises*. Department of Statistics, Government of India. National Sample Survey Organisation, Fourtyfifth Round, Number 396/1.

Ogaki, M., J. D. Ostry, and C. Reinhart (1996, March). Saving Behaviour in Low- and Middle-Income Developing Countries: A Comparison. *IMF Staff Papers 43*(3), 38–71.

Ohyama, M. (1972). Trade and Welfare in General Equilibrium. *Kieo Economic Studies IX*(2), 37–73.

Pereira, A. M. and J. B. Shoven (1988). A Survey of Dynamic Computational General Equilibrium Models for Tax Policy Evaluation. *Journal of Policy Modelling 10*(3), 401–436.

Perraudin, W. and T. Pujol (1991, June). European Fiscal Harmonisation and the French Economy. *IMF Staff Papers 38*(2), 399–440.

Piggott, J. and J. Whalley (1985). *UK Tax Policy and Applied General Equilibrium Analysis*. Cambridge University Press.

Powell, A. A. and F. H. G. Gruen (1968). The Constant Elasticity of Transformation Production Frontier and Linear Supply System. *International Economic Review 9*(3), 315–328.

Rodrik, D. (1988). Imperfect Competition, Scale Economies and Trade Policy in Developing Countries. In R. E. Baldwin (Ed.), *Trade Policy Issues and Empirical Analysis*, Chapter 5, pp. 109–137. Chicago: University of Chicago Press for NBER.

Roland-Holst, D. W., C. Polo, and F. Sancho (1995). Trade Liberalisation and Industrial Structure in Spain: An Applied General Equilibrium Analysis. *Empirical Economics 20*, 1–18.

Samuelson, P. A. (1986, July). Theory of Optimal Taxation. *Journal of Public Economics 30*(2), 137–143.

Sarkar, H. and M. Panda (1991). A Short Term Structural Macroeconomic Model for India: Applications to Policy Analysis. *Development Papers: UNESCAP 9*, 177–207.

Scarf, H. E. (1973). *The Computation of Economic Equilibria*. Yale University Press, New Haven.

Scarf, H. E. (1984). The computation of equilibrium prices. In H. E. Scarf and J. B. Shoven (Eds.), *Applied General Equilibrium Analysis*, Chapter 1, pp. 1–49. Cambridge University Press.

Serra-Puche, J. (1984). A General Equilibrium Model for the Mexican Economy. In H. E. Scarf and J. B. Shoven (Eds.), *Applied General Equilibrium Analysis*, Chapter 11, pp. 447–482. Cambridge University Press.

Shashkin, Y. A. (1991). *Fixed Points*. American Mathematical Society.

Shoven, J. B. and J. Whalley (1972, November). A General Equilibrium Calculation of the Effects of Differential Taxation of Income from Capital in the U.S. *Journal of Public Economics 1*(3/4), 281–321.

Shoven, J. B. and J. Whalley (1984, September). Applied General-Equilibrium Models of Taxation and International Trade: An Introduction and Survey. *Journal of Economic Literature XXII*, 1007–1051.

Shoven, J. B. and J. Whalley (1992). *Applying General Equilibrium*. Cambridge University Press.

Stiglitz, J. E. (1973, February). Taxation, Corporate Financial Policy and the Cost of Capital. *Journal of Public Economics 2*(1), 1–34.

Storm, S. (1993). *Macroeconomic Considerations in the Choice of an Agricultural Policy*. Aldershot: Avebury.

Summers, L. H. (1972, September). Capital Taxation and Accumulation in a Life Cycle Growth Model. *American Economic Review 71*(4), 533–544.

Tait, A. A. (1988). *Value Added Tax: International Practice and Problems*. International Monetary Fund.

Taylor, L., H. Sarkar, and J. Rattso (1984). Endogenous tariffs, the political economy of trade restrictions, and welfare. In M. Syrquin, L. E. Westphal, and H. B. Chenery (Eds.), *Economic Structure and Performance*. New York: Academic Press.

Tobin, J. (1965, December). The Burden of Public Debt: A Review. *Journal of Finance XX*, 679–682.

Tobin, J. (1969, February). A General Equilibrium Approach to Monetary Theory. *Journal of Money, Credit and Banking 1*, 15–29.

Tørmä, H. and T. Rutherford (1992). A General Equilibrium Assessment of Finland's Grand Tax Reform. Technical Report 15, Department of Economics and Management, University of Jyväskylä.

Venables, A. J. (1985, August). Trade and Trade Policy With Imperfect Competition: The Case of Identical Products and Free Entry. *Journal of International Economics 19*(1/2), 1–19.

Whalley, J. (1985). *Trade Liberalisation Among Major World Trading Areas.* The MIT Press.

Whalley, J. and B. Yeung (1984). External Sector Closing Rules in Applied General Equilibrium Models. *Journal of International Economics 16*, 123–138.

Yano, M. (1983, November). Welfare Aspects of the Transfer Problem. *Journal of International Economics 15*(3/4), 277–289.

Zangwill, W. I. and C. B. Garcia (1981). *Pathways to Solutions, Fixed Points and Equilibria.* Englewood Cliffs, NJ: Prentice-Hall.

Name Index

Subject Index

For Product Safety Concerns and Information please contact our EU
representative GPSR@taylorandfrancis.com Taylor & Francis Verlag GmbH,
Kaufingerstraße 24, 80331 München, Germany

Printed and bound by CPI Group (UK) Ltd, Croydon, CR0 4YY
08/05/2025
01864399-0003